Steve,

    All the best of luck and
success in the future
change challenges you
undertake. We hope the
program and the book are
helpful on that front.

                    Peter Robinson
                    and

                    Elspeth Murray

                    2006

# FAST FORWARD

# FAST
# FORWARD

Organizational Change
in 100 Days

Elspeth J. Murray
Peter R. Richardson

OXFORD
UNIVERSITY PRESS

2002

# OXFORD
UNIVERSITY PRESS

Oxford   New York
Auckland   Bangkok   Buenos Aires   Cape Town   Chennai
Dar es Salaam   Delhi   Hong Kong   Istanbul   Karachi   Kolkata
Kuala Lumpur   Madrid   Melbourne   Mexico City   Mumbai   Nairobi
São Paulo   Shanghai   Singapore   Taipei   Tokyo   Toronto

Copyright © 2002 by Oxford University Press, Inc.

Published by Oxford University Press, Inc.
198 Madison Avenue, New York, New York 10016

www.oup.com

Oxford is a registered trademark of Oxford University Press

Library of Congress Cataloging-in-Publication Data

Murray, Elspeth J., 1961–
   Fast forward : organizational change in 100 days / Elspeth J. Murray
and Peter R. Richardson.
      p. cm.
Includes bibliographical references and index.
 ISBN 0–19–515311–1
 1. Organizational change. 2. Strategic planning. I. Richardson,
Peter R., 1947– II. Title.
   HD58.8 .M875 2002
   658.4'02—dc21
2002004749
Rev.

9 8 7 6 5 4

Printed in the United States of America
on acid-free paper

*To our greatest supporters*
Alan, Bob, David, Patrick, Sheila, and Stephanie

# Preface

The central concepts of this book are deep organizational change, shared understanding, speed, and momentum. How did these all come together? As an actor was fond of saying in *Shakespeare in Love*, "It's a mystery."

This book might never have been written but for several seemingly unconnected events. In 1991, Peter was on sabbatical in Australia and had the great pleasure of working with Roger Collins, Australia's most distinguished professor of business, beef farmer, and wine expert. Roger, a leading authority on organizational change, had already developed a framework around deep change, which, when worked around a bit, became the operational framework for the central concept of deep change that we present in chapter 2.

Four years later, Elspeth was writing her thesis, in which she developed an operational definition of shared understanding. Over a good bottle of wine one evening, we realized that a central purpose of strategic planning, which both of us assist public and private sector organizations with from time to time, was to develop just this for executive teams—a shared understanding of the change challenge that they face.

So, now we had deep change and shared understanding. Speed and momentum came from a combination of our teaching, research, and work with companies. In our teaching, we continually hear from executives and managers who tell us that change happens far too slowly and that there never seems to be a critical mass of resources available to drive it. Our research clearly showed that the fewer major change initiatives organizations drive at any one time, the more successful they are.

In our work with companies, we were struck by two additional observations. First, change is by far the biggest challenge faced by executives today, and second, not all change is created equal.

Our belief is that to be successful today and in the future, organizations should not be built to last; rather, they have to be *built to change*. This concept is something that makes this book different. Another unique aspect of our book is that we not only discuss *what* to change, but more important, *how* to accomplish this enormously difficult task, something very few books on change attempt to do.

We have been very fortunate as academics to have worked over extended periods of time with large and small organizations that were trying to make change happen fast. We've had the opportunity to see what works and what doesn't. We've also helped many organizations design their change processes and followed their progress over a period of several years.

The exceptional executives we have worked with were willing to pilot some new ideas on our behalf. From this work, we came to realize that there are many truly outstanding executives in the world whom one rarely hears about—people like Diego Hernandez, who led the team that developed Collahuasi, one of the world's great new copper mines in Chile; Doug Harrison, who made deep change happen fast at Acklands-Grainger, one of Canada's leading industrial distributors; and Paul Tellier, who turned CN into the leading North American railroad within a decade. We felt that we wanted to write about these individuals, their organizations, and the processes they used to rapidly bring about deep change in their organizations.

To a certain extent, we've been "outsiders on the inside," looking objectively at the process of change. This has proven to be an ideal position for two academics interested in sharing their experiences and observations by writing a book that covers both the *what* and *how* of organizational change. We hope our musings, insights, and pragmatic approach help you and your organization with your challenges around change.

Elspeth J. Murray
Peter R. Richardson

# Acknowledgments

As colleagues it has been great fun, and a lot of hard work, writing this book. We would not have enjoyed the process so much, and the effort required would have been much greater, had it not been for many people who helped us in so many different ways.

Much of the book is drawn from work we have done with innovative executives since the 1980s. In particular, Doug Harrison, president of Acklands-Grainger; Diego Hernandez, executive director of Compagnia Vale do Rio Doce; Andrew Waitman, managing director of Celtic House International; Bill James, former CEO of Falconbridge Limited; Sam Hayes, CEO of Canada Steamship Lines; Gillian Lynch, formerly of Health Canada; Marion Crane, of the Ministry of Finance, Government of Ontario; and Mike O' Sullivan, Surveyor General of Canada Lands, to name just a few, have shared with us a wealth of experience.

We would also like to thank Stephen Miles, of Heidrick and Struggles, for his continuing support and assistance in writing this book. He helped immensely on a number of fronts, from acting as a sounding board for some of our ideas to interviewing several of the CEOs we discuss in the book. His sense of humor came in handy many times.

The book is based on research conducted over five years with a range of different firms and leaders. We have many people to thank for spending their valuable time sharing their change-related experiences with us, too many in fact to list here. In addition, there are literally thousands of students in our Queen's Programs who have shared with us their frustrations and their successes in the change arena. All of these people should know that their time and insights have added immeasurably to the content of this book.

The book has also come together through the efforts of several people who have supported us directly in our writing efforts. These include Debbie de Lang, who carried out a painstaking literature search for us, putting her MBA skills to good use. Moira Jackson first suggested Oxford University Press as a publisher, and she was excellent in helping us to draft the final document. Special thanks go to Martha Cooley at Oxford University Press, who not only took the risk of championing our book, but who also dealt with us with great patience and understanding.

# Contents

# FAST FORWARD

# Introduction

## The Challenge of Organizational Change

It's a common scenario: You've mapped out what you believe is a great game plan to move your organization forward. You think everyone is on board. You believe you've allocated the right resources and enough of them, but nothing's happening. There's no sense of urgency, no pressure to move more quickly on initiatives that are critical to the organization's future viability and profitability. In the face of a seemingly endless stream of disruptive technologies, increasing customer expectations, new competitors coming out of nowhere, unrelenting globalization, and increasing shareholder expectations, you are trying to change your organization to meet new demands, and you're not making any progress. In fact, no one seems to understand what they have to do.

How to make major organizational change happen quickly and how to make it last are challenges that have bedeviled managers for decades. There can be no argument that change of this kind remains one of the most important and difficult leadership and managerial tasks in any kind of organization—public, private, or not-for-profit. Nevertheless, it is still not well understood.

A substantial body of knowledge is being developed on implementing change, and there are many books on the subject, but they tend to focus on the particular interests and expertise of their authors. Business leaders can learn a great deal from these authors, who have contributed significantly to our understanding of change. There is little doubt that following their advice will enhance the likelihood of successful change and, for the reader who is interested in learning more about particular aspects of change, we make frequent references to the work of leading scholars in this field.

What makes our book different is that it presents a holistic, pragmatic perspective on the subject of change—not only *what* to do, but more important, *how* to do it. Although we build on the foundations laid by the work of scholars and practitioners and incorporate much of what they have learned on the subject over twenty years, we believe that there is no generic recipe for change because the circumstances cover such a broad range and mixture. Rather, we offer guidance for developing suitable frameworks for different types of deep change, those common in many corporations today.

Our objective is to help you design a practical, customized framework that clearly establishes the Winning Conditions for your particular change initiative. These are the fundamental preconditions of any change process that, when brought together in an integrated manner, provide a high probability of a successful outcome.

Our approach reflects twenty years of experience with organizations around the world as they've faced the often daunting task of effecting major organizational change. Through this work, we have developed an understanding of what separates the winners from the losers in tackling these challenges, and that's what this book is about. We have researched and worked with organizations in Europe, North and South America, and Australia. Our research methodology has included a series of longitudinal studies lasting up to five years with the senior executive teams of thirty organizations in both the public and private sectors. These studies represent instances of both success and failure. The private-sector corporations, which make up over two-thirds of our sample, cover the industrial spectrum from high technology to mining, and from manufacturing to financial services.

The change initiatives in these organizations encompassed the entire range of the change activities discussed in this book. The organizations launched major corporate change initiatives, as well as new ventures. They made acquisitions and divestments. Some of them went through financial and strategic turnarounds, while others proactively drove deep cultural change. We learned that change activities may share characteristics within various categories, but it is a mistake to rely on general lists and formulas to manage them.

We were also able to hold a continuing series of candid discussions with executives on their processes, activities, frustrations, successes, and failures. We found out what worked for them and what did not. As one aspect of these discussions, we carried out a series of interviews with twenty executives who have succeeded in rapidly implementing deep organizational change. Like the executives in our studies, many of those we interviewed also discussed prior examples of failure and the lessons that they learned from them.

Before going into the details of successful change, it is worth reviewing why and where corporations fail in their plans for these journeys. Often, these journeys not only fail, but they also end up taking the organization in entirely the wrong direction. A recent study found that along with—or instead of—the intended benefits, change initiatives have produced cynicism and burnout, damaged working relationships and people, and reduced loyalty and trust.[1]

## Change Has Many Faces

How do companies like 3M and Hewlett-Packard repeatedly bring new products from concept to market in as little as ninety days? In less time than it takes most companies to even make a decision, these companies are able to make decisions on a new product or service, assemble and focus the required resources, and commercialize the innovation.

Are you faced with creating value through and from acquisitions? Are your shareholders disillusioned at your corporation's inability to generate the value that was initially envisaged when the deal was struck? How can companies like GE Capital and Cisco acquire, integrate, and secure value from a continuing stream of acquisitions that would swamp most of their competitors? In the case of these two companies, it's what they do in the 100 days before the deal is finalized and the 100 days after the acquisition that makes the difference.

Are you grappling with becoming a customer-centric organization, knowing full well that such a shift represents a deep cultural change in your corporation? The prevalent myth is that deep cultural change takes time, lots of it. Yet, if that's so, how did Ford manage to transform its strategy and its culture in less than thirty-six months? How can Acklands-Grainger, a stodgy Canadian Industrial supply company, move in less than twelve months from an outlook of complacency and a 4 percent growth rate to an exciting place to work with a 20 percent growth rate and higher profitability?

It's clear from these examples that change initiatives are not all the same. They differ in a number of respects: the reason for initiation, the time frames over which they must be accomplished, and the breadth and depth of impact.

A significant differentiator among change initiatives is the reason for the initiative. Is change being undertaken in an anticipatory manner? Or is "fur flying" because the organization is in a full-blown crisis? Depending on the answer, the approach to the initiative can be very different. There are many reasons to contemplate change in an organization, and each type of initiative requires a different set of changes and a specially tailored approach if the initiative is to succeed.

Consider mergers and acquisitions as an example. Almost all of them involve cultural change either for the acquired company or for both companies, and the outcome of the entire process is often determined by how well this is addressed. This kind of change is substantively different than that involved in launching a new product or service internally, which requires innovation, cross-functional integration, and, most likely, significant customer involvement. In turn, both of these initiatives are very different from the implemention of a turnaround, which almost certainly requires cash management, cost reduction, and rationalization skills.

## Time Frames

Change initiatives vary widely by the time frames over which they must be accomplished. If the challenge is a corporate turnaround, the first 100 days may be all you have to work with because the second 100 days don't really matter if you have not survived the first 100. Forget taking a year to diagnose what's required and to develop a game plan. For these initiatives—and others that involve a time imperative, such as the rapid launch of a new product or service—

there is a need to compress the entire change process, take tangible action, and achieve outcomes exceedingly rapidly. Alternatively, you may believe that time is on your side and that you have a couple of years to make things happen. The risk in this situation is that you fail to move fast enough, for a variety of reasons, and the process stalls.

Despite significant differences among the various types of change, how can some organizations make each and every one of these very different changes happen and happen quickly, while others have outcomes that are hit and miss? It depends on what gets accomplished in the first 100 days, the first 200 days, and the first twelve months. In the first 100 days, the winners ignite the fuel, achieve liftoff, and accelerate the process. By the end of the first 200 days, they achieve escape velocity and a stable trajectory. By the end of the first year, they're in orbit.

This book articulates what has to happen in each of these stages of flight, often taking organizations where they have never been before. More important, however, it explains how to execute the flight plan for these journeys. To take our analogy one step further, we not only provide a pilot's manual, but we also describe specific approaches for executing the flight plan for different types of corporate journeys.

## The Breadth and Depth of Change

The breadth of impact of change initiatives differs significantly from situation to situation. There are change activities that span the entire organization, and demand for their success is an agenda shared by the entire employee group. For example, the launch of a new corporate or business-unit strategic plan for the whole corporation should engage everyone on the leadership team and, ultimately, all employees. On the other hand, an initiative such as the development and launch of a breakthrough product or service may involve only certain departments and divisions, even though it has a bearing on the future success of the entire corporation. Both are strategic in their own way, and although there are some common elements in the approaches, the specific nature of each process is quite different.

Change also varies in depth. We have observed that the deeper the level of change required, the more difficult it becomes. Some change initiatives are relatively shallow, dealing with operational and possibly some strategic elements of the business. You may need to do things better, improve efficiency and productivity, and perhaps realign the organization. However, the basic business paradigm remains unchanged, core values and beliefs really don't need to be challenged, and for the most part, leadership change is not required. Appropriate, well-developed tools for this type of change include reengineering, restructuring, and rationalization.

Have you ever observed, though, that there are organizations that seem to cycle through change activities every eighteen or twenty-four months with few desired outcomes to show for all the activity? They seem to be continually restructuring and changing business processes. A company in this mode of non-productive change has probably noticed that morale isn't very good, customers aren't particularly satisfied, and elusive outstanding financial performance appears to be another twelve-month "hockey stick" projection away. It's likely that the executive team has failed to make the correct diagnosis of the depth of change that's required. Restructuring and reorganization by themselves won't cut it. Like a doctor who treats a patient's symptoms without looking for their cause, you've failed to diagnose the real problem that ails your organization and to find the correct treatment that is required.

Robert E. Quinn defined the state of many organizations failing to deal with change effectively as one of slow death, and he asked his readers whether they want to be part of the problem or part of the solution. In the latter case, Quinn introduced the notion of deep change, a concept that we operationalize in our book. Deep change occurs when an organization has to realign its fundamental values and beliefs, as well as its strategy, if it is to move on to future success. Slow death is that state that many organizations enter when they fail to muster the courage to address their fundamental cultural problems.[2]

Culture is a major challenge in organizational change and has been recognized for some time. Rosabeth Moss Kanter addressed the problem of organizational change in general, and innovation in particular, in large organizations and concluded that the largest barrier to change is cultural. She identified four particular building blocks of change:

- The ability to break with the past.
- A crisis or "galvanizing event" to initiate the process.
- Strategic decisions that move innovation to the top of the corporate agenda.
- The role of individual sponsors and champions, and the need to embody changes in action.[3]

Changing culture is, in fact, one of the most challenging change tasks faced by any organization.

Diagnosing the need for deep change involving cultural and even paradigmatic change is difficult and inherently threatening for leadership teams. When you go beyond pure strategic change, in which you primarily deal with "things," into the realm of cultural and paradigmatic change, you start to deal with emotions, beliefs, values, and states of mind, all of which are much more challenging to change than "things." It's relatively easy for a company to change its product line, but it's a lot more difficult to change the culture of its entire sales force.

Some companies regularly introduce new change programs that don't seem to go anywhere. The failure of the programmatic approach to change has been well documented by Michael Beer.[4] He has concluded that, for the most part, many change programs don't produce change. He attributes this to a failure of leadership, noting that in a deep change mode, executive teams cannot preach change; rather, they must lead by example and inspiration. At these deep levels, either the leadership has to change or the leadership team has to change; these are two options that many executives don't like to contemplate. Yet, we know that deep change won't happen unless executives demonstrate the behaviors, attitudes, and values that the required approach demands.

There is no doubt that change, particularly deep change, is a human problem, and a major school of thought around the subject can be characterized as the behavioral school. Authors adopting this approach focus in on the human aspects of change. Because of its uncertainty, they tend to characterize the process as inherently threatening and destabilizing. This is certainly the case for many people, but what about those who welcome change and want to make it happen?

Recently, Kanter, writing with Barry Stein and Todd Jick, presented a behavioral model of change developed around the concepts of external and internal driving forces, the form it takes, and its execution. One of their key findings is that no one person or group can make change happen alone. Rather, the success of the process depends on relationships among the key players or stakeholders.[5] This is a critical insight about deep change. Making it happen requires the development of a human flywheel within the organization, spanning levels, functions, and disciplines, that creates an unstoppable momentum for change.

## Speed, Critical Mass, and Intelligent Momentum

Organizations that make major change happen are actually putting into practice several of the basic laws of physics. They recognize that successful change builds momentum fast and obtains results quickly. They understand that the product of acceleration and mass is driving force, and that speed combined with mass produces momentum. This notion has received almost no attention by writers on the subject.[6] One of the leading authorities on the topic, Andrew Pettigrew, commented, "Until very recently, scholars of innovation and change have been curiously uncurious about the pace and sequencing of change."[7] Successful change leaders recognize that both are critical to success.

Although it is one of the most critical elements of any corporation's competitive edge, some aspects of management theory actually argue implicitly against taking rapid action. One of the few writers who has adopted a dynamic process orientation to the subject of change, James Brian Quinn introduced the notion of logical incrementalism.[8]

By viewing change as an evolving process, Quinn advanced our understanding of change considerably. Typically, change has been viewed from a more static perspective, as scholars have sought to find the key ingredients of a successful change recipe. For example, one prevalent approach to the subject has been the notion of a pilot's pretakeoff checklist. This approach does have merit, though, because it increases the likelihood that something critically important has not been overlooked.

Perhaps the best-known writer in this vein is John Kotter, who has identified many key elements of change but places them in a static rather than dynamic context. Among eight key elements of change strategies (see table I.1), he identified the importance of a sense of urgency, power and coalitions, and the need for strong champions.[9] These are important insights that have made an impor-

**Table I.1** Kotter's Eight Elements of
Successful Strategic Change

- Develop a vision and strategy
- Communicate the change vision
- Establish a sense of urgency
- Empower employees for broad-based action
- Generate short-term wins
- Consolidate gains and produce more change
- Anchor new approaches in the culture
- Reward success

tant contribution to our understanding of *what* is required to drive change. But we have found that checklist elements are not enough. For example, Kotter mentioned the need for strategy, but he did not address *how* this can be accomplished expediently. Our intent in this book is to shed light not only on *what* to do, but also on *how* to do them in combination to create a dynamic change process.

Returning again to James B. Quinn, his first premise, building on the behavioral school of thought, is that because radical change is usually overwhelming for most people, change should be implemented as a series of small steps. Building on this notion, he developed a three-stage linear process for implementing change that moves from building awareness through generating understanding and finally moving to action.[10] The modern world, however, does not usually allow the time that the incrementalism of his linear model requires to produce results. In addition, change cannot always occur in small, logical steps; increasingly, the corporation must take a big step and do it fast.

Failure to develop its own internal source of energy is devastating for any change initiative. To add to our space analogy, the spacecraft never reaches a speed at which it can escape the pull of gravity, and it will ultimately fall to earth. All too often, big initiatives move at a snail's pace and eventually die a slow, lingering death, often destroying careers and hard-earned reputations in the process. Even if they eventually succeed, they do so at a disproportionate cost to their eventual benefits.

Of course, in addition to momentum, change needs direction. If nothing else, change is about learning. Robert E. Quinn describes this process in *Deep Change* as "building the bridge as you walk on it."[11] Studies suggest that organizations fail to learn from their experiences of managing change, thus inhibiting further development of the process and organization capabilities.[12] Change appears to be a very ad hoc kind of process, but it really isn't. You start out with a vision, and you know what you want to build, but along the way, there will be surprises; as you find out more, there may be opportunities to improve the outcome. The leadership team needs an initial game plan, but it also needs a continuing process that allows new insights and understandings to be shared and incorporated into the process to create intelligent momentum.

## What Not To Do

As much as it is important to present what we believe are the key elements of successful strategic change, it is important for you to understand what is not being advocated in our book.

Although speed and momentum are important considerations, we do not advocate changing everything at once. In fact, we believe that change will go better and faster with fewer key initiatives under way at any one time. Too many changes all at once can be a recipe for chaos. Rule number one for us is never to forget that there is a business to run and customers to satisfy even as changes are under way.

We believe that there are dynamic frameworks and concepts that are common to many aspects of strategic change, but we also believe that every change initiative must be designed specifically for the context in which it is to be implemented. For us, context includes the business environment, industry and market factors, and the unique strategy, structure, and culture that define any organization. Rule number two of change is that each initiative must be custom designed, yet based on some good design principles.

We are not advocating slipping into a mode of knee-jerk reaction. Although there is undoubtedly a need for speed, corporations that react to every blip in the market, every negative analyst's report, and every competitive maneuver usually don't do well in the end. Instead, we argue that companies need to be responsive to forces influencing change. In a fast-paced environment, the need for strategy is greater, not less, than in a slowly evolving one. However, the strategy has to be of such a nature that it can respond to the need for changes while maintaining its overall direction and integrity.

Most important, we are not advocating change for change's sake. Jack Welch is quoted as saying, "Change before you have to." We doubt that he means you should always be implementing radical change. Successful corporations will change and evolve continually, but revolution is not needed all the time. Nevertheless, change is a constant, and the need for revolution might be lessened if, as Welch suggests, you change before you have to.

What all this implies is that, at any time, there are likely to be two or three or four major undertakings under way in any well-resourced and quickly moving organization that are repositioning the organization for the future. The challenge for an executive team is to make the tough choices as to the appropriate areas for these to be in.

## Establishing the Winning Conditions

Our work has led us to understand that change is a *continuing process* based around establishing a set of Winning Conditions. The following ten elements of the change process establish the Winning Conditions for successful organizational change.

1. Correct diagnosis of the change challenge.
2. Early development of shared understanding.
3. Enrichment of shared understanding.
4. Establishment of a sense of urgency.
5. Creation of a limited and focused strategic agenda.
6. Rapid, strategic decision making and deployment.
7. A human flywheel of commitment.
8. Identification and management of sources of resistance.
9. Follow-through on changing organizational enablers.
10. Demonstrated leadership commitment.

The first three of these provide initial, as well as continuing, guidance for the process through creating *shared understanding*. The second three generate *speed*. The final four create *critical mass*. All ten are crucial as parameters of a successful change process, and they must be established to critical levels within the first 100 to 200 days of the change process. Together, they produce the momentum that makes the process unstoppable, and the desired changes become inevitable.

Not only are these Winning Conditions applicable to specific change initiatives, but, as we will show toward the end of the book, they also provide a framework that defines an organizational culture capable of sustaining continued rapid change, a competitive advantage for any corporation in a world in which speed is critical.

## Reading On

This book is structured in two parts. The first part develops a powerful and dynamic model of rapid change, drawing on the writings of other authors and our own research and practice, as well as the experience of many executives. In chapter 1, we elaborate on the contemporary challenge of organizational change and provide our rationale for the development of our Winning Conditions. In chapters 2 and 3, we talk about speed and momentum and how to build them. First, we address the overall process required to deploy strategy rapidly by explaining why the first 100 and 200 days are so critical. We then describe the ten Winning Conditions in detail and provide the key concepts and frameworks associated with each. Key elements in this model are the parallel deployment of a limited set of initiatives and the makeup of each of these initiatives. In Chapter 3 we define a streamlined, flexible approach to developing strategy that fits well with the fast-paced requirements of the contemporary corporate environment. As we will explain, a great strategic plan—concise, focused and evolving—is the flight plan for change and growth.

In chapter 4, we examine a critical enabler of rapid change—the speed of decision making and resource deployment. Second, we examine a critical enabler of rapid change—the speed of decision making and resource deployment. Using some simple analytical tools, we demonstrate how the strategic decision-making process in most companies is actually made up of white space, periods in which nothing is happening, and the decision process simply stalls. With some process analysis, and some common sense, any organization can slash the time it takes to make major decisions and deploy resources to support them.

We conclude part I in chapter 5 with a number of thoughts on implementation, or making it happen. We discuss the launch of a new strategic plan that demands deep organizational change, probably the most ambitious undertaking for any organization apart from a complete paradigm shift in the business. We point out the weaknesses common in many such launches and develop a framework for rapid deployment. Change will not happen without effective implementation skills and methodologies. In this chapter, we reflect on some of the personal styles and habits required of change leaders, as well as the organizational enablers that support and reinforce the activity.

Part II examines types of change initiatives that are substantively different, using the frameworks developed in part I as a reference point. Based on our research and experience, we have identified five different types of change that experience high failure rates, ones that executives most want to learn about in order to improve their chances of implementation success:

- *Integrating a new acquisition.* The executives we interviewed indentified this as the second greatest challenge they face in making change happen. Given the pace of acquisitive activities today, this subject is of critical importance to many companies, and chapter 6 shows how a few companies seem to be able to accomplish this task successfully on a continuing basis.
- *Launching a new venture.* Creating shareholder value eventually comes down to the corporation's ability to generate profitable growth initiatives. Chapter 7 examines how some companies appear to be able to quickly launch a continuing stream of new products and services and provides a powerful framework for leading this activity in your own organization.
- *Establishing an information technology platform.* Recent corporate history is littered with disastrous information technology initiatives that have destroyed massive amounts of shareholder value. What does it take to make these initiatives work successfully? How can you deploy an e-business platform within 200 days and secure tangible results within the year? Chapter 8 provides some of the answers.
- *Leading an organizational turnaround.* This is an activity in which speed is essential, the choices often appear limited, and executives often wield an ax with brutal force yet fail to achieve lasting results. In chapter 9, we describe an approach that we characterize as "lean and keen." It has been successfully employed by a few leading turnaround executives, and it can get fast results, and leave the corporation in good shape for the long term.
- *Implementing deep cultural change.* This task is probably the most challenging faced by any leadership team, and a fast start is essential. You don't need ten years to change culture, and chapter 10 develops a framework that will help you make real progress even within the first twelve months.

For each type of change, we describe the elements of the 100-day and 200-day action plans that are needed to launch such an initiative successfully. In addition to frameworks and specific examples, you'll hear directly from executives with a proven track record in each of these areas.

In our final chapter, we address what comes after the first 200 days. Although it is possible to initiate and largely complete some major change initiatives in this time period, others will take much longer. The initial period is critical, but change initiatives must retain their vitality and momentum for an extended period that may last for several years. Of course, the reality for almost all organizations is that change never stops. This demands a culture that increasingly becomes change oriented. In this final chapter, we examine what's required to maintain momentum on continuing change initiatives and demonstrate that adherence to the ten Winning Conditions can provide a framework for building change management into the organization as a continuing core competence.

# PART I
# UNRAVELING THE MYSTERY

# 1 _____

## Making Change Happen Fast

In his groundbreaking book, *New Directions for Organization Theory*, Jeffrey Pfeffer identified one of the major challenges facing organizations as eliminating inertia, which he defined as an inability to change as fast as the environment.[1] In today's world, you don't have ten or even five years to implement a major strategic change. Most executives agree that in any major change initiative, substantive results must be secured within the first twelve months. Hence, speed is of the essence.

It is not just about speed, however, because an object that has speed and no mass is easy to stop in its tracks. Driving force is needed to create change, especially in a rapid time frame. If we believe the laws of motion and that force is the product of mass and acceleration, then it is easy to see that organization change requires a critical mass of resources applied to a rapid implementation schedule to produce change. All too often, these are lacking.

Thinking again about the laws of physics, it is well known that the same force distributed over a small surface area will move an object much more quickly than if it is distributed over a large one. In fact, if the object is at rest, it won't move unless a sufficient force is applied to overcome any friction or inertia that may be present. Corporations are much the same. In large ones, particularly, change efforts are diffused throughout the organization, and nothing much seems to happen fast. By contrast, in companies that focus their change activities, more movement occurs, and it occurs faster.

### Speed: The New Reality

Our framework for change emphasizes speed of deployment, which we believe can be a major competitive advantage in all industries. We propose a change process that is dynamic, iterative, and fluid. A central conclusion from our research is that the more focused the process, and the faster deployment occurs, the greater the likelihood of success. In the past century, some of the most successful military campaigns have been based around speed and mobility. The German invasion of France at the outset of the Second World War and the successful Allied campaign to close the Gulf War come to mind in this respect. There are parallels in business. For example, the beauty of acquisitions is that if they work, they can rapidly produce profitable growth. The deal can be concluded within the first 100 days and initial benefits can be secured within the second 100 days. That, at least, is the theory. However, many corporations can move fast to make the deal but move slowly when it comes to integration and generating value from the acquisition.

The unfortunate reality is that many corporations are neither organized nor structured to move at the necessary pace. This poses particular challenges when change arises not from a comfortable, slowly evolving environment, but from abrupt, discontinuous change, the cause of which may be either external or internal.

True, there can be important developments that happen overnight and demand a strategic response, such as the surprise launch of a new product by a major competitor or a major acquisition that restructures the industry. The reality in many large corporations, however, is that external developments that give rise to the need for significant changes in strategy all too frequently do not even appear on the radar screen of the executive team until there's no time to react thoughtfully. Sometimes, of course, the developments are internal; for example, the sales force may come up with a major new market opportunity or the research and development team may develop a breakthrough product or service opportunity. However, by the time the corporate bureaucracy has worked through its ponderous decision and resource allocation processes, a smaller, nimbler competitor is already established in the market.

This kind of experience has given rise to a common misconception that you have to be small to be fast.[2] And there is a certain truth that many large organizations are beaten to the market by smaller, more nimble competitors. In smaller firms, or in companies that focus their change activities, more movement occurs faster. We have already referred to some large organizations, such as 3M and Hewlett-Packard, which are quick to respond. As they get bigger, they do not lose this ability to focus. What makes them different? Our research has shown that they develop processes that specifically enable them to make decisions, commit resources, and achieve results quickly.

In addition, these types of companies are not afraid to make mistakes. As Gerald Schwartz, the chief executive officer of Onex, one of Canada's leading diversified corporations, said, "We try and get people to move with speed. And one of the things we say is when you move with speed, you're going to make some mistakes, but that's okay because the good things will work and the bad things will show up and we'll go and fix them." It's not necessary to have the ship pointed in precisely the right direction at the outset; course corrections can be made as you go as long as you don't start out in entirely the wrong direction—a mistake most management teams are unlikely to make.

In this respect, a key element in building speed is a set of measures that lay out clearly, early on, the parameters, particularly temporal, that define successful change. These should define clear, measurable objectives, the outcomes of the process, as well as milestones that indicate progress toward these ends, all with associated time frames. Unlike some practitioners who advocate taking a considerable amount of time to construct some kind of rational scorecard, we believe that if change is to be implanted fast, these measures have to be developed with expediency and refined as the process moves along.

## Mass: Creating the Driving Force

Many of the executives with whom we discussed change commented that change happens slowly when initiatives lack a critical mass of resources to drive them. Very often, these are human resources—change may be a part-time activity in the corporation—but not infrequently, the tools are lacking as well. Establishing the Winning Conditions for successful change means that a critical mass of resources must be brought together quickly to build momentum.

Continued downsizing in the 1990s has left many organizations without the resources they need to deal with change. In fact, most executives and managers spend most of their time simply running the business, and they have very little time to devote to change activities. One clear message about change that this reality underlines is that few major change initiatives should be contemplated at one time, and they had better be the right ones!

It can take a long time for change initiatives to percolate through an organization. Our interviews with executives suggest that it is not unusual for strategic initiatives to take twelve or even twenty-four months to reach frontline employees. And if the supervisory group feels that the initiative is not in their interests, it may never reach the front line. Part of creating mass is involving a broad coalition of employees in making it happen. The faster this takes place, the better. We refer to this phenomenon as a "human flywheel" that is necessary to build and sustain momentum.

Lacking internal resources for change initiatives, many corporations are turning to consultants to drive change, leaving executives and managers free to focus on running the business. This can be fatal. Many consultants possess good analytical skills but lack experience with change and implementation. They take six months or a year just to carry out a diagnosis, far too long in today's environment. Of course, delegating change activities to consultants may cause employees to lack a sense of ownership in the initiative, sharply reducing the likelihood that the change will either be adopted or be lasting. Finally, since they don't have a tangible connection to the corporation, consultants often lack the motivation to make the tough choices and sacrifices necessary to drive the changes home. In our experience, successful change consultants view themselves more as catalysts—they are there to speed things up, not slow them down—and they work accordingly.

This lack of resources can also be attributed in part to the way in which many corporations and government organizations do their budgeting. Although most distinguish between capital and operating budgets, some types of investments are often treated as operating expenses, particularly those in employee development and training, information systems, and product and market development, which are key change enablers. Of course, these aren't really expenses at all, but they are treated as such by accountants. When executives and managers are asked to pare their budgets by 5 or 10 percent, as commonly happens, what gets postponed or eliminated first are these apparently discretionary items. Thus, for example, major new software initiatives frequently end up with only half of the training activity that is really needed if they are to be used effectively. Not only is this false economy, but it is also a root cause of failure for many change initiatives, although it is rarely recognized as such.

## Shared Understanding

Speed and mass are necessary to provide momentum, but by themselves they are insufficient to bring about lasting change. What's also needed in the process is intelligence, which provides the activity with a sense of purpose and direction. What provides this sense of intelligence in the change process is what we term *shared understanding*. This is a relatively contemporary concept that has a profound relevance for organizational change. Usually, organizational change is associated with a high level of uncertainty, disagreement, and lack of understanding about what to do. Richard Daft, R. Lengel, and L. Trevino, writing on this challenge in 1987, observed:

> Managers are not certain what questions to ask, and if questions are posed there is no store of objective data to provide an answer. . . . The organization reduces equivocality by pooling opinions and overcoming disagreement. This leads to a shared understanding and social agreement about the correct response.[3]

When operationalized, what a powerful concept this can be for driving change.

What, then, is shared understanding? Executives have understood for some time that one of the elements of successful change is an inspiring vision of some kind. By creating either a picture of a desirable future state or the motivation to close a gap between today and the future, a powerful vision can be a key element in convincing people of the need to change. Sometimes, the vision can be stated simply, although in our experience, the more substantive and concrete it is made, the easier it is for many people to buy into. Of course, visions alone are not sufficient to drive change; you may be one of the many employees who have seen visions come and go with succeeding CEOs, with nothing much changed. Repeated failures of this type have bred considerable cynicism about this approach.

Our experience has led us to the realization that the problem is often not with the vision itself. We have met many executives with powerful and articulate visions. The challenge has been to turn these into tangible actions. For example, the CEO of one corporation that we have worked with had a truly revolutionary vision to turn his corporation from an engineering consulting firm into a "one-stop" supplier of engineering services for its large clients, many of whom wanted to get out of doing these activities themselves. His company would design the plants, build them, and then use technology to create a maintenance infrastructure that they would provide on a continuing basis to the client once the plant was in operation. Everyone, even customers, was excited by this vision. However, like many inspirational visions, this one never became reality.

Why is this? In retrospect, it was very easy to get people excited about a powerful vision and to get an intellectual commitment. However, bringing a vision to life also requires an operational commitment that rests on a growing foundation of shared understanding, which goes way beyond vision, incorporating three other elements:

- Agreed-to measures of success.
- Clear definitions of the projects and programs required to bring the vision into reality.
- A set of enabling processes that continually deepen the team's understanding of its challenge and what needs to be done.

Along with critical mass and speed of deployment, our process emphasizes the development and continual enrichment of a broad and deep level of shared understanding. All of our research and experiences indicate that the more widely understood and focused the process, and the faster deployment occurs, the greater the likelihood of success.

## Why Change Programs Don't Produce Change

In our work over the years with numerous CEOs and senior managers across a wide variety of industries and firm sizes, we have been struck time and again by commentary that points to a lack of speed as a major issue associated with an organization's inability to make change happen successfully.[4] Lack of speed is only the end result, however, of more insidious root causes. Consider the following three comments from people we have interviewed; they are typical of many we hear periodically.

The CEO of a major telecommunications provider observed:

No matter how hard we try, it seems to me that on many significant opportunities, where I thought we had alignment, we obviously didn't. Promised commitments never materialized, and agreed-to high-priority projects were starved of necessary resources. We're still finalizing the design specs and we find out that one of our smaller, nimbler competitors is actually getting ready to go to market.

An entrepreneurial division manager in a major packaged goods company complained:

We're stuck in the Stone Age. Halfway through the year, one of my brand managers comes up with a great new product idea, and we're told to stick it in next year's budget. It's the twenty-first century and my company has yet to realize that great ideas don't coincide with budget cycles.

Another theme that we have heard countless times in many different forms was neatly characterized in the following cry from the heart:

We don't make the tough calls. We try to accomplish far too much, spread our resources way too thin, and then we wonder why everything moves forward at a snail's pace.

These quotations reflect specific instances of several of the many and diverse factors that appear to militate against successful change. In reality, these factors can be grouped into two broad categories: commitment and resources.

Failures of commitment result from an inability to develop shared understanding and a lack of a powerful multilevel coalition in support of change initiatives. Typical of these problems are:

- *Lack of shared understanding* among executives and managers, resulting in a failure to act decisively. Although there may be a shared vision, little progress is made. Lip service is paid to commitment. Everyone is rowing the boat, but at different speeds and perhaps in different directions. As we will see, shared understanding requires much more than merely sharing a vision for the future.
- *Inability to build support and a critical mass* among employees who actually want to implement new initiatives. A small select group is informed, but broad support never materializes.
- *Failure to understand and deal with opposition.* Individuals and coalitions, usually a small minority, who do not support the proposed direction are allowed to voice their opposition unchallenged, and they may, in fact, build opposition among those previously uncommitted.
- *Absence of accountability for outcomes.* There is no follow-up and attendant consequences, positive or negative, for failure to fulfill strategic change commitments. People know that operational performance is much more likely to be questioned than strategic performance, especially if there are no detailed action plans developed around high-level strategies.

Failures of resources arise from an inability to adequately support key initiatives. This can occur for one of any number of reasons, but we have found the following to be common issues:

- *Lack of human resources*, particularly those dedicated to the process. Executives are unwilling to make the tough decisions to commit people full-time to change initiatives. Unfortunately, employees have the best of intentions but just too many daily tasks. As we will show, although everyone has to be involved in change, for some people, it has to be a full-time commitment.
- *Failure to focus* and make the tough decisions, thus developing too many

initiatives that lack a critical mass of resources and spreading people and budgets too thinly. People can mentally and physically handle only so many change activities at one time, particularly if there are ongoing operations to handle as well.

- *An overwhelming preoccupation with operations and short-term crises* in many organizations in which most executive and managerial time and debate are devoted to current issues, with little devoted to strategy and change. Our surveys of executives suggest that most spend less than 20 percent of their time on these matters. This failing is common in high-growth environments in which executives believe that they have no time for planning and strategy. This may be expedient in the short term, but sooner or later the negative consequences of this lack of future orientation become apparent.

Taken together, these individual failings actually add up to a much more critical problem for change: lack of intelligent momentum. In addition to sustaining forward movement, momentum is required to overcome organizational barriers to change that are present in every corporation. The best of intentions will be futile if these are not dealt with. They can be such things as restrictive or inappropriate organization structures and reporting relationships. They can take the form of disabling information systems. They can derive from lack of skills. In fact, they can be simple policies and procedures that work against the new direction. Changes in these organizational elements must proceed in parallel to changes in business practice before any significant momentum can be achieved. In today's rapidly changing environment, for change to happen fast, intelligent momentum must be achieved very quickly.

## The First 100 and 200 Days

Our research and experience have demonstrated that the first 200 days of a major change initiative largely determine its outcome. The first 100 days should be used to create speed and a sense of urgency, and the second 100 days should build the critical mass required to achieve breakthrough momentum.

In many change initiatives, virtually nothing happens in the first 100 days, often because people demand time to study and validate the concept. That would be like the pioneers refusing to move west until they had the entire map of the continent in hand. People who don't want to change successfully use this approach to stall the process. Executives in one low-performing packaged-goods company told us of the breakthrough strategic plan that was derailed by one senior vice-president of marketing who insisted for nearly a year on market studies to "validate" the new strategy. By the time these studies were complete, the window of opportunity had passed.

On the other hand, in those initiatives in which the first 100 days is used to create understanding of the need for change, build initial momentum, and perhaps even secure some initial successes, then overall success is far more likely.

Consider Cisco's approach to acquisitions. The company aims to have the products of an acquired company integrated into its own product line as soon as the deal is closed. A predetermined integration team, often headed by an employee of the acquired company, swings into action immediately. The new employees are made to feel as though they are Cisco employees as fast as possible, and they are often given enhanced benefits. Major systems integration projects are completed within the first 100 days. Little wonder that Cisco is relatively more successful than its competitors at deriving value from its acquisitions.

The second 100-day period is important in terms of consolidating the progress made during the initial 100 days. This is the critical time during which momentum is built. Together with the critical mass of resources now in place, the accelerating speed builds momentum to the point at which it cannot be stopped. By the end of 200 days, tangible results should start to flow.

Take, for example, Acklands-Grainger, the industrial distributor we mentioned in our introduction. In the first 100 days following the launch of a new strategic plan for the company, several major steps were implemented. One of them was a communications initiative in which over five hundred of the company's employees participated in one-day sessions during which they reviewed the new strategy, had an opportunity to ask questions of CEO Doug Harrison and his executive team, and thought through the implications for their own operations. They overwhelmingly expressed enthusiasm for the new approach.

However, across the company, there was still a palpable sense of wonder: "Is this all talk, or are things really going to change?" Although Harrison could report that the company's growth rate had risen to nearly 20 percent on an annualized basis, there was little that frontline employees could point to as being different. Recognizing the understandable skepticism in the organization, the Strategy Team committed to five deliverables for the end of the first 200 days that would demonstrate to all employees that things were changing. These included specific changes to branch operations, improvements in logistics, and implementation of training. Although their delivery was not perfect, the outcomes, each first steps in one of the organization's five key initiatives, consolidated the momentum felt throughout the organization and provided employees with specific developments to point to and talk about.

## The Winning Conditions: Building Intelligent Momentum

In Canada in recent years, there has been continuing concern that the Province of Quebec might separate from the rest of the country. However, after several referendums, the province remains part of Canada. Speaking about this failure, the separatist Premier of Quebec Lucien Bouchard remarked that he would not hold another referendum on the subject until he had established what he called the "winning conditions."

Bouchard's failure to bring about deep change in his province, in spite of a passionate and committed following, led us to reflect on the notion of winning conditions and ask what these might be for organizational change. As we reviewed our experience over the last twenty years, we were able to identify that change seemed to be more successful when the process exhibited the ten characteristics that we outlined at the end of our introduction. Together, these Winning Conditions contribute greatly to an organization's ability to generate speed, critical mass, and ultimately unstoppable momentum around its key change initiatives.

## Guiding the Change

The first set of Winning Conditions relates initially to the leadership team, and ultimately to the entire organization, and their awareness of the need for change, their understanding of its nature, and the magnitude of the challenge. As the process unfolds, this understanding has to become deeper and richer.

### 1. Correct Diagnosis of the Nature of the Change Challenge

The importance of diagnosis as a key step in organizational change has been recognized for some time.[5] Without correctly diagnosing the nature of the change required—its depth, breadth, and likely acceptance—it is virtually impossible to properly map out a plan of action. Equally important is that the executive team shares the same view of this diagnosis. In our approach, we differentiate among four distinct depths of change:

- Operational changes that "tweak" the organization.
- Strategic changes that reposition or refocus the business.
- Cultural changes that reorient values and beliefs such as those related to quality and customer service.
- Paradigm changes in which the organization is re-created.

In addition to depth of change, diagnosis of the breadth of impact is critical. Is the change confined to a business unit or work group or does it span the entire organization? The complexity and difficulty of the process increase significantly at each new level of depth and breadth, and diagnosis requires its own techniques to drive the change. It's akin to the differences among putting a satellite into orbit, going to the moon, traveling to Mars, and taking a trip outside the galaxy.

### 2. Early Development of Shared Understanding

Shared understanding is a necessary antecedent for initiating change. If key decision makers and champions are not on the proverbial same page, then the change activity will likely experience any number of challenges. It is not enough, however, to merely have a shared understanding of some inspirational vision for a future state for the organization. A vital element of this shared understanding is agreement on what we term the *critical few* make-or-break programs and projects around which future strategy must focus. Shared understanding is a multifaceted enabler for change. Too often, as we discuss in chapter 2, change initiatives are launched with a great sense of vision and the best of intentions, but a woefully limited shared view of the operational aspects of the change initiative itself and the issues that must be addressed to achieve a successful outcome.

### 3. Enrichment of Shared Understanding

Learning is a key part of strategic change, and change initiatives need processes that allow learning to be shared across the organization.[6] Over time, this results in a deepening and enrichment of shared understanding, particularly among the executive team, but often throughout the company as well. To use a favorite book analogy, in any major change, many organizations start off on the same page, but very soon after, individuals begin reading at different rates. Before you know it, key sponsors, champions, and participants in the change are all on different pages. Some mechanism must be developed to bring them all back to the same page to review the story, then continue reading.

As chapter 3 describes in greater depth, organizations need a continuing review process that will work in rapidly changing environments. One element of this process is a continuing assessment of changes in the organizational context—the overall business environment, markets, competition, and perhaps even the overall corporate strategy. A second element is periodic review, updating, and action planning of the strategy for change, perhaps as frequently as every 60 days, but certainly every 90 or 120 days. This process is often complemented by other forms of learning, such as in-depth studies, focus groups, seminars, and even change workshops. There may be other approaches, but it is key that mechanisms exist to maintain and enrich the shared view of the change challenge throughout the organization.

### Speed

One of the two elements of momentum is speed, and this is what has to come first when implementing organizational change. A sense of urgency is necessary for this, but it is not sufficient. Other Winning Conditions such as focus and the ability to make decisions quickly are the other key enablers of speed.

### 4. Establishment of a Sense of Urgency

John Kotter, in his book *Leading Change*, argues that creating a sense of urgency is the first step in successful organization change.[7] He comments, "Visible crises can be enormously helpful in catching people's attention and pushing up urgency levels." There is no doubt that the presence of a crisis sharpens the mind and imbues the change process with a sense of urgency right from the outset. However, we believe that reliance on crisis-driven change may not bring about the desired results, may not bring lasting results, and ultimately has negative consequences. Deep change can be brought about in an anticipatory mode, in which there may not be an initial crisis around which to build the change initiative. The most difficult of these cases is in organizations that are experiencing record earnings and have a strong culture, but not all of the executives realize that major change is necessary. Such situations require, within the first 100 days, a major communications exercise designed to build awareness and understanding of the need for change. Although this is unlikely to win everyone over, as long as a significant percentage of employees, perhaps 20 percent, accepts the need for change, its purpose has been served, because it will then be possible to build momentum rapidly.

## 5. Creation of a Limited and Focused Strategic Agenda

One of the worst mistakes organizations make while undertaking change initiatives is to try to change everything at once. This does not work and never has worked. In our research, we found that organizations that limit their strategic change agenda to two or three major initiatives at any one time make the fastest progress overall.[8] Thus, the planning activity must develop a focused agenda for change, one that provides the following:

- A sense of vision embodying desired outcomes.
- A clear statement of the change mission, with an associated time frame.
- Clear, unambiguous objectives that capture the essence of the mission.
- A statement of the three or four make-or-break challenges and opportunities inherent in the change.
- A set of tactical action plans for initial deployment, with appropriate accountabilities.

## 6. Rapid, Strategic Decision Making and Deployment

Change won't happen fast if it is introduced in a traditional linear, sequential manner. A parallel-deployment methodology is the only effective approach. By this, we mean that organizations can't wait until major communications exercises are complete before undertaking substantive initiatives, such as lead customer testing in the case of new ventures. Similarly, executives who make symbolic gestures around cultural changes, such as "Quality is Job 1," cannot then delay benchmarking activities associated with defining just what "quality" means. In short, these activities must occur in a parallel fashion to shorten the time frame for change.

Enabling these parallel activities, is a strategic decision-making process that can produce major decisions, resource reallocations, and action in days or weeks, much faster than many companies appear capable of, even today. For example, if board approval is required for major financial reallocations, the board's decision-making process must be in sync with the time frames driving the change activities. The reality is that many of the approval processes are cumbersome and lengthy and work against building speed into the change process.

## Momentum

The last four winning conditions are concerned with building and sustaining momentum. Securing a critical mass of resources, overcoming resistance, aligning organizational structure and processes, and demonstrating leadership throughout the organization are key in this respect.

### 7. A Human Flywheel of Commitment

Change affects everyone differently. In most organizations, relatively few employees are willing to engage in early-stage change activities, even when the change is perceived to be positive or nonthreatening. At the same time, there are always a few "gung ho" true believers to be found. As Larry Weinbach of Unisys observed:

> Make sure that you recognize not everybody is going to come on board on day one and that it's going to take a lot of face time to ensure that people understand where you want to go and why. . . . The why becomes a big issue because, it may seem surprising, but a lot of people may not understand why you want to make the strategic change, even if the company is not doing well.

In our work with organizations, we have observed that approximately 20 percent of employees can be initially motivated to become active in driving change. This realization is key to successful change because executives often waste far too much time at the outset trying to get a majority of employees on their side before taking action. Jack Welch has commented that in his early days as CEO of General Electric, he spent far too much time trying to gain acceptance from a broad cross section of employees. John Kotter said, "A majority of employees, perhaps 75 percent of management overall, and virtually all of the top executives, need to believe that considerable change is absolutely essential." In our view, *all* of the executives and 20 percent of employees need to believe in the need for change at the outset for an unstoppable momentum to be built.

Approximately 70 percent will remain neutral, "sitting on the fence" to see what transpires. Roughly 10 percent will actively, and possibly vocally, oppose the new direction. To build speed and momentum, it is critical to rapidly identify and mobilize the 20 percent, wherever they are in the organization. The real power of this group lies in their ability to convince the fence-sitters to become engaged. Once this happens, a human flywheel develops, usually one that possesses the required critical mass.

### 8. Identification and Management of Sources of Resistance— Securing a Favorable Balance of Power Throughout the Organization

Resistance to change is almost inevitable. This aspect of change has been explored in many books and articles.[9] What is apparent from this literature is that the causes of resistance are numerous and often imperfectly understood by executives. For example, a considerable proportion of perceived resistance arises simply from lack of awareness and understanding. In addition, those employees who are deeply opposed to change are not always apparent at the beginning of a new initiative. Many of them, the passive-aggressives, do not declare themselves openly. The reality is that in too many change initiatives, executives spend all of their time dealing with the 10 percent who will never get on board and underutilize the 20 percent who want to be actively involved.

Failure to deal adequately with opposition, particularly employees who are actively trying to sabotage the initiative, has derailed more than a few major change efforts. Tough decisions have to be made regarding those who don't or won't engage. At the very least, these individuals have to be put on notice that opposition is not acceptable. One CEO we have worked with refers to his "I respect your decision to not come on this journey with us" conversations in which he tells employees that if they cannot support the new direction, then they have to accept that they do not have a future with the organization. At some point, one is either for or against a new direction, and if someone is holding up the train, it is time for them to either get off or be helped off.

## 9. Effective Follow-through on Changing Key Organizational Enablers

"If You Want to Change Strategy, Change the Performance Measures and the Corresponding Recognition and Rewards." This was the message we heard from a number of senior executives. It's not quite as simple as that, but there's no doubt that many change initiatives fail because these two elements, as well as other key enablers, are misaligned with the new direction. Other key enablers include communication, policies, information reporting, and employee learning. These are so badly misaligned in some cases that employees who are early to embrace the new direction may get penalized by the old systems, formal and informal.

There is little doubt that if opponents to a new direction have the opportunity, to use an existing reward system to penalize the innovators they will do so. In addition, individuals opposed to change may use other enablers, such as existing policies, control of information, and communication vehicles, as barriers and obstacles to progress. Therefore, it is imperative within the first 100 days of a new change initiative to start to realign these key enablers with the new direction.

## 10. Demonstrated Leadership Commitment

Leadership is probably the most studied aspect of change, yet it is only one element of a complex process. It is a requirement, but alone it is not sufficient to guarantee success. Napoleon, even with the passionate support of his imperial guard, was eventually defeated by the discipline and organization of Wellington's soldiers. There have been many attempts to identify appropriate leadership styles and attributes that correlate with successful transformation, and although certain traits can be identified, no single model emerges. It appears that transformational leadership is highly situational and that widely differing approaches can be successful.[10] Also, studies of change leadership have tended to focus on executives and managers, but it is clear that success demands leadership at all levels of the organization. Relatively little attention has been paid, for example, to the leadership styles required of supervisors.[11]

In adopting a leadership style for successful change, an executive must both recognize which approach is appropriate and understand the key tasks involved. For example, change in a crisis situation often fails because senior executives abdicate their responsibility for tough decisions on nonperforming employees, resource allocations, or "sacred cows" that are paralyzing the organization. By contrast, poor anticipatory change frequently results from a top-down, directive leadership style, which fails to build broad commitment, as well as excessive secrecy about the new direction. Together, these result in a lack of awareness and understanding of the need for change and an inability to build a sense of urgency and momentum. Whatever the nature of the change, it is almost certain that the deeper it becomes, the more critical it is for an executive team to reflect on their leadership style and to demonstrate new behaviors and values appropriate to the future direction.

## Summing Up

So how do you make change happen fast? Whether you are an executive leading a large global corporation, the head of a business unit within one of these firms, or the entrepreneurial CEO of a rapidly growing company, the challenge is to establish the Winning Conditions for change and to do so early in the change process. Our research and experience indicate that it is what happens, or doesn't happen, in the first 100 days and 200 days of any major change initiative that largely determines the outcome of the change process—success or failure. The Acklands-Grainger example, and many other success stories that we will describe throughout the book, demonstrates that the key parameters—the Winning Conditions—for the change initiative were established within the first 100 days and consolidated within the second 100 days. These Winning Conditions, which are common to all types of strategic change, form the elements of a dynamic change process that we develop in chapter 2.

# 2

## Establishing the Ten Winning Conditions

One of Jack Welch's sage pieces of advice is: *change before you have to*. Crisis-driven change, although easier to initiate, tends not to be lasting. Lasting change comes more from a proactive approach, but it is much more difficult to create because of a lack of a sense of urgency. Proactive change tends to occur much more slowly, if at all, especially in an organization with an apparently sound operating performance, a strong culture, and no crisis to help create awareness and understanding of the need to change. In these situations, executives hoping to introduce change in an anticipatory mode are frequently stymied by complacency and inertia even when they make a sound case. Thus, one tough question for many organizations is not how to undertake major change in the face of a crisis, but rather how to effect major change without the impetus of a crisis. Paul Tellier, CEO of CN, had the following experience:

> When I joined CN, I found no sense of urgency. There was no crisis, no threat, no customer focus. . . . The Business Plan was a short document that the company was required to prepare for financial administration purposes. . . . In the early days, whenever I wanted to change something, I was given seventeen reasons why it could not be done.

Why is crisis the most common driving force for organizational change? Very often, it's because executives have failed to act in a timely manner—before a crisis arrives. Crisis works in the short term because it creates a sense of urgency and a powerful, unarguable logic for change within organizations. In fact, many executives appear to be incapable of bringing about change without this sense of immediacy. However, crisis is often accompanied by feelings of panic that may result in poor decision making, confusion, and failure. In addition, though this form of change is the easiest to implement rapidly, many executives report that organizational changes, particularly behavioral, are difficult to maintain once the crisis is perceived to have passed. To sustain change initiated in this manner, leadership behavior and organization processes such as performance evaluations, rewards systems, and communications must be modified to reinforce new approaches and directions, something many organizations fail to bring about.

This chapter begins the development of a framework for avoiding this state of affairs. We have found evidence of a fundamental malaise affecting the change process in many organizations that stems from the fact that executives are often unable or unwilling to diagnose how deep a change intervention is required. Or, frequently, the diagnosis is made too late. Even though leading indicators of the need for change are evident, the executive team either ignores them or cannot reach agreement on the need for change. Also, the diagnosis is often too "shallow"; in other words, the change challenge is identified as one in which operational issues must be addressed, when in fact change is required at a much deeper level involving cultural, and possibly even paradigm, change. Perhaps a major reason for this is that it is far less threatening for executives to diagnose operational or strategic changes that will allow their own behavior to remain largely unchanged. It is a far greater personal challenge to diagnose a requirement for profound cultural or paradigm shifts, which demand changes in leadership style, behavior, and beliefs. The first step toward successful change, then, is a timely diagnosis of the *depth* of change required.

Employees often comment on the failure of executives to identify and overcome opposition to change that results in delays and, not infrequently, the collapse of the whole initiative. Significant organizational change is an exercise in power. It's the good guys versus the bad guys, the forces of light versus the forces of darkness, and usually, the stronger side wins out. In many cases in which change fails to take hold, either a favorable balance of forces to drive the process is not created in the first place, or the voices of opposition and dissent are not dealt with and increasingly become a rallying point for forces opposed to the new direction. A key part of the diagnosis is an understanding of who the stakeholders are in the change process, how they view it, and how power and influence are distributed among them.

## The Starting Point: The Flight Preparedness Assessment

For many organizations, change is multifaceted and the challenges are many. For some, commitment is lacking but resources are plentiful. In others, resources are scarce and commitment is strong, but people are unintentionally working at cross-purposes. As a way of better understanding the areas in which you have the most work to do, and what you should seek to take from our book, it is useful to assess just how well your organization is positioned to undertake a significant change initiative. Better yet, ask a group of your senior managers to undertake the same assessment and see if they agree. The ten questions posed in table 2.1 highlight some of the key items related to successful change initiatives. Score each item on a scale of 1 to 5, with 1 being no or poor, and 5 being yes or very good/well.

**Table 2.1** Strategic Change Assessment

1. Do members of the leadership team have a strong shared understanding of the nature of the change challenge?
2. Are change initiatives clearly understood throughout the organization?
3. Is there a limited number of change initiatives under way at any one time (maximum of five is acceptable)?
4. Do you move rapidly, (i.e., within a few days) from making a decision to proceeding with deployment of resources and initial actions?
5. Are sufficient resources allocated to get the job done in the required time?
6. Is there a detailed 100-day action plan for each initiative?
7. Do all major initiatives have dedicated human resources, including an executive sponsor and a full-time champion?
8. Do people not involved in specific initiatives obtain periodic updates on progress and successes?
9. Are specific outcomes secured from key initiatives within 200 days of start-up?
10. Does your organization have tangible recognition and rewards for employees who deliver successful change initiatives fast and well?

How did you do? If you scored 35 or more, your change process is probably working pretty well, particularly if you scored high on outcomes in questions 8 and 9. However, even at this level, the 1s, 2s and 3s in your score indicate areas for improvement. A score under 35 suggests that there's considerable room for improvement in the process, and a score under 25 indicates a need for the whole executive team to review your organization's entire change approach.

This quick assessment has provided an indication as to how well your current approach to change matches up against our ten Winning Conditions. Is there sufficient shared understanding of the nature of the challenge throughout the organization to provide guidance? Is there a sense of urgency and a propensity for action and decision making that create speed? Are there adequate resources to provide momentum? We will now explore each of the Winning Conditions in some detail and discuss the key frameworks and concepts associated with each.

## Guiding the Change

Our first three Winning Conditions provide and maintain guidance for the change effort: What is the change challenge? What is the desired outcome for the change effort? How will the change journey unfold? To answer these questions, three conditions must be established right at the outset. It is vital to correctly diagnose the nature of the change intervention required and to develop among the executive team a shared understanding of the change required. Both of these need to be established very early on in the process, within the first few weeks. A third critical step is to create a process that will be used all the way through the change initiative to enrich this shared understanding and ensure its dissemination and acceptance throughout the entire organization.

## 1. Correct Diagnosis of the Change Challenge

Most books on organizational change treat the concept as homogeneous. This is simplistic, because there are many different types of organizational change. Without correctly diagnosing the nature of the change required, it is virtually impossible to properly map out a plan of action. Equally important is that the executive team shares the same view of this diagnosis. A physician noting that you have a pain in your knee doesn't get far with prescribing an effective treatment without digging further. A great physician will ask a set of questions to identify not only the type of pain—where it hurts and how much—but the true source of that pain. Only then is the real extent of the problem understood, and only then can an effective course of treatment be prescribed.

Drawing the analogy back to the organization context, the "type of pain" relates to the signals for change and the urgency of the change challenge. For instance, is it painful that the patient can't walk? Painful, but the patient is still mobile? Uncomfortable, but no significant impact on functioning? Or, most difficult of all, no visible symptoms? As we know with cancer, by the time visible symptoms appear, it can be too late. Hence, there is great value in periodic examinations to detect latent problems. The best diagnoses are those that are made quickly and are based on correct information. One must start with a general set of questions designed to lead to an ever more specific and focused diagnosis and subsequent course of treatment. Of course, treatment takes time, and it must proceed in a prescribed, ordered manner to be most effective. Sometimes, treatment only requires taking a few antibiotics, and all is well. However, when the malady may be disabling, a complete change in lifestyle might be necessary.

The same is true with respect to organizational change. First, there is the need to make a correct diagnosis of the problem or challenge at the outset, and depending on this assessment, the course of treatment can be quite different. In figure 2.1, we characterize four distinct levels of change, or categories, of diagnosis:

*Operational:* a relatively shallow form of change in which the diagnosis is that what's currently being done in the organization is right, it simply has to be done better, largely by focusing on operational and efficiency improvements.

*Strategic:* a deeper diagnosis suggesting that both effectiveness and efficiency need improvement through a strategic repositioning and refocusing. However, the basic business paradigm and attendant values and behaviors are sound and do not need to change.

*Cultural:* a relatively deep level of change in which not only strategy, but also organizational behaviors, values, and beliefs need to change.

*Paradigm:* the deepest level of change—the fundamental business paradigm has to change or the organization will collapse. This level almost certainly involves cultural, strategic, and operational change as well.

**Figure 2.1** Organization Change—Depth of Intervention

A common misdiagnosis is to assume a need for strategic change when in fact the change is culturally based. In our work, we encountered a large government department that, in response to politicians' promises to improve customer service and the quality of internal processes, undertook a strategic planning exercise as a vehicle for mapping out how to deal with these political imperatives. The agreed-upon course of action centered on the need to undertake process mapping and redesign, provide employees with training in customer service, and establish a performance-measurement system to track progress against both.

The plan was finalized and agreed to, and implementation began. At the first executive team review, however, it was clear that, just as in many previous attempts to change the organization, real progress was absent. Employees simply were not buying in to the new approaches. In the end, one brave and frustrated middle manager voiced the reality of what the executive team was ignoring—an overwhelming belief throughout the organization that what they had been doing for years was the right approach and that the new approaches would compromise the basic values of the organization. Comfort with day-to-day operating issues was defeating future-oriented, change-related initiatives. The manager went on to say that, in her view, the real change challenge was cultural. Only if a cultural change could be brought about would there be any hope of implementing the new approaches. That's when the lights went on for this executive team.

Surfacing the true change challenge is never easy. Drawing on the medical analogy once again, a physician, even one who asks the right questions, is challenged in diagnosis by the following:

- Patients who try to diagnose themselves.
- Hypochondriacs who inflate the slightest ailment into a life-threatening disease.

- Stoic patients who don't like to "complain" or don't feel comfortable "complaining" for fear of being labeled a hypochondriac.
- Patients who simply don't tell the truth for fear of the treatment implications.

In organizations, self-diagnosis of a change situation is the most difficult to do well. Self-diagnosis of a cold is one thing, but most people would be reluctant to take the same approach with a life-threatening disease. Similarly, executives often misdiagnose the change challenge, by leaning hopefully toward an operational or strategic change, when in fact the real challenge is at the level of culture. When this happens, organizations are usually subjected to a depressing continuing cycle of downsizing, reengineering, and reorganization. The solution to this propensity for self-diagnosis is to engage outside objective views in the diagnosis process from individuals who can ask the right questions.

Patients who are hypochondriacs and those who believe the cure to be more painful than the disease are the most problematic. Organizations always have employees who continually preach "doom and gloom," obscuring the true nature of the change agenda through rumor and innuendo. Here, simple questioning and persistence in that questioning will not work. Hard, cold, indisputable facts are called for, and only those that can bring out the truth. It is difficult to argue with visible test results.

Another challenge for organizations is that many employees, for a variety of reasons, simply will not speak openly about the problems that they are facing. Stoic patients are somewhat more challenging because the doctor has to convince them that comments will not be taken as complaints but rather as valuable inputs in the diagnosis process. It's the same in organizations—messengers have to be convinced that they will not be shot!

In organizations, a diagnosis that indicates a need for deep change can be inherently threatening for executives because it often involves dealing with unpalatable truths and the likelihood that the probable cure will be very painful and may even involve unacceptable personal risks. We call these hard realities "mooses." Like moose, these ugly realities are big, dangerous, and destructive. If not dealt with, such issues ultimately wreak havoc within organizations and derail the best of plans and intentions. However, people are reluctant to "put the moose on the table" because it threatens either themselves or other employees. The "moose" for the government ministry was that managers lacked the understanding and approach necessary for fulfilling their role in managing and leading deep change initiatives. To put it bluntly, they were managing but not leading. Before they could move forward with their change initiative, they had to look at their own motivations and leadership style. Since their challenge not only encompassed operational and strategic issues, but, more important, demanded a cultural change from the organization, they had to demonstrate a changed set of behaviors themselves. The stark reality is that when cultural change is involved, either the leadership has to change or the leadership has *to be changed*.

The complexity and difficulty of change increase significantly with greater levels of depth. In part, this is because the layers accumulate as the depth in-

**Table 2.2** Change Vehicles—Different Levels of Intervention

| | |
|---|---|
| Operational | |
|     Restructure | |
|     Reengineer | Focus on efficiency |
|     Downsize | |
| Strategic | |
|     Improve business planning | |
|     Restructure product portfolio | Focus on effectiveness |
|     Realign facilities/processes | |
| Cultural | |
|     Change leadership | |
|     Change vision and values | Focus on attitudes/beliefs |
|     Change performance drivers | |
| Paradigm | |
|     Redefine the business | |
|     Change definition of success | Focus on survival |

creases. For example, cultural transformation almost inevitably requires elements of both strategic and operational change. This means a noticeable rise in the challenge—and in the failure rate—when the change involves either culture or paradigm shift. We attribute this increased degree of difficulty to the fact that at these levels, there are personal consequences for all involved that usually generate a substantially higher level of resistance, unless the process is exceptionally well led.

Table 2.2 provides some appropriate tools and approaches for each level of change. Reengineering, restructuring, and downsizing are relatively shallow approaches that, by themselves, will not bring about deeper levels of change. At the deepest level, a complete redefinition of the business model, as well as of success, will be required that will almost certainly involve behavior change and a completely new strategy.

In addition to diagnosing the depth of change, it is important to understand its breadth of impact. Does it affect the entire organization, or is it principally confined to certain groups and functions? The challenge facing executives who intend to implement a complete corporate paradigm shift is considerably different from the integration of a major acquisition or the implemention of a new technology platform (for example, an Enterprise Resource Planning System such as SAP). It is important to understand this distinction because it has implications for who should be involved, the resources required, and how the process should be led.

Two other key elements need to be assessed during an initial diagnosis. First, the stakeholders in the change need to be identified. How will they be affected? What will be their likely response? In many ways, this is analogous to a market segmentation analysis. For example, although certain types of changes, such as a greater degree of involvement or cross-skilling, may be received positively by many rank and file employees, supervisors may feel threatened *and unions may raise hell.* Other changes, such as cost reduction, may be great for shareholders in the short term but have negative consequences for customers.

**Table 2.3** Force-Field Analysis

|  | External Forces | Internal Forces |
|---|---|---|
| Driving Forces | • Customer demand<br>• Competition | • Profitability<br>• Low morale |
| Restraining Forces | • Distributor inertia<br>• Regulations | • Passive resistance<br>• Resources |

This understanding can then lead to insight into the probable balance of power at the outset of the process. Does a coalition exist that is likely to be able to drive change to a successful conclusion? Or are there substantial opposing forces that must be neutralized lest they defeat the entire process? We call this a *force-field analysis*, a simple example of which is shown in table 2.3.[1]

## 2. Early Development of Shared Understanding

Shared understanding is a necessary antecedent condition for initiating change. At a minimum, key members of the executive team need to have the same understanding of the change challenge. Beyond this, however, these same people must also be on the proverbial same page with respect to other critical elements of the change initiative. The questions remain, however: Shared understanding of what? And among whom?

Before answering these questions, it is worth stepping back to review the importance of shared understanding as a concept, particularly at the executive level. Of relevance to implementing strategic change is an accumulating body of knowledge in the strategic management area centered around top executives and their effects on organizations. The roots of this can be traced to one of the earliest influential writers on management, Chester Barnard,[2] whose work was built upon most recently by Donald Hambrick and Phyllis Mason, who maintain that "the performance of an organization is ultimately a reflection of its top managers."[3] This has never been more true than in the context that is driving organization change.

### The Importance of Shared Understanding

Research in this field has established numerous significant relationships between executive characteristics and organizational outcomes, such as strategic choices and performance.[4] In consequence of the diversity of experiences and values that executives possess, it is reasonable to infer that unless there is a well-defined strategy-making process to bring executives to a clear focus, there will be a considerable divergence of opinion on what really matters in the future. Hambrick, a leading researcher into the behavior of executive teams, noted:

> In the face of the complex, multitudinous, and ambiguous information that typifies the top management task, no two strategists will identify the same array of

options for the firm. They will rarely prefer the same options. If by remote chance, they were to pick the same major options, they almost certainly would not implement them identically.[5]

We believe that this is a particularly important observation with great significance for organization change, especially in the proactive or anticipatory mode, because one of the problems here is the inability of executives to agree on what changes are necessary, if indeed they can agree that change is required at all.

Beyond the executive team, however, lies the issue of creating shared understanding across the organization. How can the required alignment and understanding be achieved, especially if the news is not good? CN's Paul Tellier noted the following about the massive change he undertook:

> Even when the organization didn't like the message I had to communicate (in this case, major downsizing and realignment of resources), it was critical that everyone throughout the organization understood that we had no choice and that the future of CN was at stake.

Several notable academics[6] have suggested that alignment can be achieved through a hierarchy of integrative mechanisms and structures. They do not offer any views, however, as to how these mechanisms and structures "work their magic." It is possible that these mechanisms and structures work because they create, facilitate, and direct the kinds of understandings among the different parts of the organization in a way that leads to integration at a different level, an interpretive one. Thus, alignment might be not so much the result of a structure, but rather an outcome of a process whereby *shared understanding* is created.

### Shared Understanding of What?

If shared understanding is a necessary antecedent condition for initiating change, the next logical consideration is what you want everyone to understand. Clearly, recent corporate history has proved that it is not sufficient merely to have a shared understanding of some future vision for the organization. In the 1990s, extensive corporate-visioning exercises resulted in many wonderful declarative statements by executive teams, but these statements were followed by little in terms of realization of the visions. It appears to be relatively easy to create *intellectual acceptance* of an inspirational future state, but it is far more difficult to create a realistic *operational commitment*. A growing body of evidence suggests that, for organizational change to be effective, shared understanding is necessary across a broader array of organizational functions and processes.

As a case in point, the concept of shared understanding and its effects on organizational success have been studied in the context of implementing information systems. Research into the development of shared understanding between information systems and line executives confirmed four distinct categories as relevant in that particular context.[7]

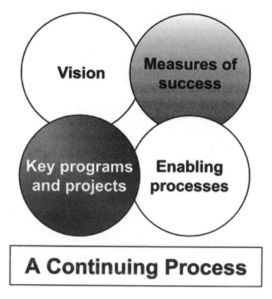

**Figure 2.2** Four Key Elements of Shared Understanding

1. A vision for information technology.
2. Critical investments necessary for achieving that vision (i.e., doing the right things).
3. Key activities in managing those investments (i.e., doing things right).
4. Measures of performance.

Shared understanding around a vision for information technology (IT) did not by itself identify those firms that were ultimately successful in their deployment of IT within the organization. It was a shared understanding of *critical* investments and the few, *key* activities required to manage these investments that was most strongly linked to success in deploying IT strategies.[8]

What does this mean for strategic change in organizations? We extended this research to the realm of strategic management and found the following to be key elements of shared understanding within an executive team (see figure 2.2):[9]

1. Measures of progress toward, and ultimate achievement of, the organization's vision and mission.
2. What executives see as the vision for the organization's future changed state.
3. What they consider to be the key objectives and strategies for achieving that vision.
4. What actions they understand to be required to execute the strategies.

Our experience indicates that, for anticipatory organization change, measures play a role in creating shared understanding that is at least as important as vision. In crisis-driven change, there is usually little argument about the need to take action because there are clear indications, often financial, that dramatic action is required. At the initiation stage of proactive change, however, most firms do not have a compelling set of measures that establish a powerful logic for change, especially deep change. Consequently, one of the critical precursors for initiating action is lacking. This is particularly pernicious if it is the most senior and powerful executives in the firm who are the most blinkered in their views.

How, then, do executive teams create the necessary level of shared understanding to initiate change, particularly a deep, anticipatory activity? In our experience, this is one of the roles that can be played by an effective, strategic management process. To accomplish this end, strategic management has to be considered an ongoing and dynamic process, rather than a one-time annual event, and it also has to be a creative, learning activity.[10] The process, while creating a vision for the organization, must also establish a focused agenda of key initiatives that serve to guide and prioritize implementation activities.

Specific, measurable outcomes and appropriate accountabilities ensure that implementation progress is tracked and owned. The measurement process can serve several functions besides simply tracking performance and implementation of existing initiatives. Most important, if properly structured with leading indicators, the strategic measurement system can give an early warning of the impending need for a significant change in strategy.[11] The executive team can use significant changes in a number of key leading indicators as its focal point for initiating serious discussions on this topic that will lead to a shared understanding of what is required.

To bring about deep and lasting change, corporations require executives who are capable of leading by creating a compelling new vision of the future, selling that vision to their employees, and articulating the elements critical to making that vision become a reality. Thus, they must create a shared understanding of where the organization is going in the future, how the journey will unfold, and how everyone will know when they've arrived.

### Shared Understanding among Whom?

At the end of the day, in any organization, employees choose to do things—for example, adopt new attitudes or take action—or they choose not to. A great deal of academic research has focused on understanding why people change their behaviors, which is the ultimate goal of many change efforts. A landmark study by M. Fishbein and I. Azjen demonstrated the relationship among beliefs, attitudes, and changes in behavior.[12] What this work, and the work of others who have built upon it, clearly demonstrates is that progress begins with shared understanding.

Initially, shared understanding has to be created among the team leading the change initiative. However, over time this understanding must be extended, at a minimum, to all those within the organization who will be affected by the change. In addition, it is often critical to ensure that other key stakeholder groups are also "in the know" with respect to certain elements of the change initiative. These external stakeholders include the board of directors, shareholders, investment analysts, customers, and suppliers. Such parties often become key enablers of the entire change process and need to be kept informed about what needs to change and why.

If the first step in developing shared understanding is to map out *what* needs to be understood and *by whom*, the second step is to ensure that appropriate communication forums are available to facilitate discussion of the right message among the right people. These communication forums can be both formal and informal. More will be said about the specific vehicles later on in this chapter.

### 3. Enrichment of Shared Understanding

Our experience shows the importance of learning as a factor in organizational change, primarily because changes in the environment and progress of the change initiative itself can affect the change process. Henry Mintzberg, one of the leading conceptual thinkers in the strategic management field, observed that an organization starts out with an intended strategy to drive its change initiative, but along the way it must be able to incorporate emergent strategies that result from either learning or changes in the environment.[13]

Thus, change initiatives need processes that allow learning to be continually disseminated and shared across the organization and among the groups as identified above. Over time, this results in a deepening and enrichment of shared understanding, particularly among the executive team but, more important, throughout the organization as well. Returning to the book analogy for a moment, in a worst-case scenario, not only are people not on the same page, but also some of them have begun to rewrite the story. As environments change—sometimes precipitously—and the organization moves forward, new information becomes available, but it may not be equally available to everyone. Therefore, continuing clarification of what the new information means to the change process is critical. In the absence of this clarification, human beings create their own reality and version of events.

In the aftermath of the September 2001 terrorist attacks on the United States, New York City Mayor Rudy Giuliani and his constant updates for the citizens of his city stand as a shining example of how to meet the leadership challenge in the face of turbulence: communicate often, answer questions honestly even if the news is bad, and if you don't know the answer, say so!

But communication is not just a one-way delivery of a message. The double-loop learning feature of the communication vehicle is vital to bring issues to the surface, deal with them, and create an open and honest environment.[14] People don't have to like the messages, but they must understand clearly what they mean and have an opportunity to question the rationale behind and commitment to those messages.

Acklands-Grainger CEO Doug Harrison traveled across the country with his executive team within two months of launching the company's new strategic plan, and thereafter every six months, to ensure that every department head and every branch manager in the country had an opportunity to hear "from the horse's mouth" about the journey they were embarking upon. At each of the company's locations, he held a day-long meeting at a local hotel with key managers.

This kind of communication had never happened before in the history of the company, and these meetings alone signaled a new order of things. Harrison had multiple agendas for every meeting. The first was to communicate the change challenge in specific terms: to discuss the vision and articulate the key activities that were under way to move the company toward fulfillment of that vision. The second was to provide an opportunity for these key managers to discuss with the executive team, and among themselves, any questions or concerns they had with the journey as it had been laid out. The large-group didactic session was followed by smaller group discussions. Each small group was asked to discuss and then report on the following:

- What they liked about the proposed direction and game plan.
- Concerns they had with either of the above.
- Perceived barriers to implementation.
- Specific suggestions for addressing concerns and/or barriers.

These smaller-group discussions are an integral piece of the learning process because they provide the vehicle for double-loop learning to occur and they make the organization aware of and partially responsible for addressing concerns or barriers to implementation. They also served the third agenda item for these sessions: namely, to give the executive team an opportunity to clarify any questions and address any concerns in an open forum. Fourth, and finally, the session served as a venue for the executive team to demonstrate its commitment to the change journey.

In order to continue to enrich shared understanding, organizations need a continuing review process, one that is designed to work in rapidly changing environments. One part of this process is a continuing assessment of changes in organization context—the overall business environment, markets, competition, and perhaps even the overall corporate strategy. A second part is a review, update, and action planning of the change plan done on a periodic basis, perhaps as frequently as every 60 days but certainly every 90 or 120 days. There is then also a need for complementary communication and learning processes, such as in-depth studies, focus groups, seminars, and change workshops. The key, however, is that throughout the organization, there must be mechanisms to maintain and enrich the shared view of the status of the change and the change-related challenges that lie ahead.

## Developing Speed

To summarize up to this point, the first three Winning Conditions mobilize an intelligent process. Correctly diagnosing the change challenge and developing and enriching shared understanding around a broad array of organizational initiatives and issues provide the necessary guidance to direct organizational energy appropriately and efficiently. A process for enriching shared understanding must be defined up front to ensure that the same sense of the change initiative is maintained throughout the organization.

The next three Winning Conditions focus on getting the change process up and running quickly over the first 100 days. First, a sense of urgency must be created, focusing directly on the diagnosis and agreed-upon intervention, then maintained throughout the change process. The next step is to develop a strategic agenda that is flexible and responsive to new information and unforeseen happenings, one that will be adjusted continually as the initiative progresses. Once the initial agenda is defined, a multilayered process is needed to deploy change-related activities in parallel and keep them moving along simultaneously, a process that must be reviewed and refined on a continuing basis.

## 4. Establishment of a Sense of Urgency

Intuitively and empirically, we know that "change before you have to" is the best approach to undertaking change. In the absence of a crisis, though, how does one imbue an organization with the sense that change must happen and happen quickly? Creation of an artificial crisis, one that cannot be backed up with data, doesn't work. In fact, it will be damaging once the organization learns, as it quickly will, that things really aren't that bad. Then, credibility goes out the window and with it go many of the levers that an executive team has to drive the change. A better approach is to do your homework and present the undeniable facts of the situation.

Before taking over the helm at CN, Tellier spent countless hours poring over industry data, analysts' reports, benchmarking studies, and anything else he could get his hands on to understand how CN stacked up against the competition. CN did not compare well with the best railroads. He interviewed board members, former executives, and even competitors. As a result, Tellier had his data-driven platform for change. As a quasi-public organization, CN was not about to go out of business, so he had to use the data to convince people that by any reasonable standard, CN was not doing well and needed to change before being forced to do so.

For CN, the historical performance metrics sufficed. In anticipatory change, however, measures related to leading indicators are more effective. These are future-oriented indicators designed to provide early warning signals of the need to change. A useful part of any scorecard is an agreed-upon, limited set of measures, probably no more than five or six, that can provide an executive team with advance warning that the organization's strategy is in danger of failing to deliver the required results in the future. We have worked with a number of executive teams to develop measures such as these,[15] and they cover the spectrum from the precise, such as trends in profit margins, through the accurate, such as customer loyalty data, to the very imprecise, such as a crude ten-point assessment of the probable future value of the organization's current strategy.

Table 2.4 summarizes the various change "platforms" that we have found useful for creating a sense of urgency given certain organizational realities—

**Table 2.4** Change Platforms That Create a Sense of Urgency

| Organizational State | Change Platform |
| --- | --- |
| *Crisis*<br>Indicators are clear and widely understood | *"We must do this; our very existence is at stake"* |
| *No crisis, poor operating performance, poor leading indicators*<br>Indicators are not necessarily clear and there is no widely understood meaning attached to those indicators | *"Change ourselves before someone else does it for us—it can only get worse"* |
| *No crisis, strong operating performance, poor leading indicators*<br>Operating metrics are clear and positive, but leading indicators suggest pending trouble in the future | Ensure success<br>*"Change before we have to—excitement, challenge, opportunity!"* |

ranging from crisis all the way to anticipatory change—when operating metrics are sound.

At BLJC, a large Canadian facilities management company, CEO Dave Glass faced the unenviable task of embarking on major strategic change in the face of strong financial performance, both historic and current. There was no crisis, and in fact, the organization had been posting strong growth and profitability figures for many years. To Glass, however, the market they had created for value-added facilities-management services had attracted some formidable competitors that had begun to gain ground. BLJC had recently lost several large contracts to one particular competitor.

The success rate on bids was a leading indicator that the executive team tracked, and a decline in this rate served as a wake-up call to the executive team, although it seemed to have little effect on the rest of the organization. Analysis of the root causes of the bid failures confirmed the team's suspicions that their current strategy was losing momentum and that significant changes were required. Glass's major challenge, however, was not in galvanizing the executive team but in galvanizing the organization as a whole. With over 1,200 employees spread across the country, he needed to get the message across, find some rallying cry, and "change the organization before he had to." He could not rely on an impending financial calamity because this was nowhere in the offing—the market was growing and so was BLJC. What he did instead was to utilize the threat of competition coming into the marketplace with the express purpose of knocking BLJC from number one status. This competitive threat became the focal point for driving change, and the spirit of competition took over from there and galvanized a core group of employees into taking action.

Anticipatory change, then, requires a major communications exercise that builds awareness and understanding of the need for change and establishes that sense of urgency. This is unlikely to develop to the same level across the organization, so part of the initial challenge is to identify those early converts and convince them of the urgency of the required change. They will then influence others to sign on to the initiative.

## 5. Creation of a Limited and Focused Strategic Agenda

One of the worst mistakes organizations make while undertaking change initiatives is to try to change everything at once. This is a recipe for chaos because it creates a high level of uncertainty, reduces the focus on the business and customers, and almost inevitably means that vital initiatives lack a critical mass of resources. It never works; instead, it almost guarantees that an organization will have to pass through a period of despair, with attendant performance declines and poor morale, before it can break through to success. This need not happen.

We examined the strategy implementation rate among a sample of twenty companies and made an interesting discovery.[16] Organizations, even large corporations, that attempted to drive more than four or five major strategic initiatives at any one time were far less successful than those that focused on a maximum of three or four. One executive we interviewed told us:

> We take the tough decisions as to which two, three, or four initiatives to do in the next six, twelve, or eighteen months. We overresource them, if anything. We drive them hard and fast, nail them down, and then move on to the next set of priorities. Does this mean we do nothing else? Not at all, but these are the ones that each executive and every employee knows have to be given our absolute top priority, even at the expense of their own pet projects.

In most organizations, in addition to leading and managing change, people still have their normal jobs to do and can easily be overwhelmed by a list of additional things. Critical in establishing this focused agenda is to understand what has to happen and in what order. Better yet is to break the change journey into a series of well-defined missions, which people can grab on to and understand.

The importance of campaigns, or missions, has been well understood by the military for many years. The ultimate goal is always to "win the war," but the war will not be won without success in the various well-timed and resourced campaigns. The goal of the Gulf War was to "free Kuwait." Two campaigns, two discrete sets of activities, were critical to success—Desert Shield and Desert Storm. Desert Shield was focused on preventing any further aggression, gaining control of the airspace over the Gulf States, and paving the way for invasion. Desert Storm concerned mobilizing of ground forces, taking strategic locations, and ultimately liberating Kuwait—all of which were accomplished in a mere 100 hours. Without Desert Shield, Desert Storm might not have been successful at all. At the very least, it would have taken far longer and been successful at far greater cost.

Thus, what is needed from the up-front planning activity is a focused agenda for change, that provides the following:

- A sense of vision that embodies desired outcomes.
- A clear statement of the discrete change campaigns, with associated time frames.
- Clear, unambiguous objectives that capture the essence of the campaigns.
- A statement of the three or four "make-or-break" initiatives inherent in the change.
- A set of tactical action plans for initial deployment, with appropriate accountabilities.

## 6. Rapid, Strategic Decision Making and Deployment

To execute change rapidly within any given campaign, a number of things have to happen in parallel. One of the problems with approaches to change in many organizations, however, is that these things happen in a linear fashion—communication of the need for change, followed by a period of further study, followed by substantive shifts in resource allocation, etc. To make change happen quickly, these same activities need to happen in parallel. Four parallel streams (see figure 2.3) must be initiated, and if thought out carefully, they enable organizations to gain traction and generate speed right from the start:

- Executive actions, sometimes purely symbolic, are required to create a climate of acceptance for the new direction and demonstrate leadership.
- Multiple, continuing communication activities are aimed at creating

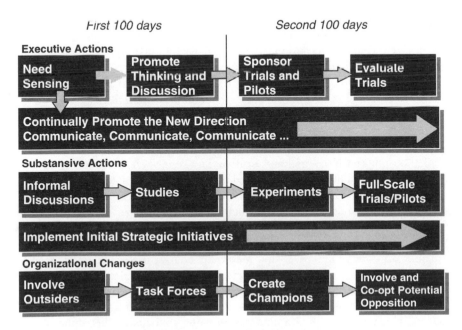

**Figure 2.3** Parallel Deployment of Change Initiatives

awareness and understanding, reinforcing the change initiative, and building commitment.

- Substantive actions are aimed at clarifying and developing the new strategic direction, including experiments and pilots. When there is no debate
  about the changes required, the implementation of initial strategic activities puts some quick "runs on the board" and builds confidence through
  demonstrating tangible results.
- Organizational changes are intended to put in place the enabling processes
  that facilitate new business approaches and to create the required alignment and cooperation within the organization.

Taking leadership first, the challenge in this respect is for executives themselves to move beyond demonstrating *intellectual commitment* and demonstrate
*operational commitment*. In tough times, taking a salary cut and reducing or
eliminating executive perquisites, such as business-class travel, are examples of
ways to focus the attention of the organization on the seriousness of the initiative. If a culture of teamwork is the desired change, then there is no better place
to start than with the executive team itself, with explicit and visible demonstrations of not just new attitudes, but also new behaviors. Changing the corporate
logo or slogan can send out powerful signals, and bringing in outsiders who can
challenge the prevailing corporate thinking and demonstrate the new behaviors
is also valuable. The organization will be watching for changes in executive
behaviors because actions speak far louder than words.

Second, it is impossible to overstate the importance of reinforcing these signaling acts through continuing communication and learning activities. From the
discussion of shared understanding, we learned what needs to be communicated
and to whom. Critical to the effectiveness of the communication, however, is the
richness of the communication medium: its capacity to change the mental models of individuals within a prescribed time frame. Researchers in organizational
learning describe the importance of the communication medium as it relates to
the development of shared understanding: "Communication media differ in their
ability to facilitate understanding. Media can be characterized as high or low in
"richness" based on their capacity to facilitate shared meaning. A rich medium
facilitates insight and rapid understanding."[17]

At the high end of the richness scale is face-to-face communication, and at
the low end is unaddressed written communication. Multiple communication
media can be utilized, but face-to-face is critical for the development and enrichment of shared understanding. This activity is essential to the success of the
change and ongoing coordination. Executives can be the all-important messengers, but the communication campaign needs full-time attention.

Third, substantive initiatives that materially change the organization need to
be implemented; for example, new products and services or changes to the operations infrastructure. At BLJC, Glass communicated the need to deal differently
with supply chain partners. Within days, he had made substantive changes to
the organization by creating a new business unit to focus on the supply side of
the business and by promoting one of his general managers to run it. In this

case, Glass and his team had studied the supply chain opportunity before making the announcement. What he didn't do, however, was dither over what the next steps should be; he took decisive action while the message was still fresh in the organization's eyes.

Some substantive decisions will require little study and can be implemented almost immediately. Others, however, will require validation and clarification, initially through the use of experiments and pilots. Studies and experiments are necessary to amplify understanding of the need for change, to build awareness, and to legitimize viewpoints. Particularly in an anticipatory change mode, these activities can be used to minimize risk through clarifying and developing the new strategic direction. In crisis or reactive situations, though, it is unlikely that there will be time available to extensively pilot new approaches.

Fourth, these substantive initiatives must be complemented by organizational changes. These are usually changes in organization structure and processes. For example, it may be appropriate to break down the "silos" or "chimneys" that limit cooperation and communication across the organization. Changes in policies, education, and training activities, as well as performance evaluation, recognition, and rewards, are important areas that need to be aligned with substantive change initiatives. For example, if the proposed change requires significantly different sales behavior, then it is likely that sales training will be required, as well as changes to the sales force compensation plan.

There is also an opportunity to bring in outsiders to demonstrate desired behaviors and to "seed" the organization with new ways of thinking. Such individuals not only signal that there are new and different ways of thinking, but they can also quickly transfer critical knowledge and skills early on in the change process. For example, at Acklands-Grainger, the new position of vice-president of logistics was created and staffed within the first ninety days of the company's new strategic plan. This signaled the importance of this area to all employees and also brought new ideas into the company. However, change agents or accelerators need not be long-term employees; it may, in fact, be desirable to portray them as temporary employees so they don't become perceived as "replacement players."

## Building Critical Mass

The first 100 days generate speed to move the strategic agenda along. To return to our space analogy, these Winning Conditions saw the guidance system put in place, the fuel ignited, and liftoff accomplished. Over the second 100 days, organizations must be concerned with developing a critical mass of employees. The final elements of our framework address how to achieve this critical mass by mobilizing those who will work most effectively toward the change objectives and by neutralizing those whose actions would retard progress. Executive leadership is one of the keys to ensuring that employees get on board and stay committed.

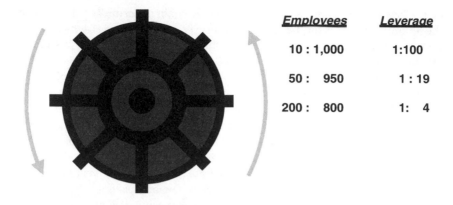

| Employees | Leverage |
|-----------|----------|
| 10 : 1,000 | 1:100 |
| 50 :  950 | 1 : 19 |
| 200 :  800 | 1:  4 |

**Leverage and momentum are built more rapidly when a critical mass of employees are mobilized across the organization**

**Figure 2.4** The Strategic Change Flywheel

## 7. A Human Flywheel of Commitment

In most organizations, relatively few employees are willing to engage in early-stage change activities, even when the change is perceived to be positive, or at least nonthreatening. Nevertheless, there are always a few "gung ho" true believers to be found. We call this the "20-70-10" phenomenon and have observed it in many of the organizations we've studied and worked with. It works this way: approximately 20 percent of employees can initially be motivated to become active in driving change; about 70 percent will remain neutral, "sitting on the fence" to see what transpires; and roughly 10 percent will actively, and possibly even vocally, oppose the new direction.

Too often, organizations focus on the 10 percent, the "saboteurs," to try to win them over, but in reality this will never occur. What happens in the meantime is that the 20 percent, the "true believers," are never leveraged to convert the 70 percent, the "fence-sitters," away from the "dark side." This 20-70-10 principle is particularly significant in large organizations, as figure 2.4 demonstrates. For example, in an organization of one thousand employees, if the executive team of perhaps ten people attempts to drive change from the center for an extended period, the leverage ratio is 1:100. In addition, the ten committed leaders are heavily outnumbered by maybe one hundred employees, some at quite senior levels, who will be opposing the change. Basic laws of mechanics suggest that momentum will be generated only slowly in such circumstances, if at all.

However, if the core team rapidly gains the active support of, say, forty out of fifty employees in middle management and senior supervisory positions, the leverage ratio decreases to 1:20. The momentum of the activity will build much more rapidly than in the first case. Building on this commitment, if the leadership team can quickly reach out into the broader organization and identify and engage a further one hundred and fifty employees in the initiative, the leverage ratio decreases to 1:5. Equally important, active supporters for the new direction now outnumber those opposed by a ratio of 2:1. In this situation, the executive team is likely to have established the critical mass and unstoppable momentum required to fulfill the vision for change.

Regardless of the nature of the change initiative, even if the situation is tough and overwhelmingly negative, there will always be those employees who are willing to give it the old college try if for no reason other than that action is better than inaction. Thus, the leadership challenges related to the 20-70-10 principle are:

- Identifying the 20 percent and engaging them as agents of change to convert the 70 percent away from the "dark side."
- Understanding the 70 percent and not treating them as a homogeneous group.
- Dealing with the 10 percent who will never accept the change and will actively oppose it.

### Identifying the 20 Percent

The true believers are usually easy to find. They are the individuals who volunteer to be part of undertakings related to early change. They are vocal supporters within small groups. They may have indicated frustration with the current state of affairs. In short, they are the people who, both formally and informally, will support and reinforce the change efforts. One looks for these people across all levels of the organization and across all positions. As an example of the importance of not being "blinded by position," in one organization we studied, a key influencer was a twenty-year veteran of the firm who just happened to be the company's receptionist. She was instrumental by reinforcing, informally and in an ongoing fashion, the importance of the change effort under way, answering key questions about progress to date, and generally ensuring that rumors were factual.

Beyond identifying the 20 percent, it is important to help these employees understand their roles in the change effort—as champions, messengers, trusted "go-to" people, and sounding boards. Any or all of these roles may be embodied in one individual, or an organization can choose to designate certain individuals for certain roles. As shown in table 2.5, there are many approaches that can be used to involve all types of employees in early-stage change activities. There are usually only a limited number of potential roles for champions of specific initiatives. However, employees can be broadly engaged in change as members of task forces or benchmarking teams, as well as in continuous improvement and proposal (suggestion) schemes in which they may be encouraged to implement their

**Table 2.5** Ways to Involve Employees in Change

- As champions for specific initiatives
- In task forces or project teams
- In training activities
- In feedback sessions or focus groups
- In benchmarking activities
- In continuous improvement or idea proposal schemes

initiatives aligned with the new direction. At a minimum, many employees can be engaged through the commencement of a two-way dialogue about what's required through participation in focus groups and feedback sessions.

### Understanding the 70 Percent

If speed and momentum are to be built rapidly, fence-sitting has to be identified and addressed early. We use this term, rather than "resisting," to clearly differentiate between those who resist for valid reasons and will eventually come onside, and the approximately 10 percent who resist for strongly personal or invalid reasons and will never come onside.

It is important to understand the root causes of fence-sitting, and these can be many. Far from feeling threatened by change, we find that most employees welcome it, and their apparent resistance stems from poor change practices. Common failings in this respect are shown in table 2.6. Lack of awareness and understanding is a frequent cause. Lack of alignment between change, performance evaluation, and rewards is also a cause of considerable fence-sitting. New behaviors are demanded of employees, but recognition and rewards remain aligned with the old way of doing things. Similarly, failure to train employees adequately can result in perceived resistance, as one company found when it introduced personal computers throughout its operations. Utilization remained low until executives became painfully aware that the training budget for the implementation had been slashed by 75 percent as a cost-saving measure. Employees simply lacked the skills to use the new technology.

Paradoxically, resistance also arises because of well-intended initiatives that are implemented poorly. A major distribution company found that its branch

**Table 2.6** Common Reasons for Perceived Resistance

- Lack of information or awareness about the need for change
- Lack of involvement in the change efforts
- Lack of leadership commitment to "stay the course"
  — Flavor-of-the-month phenomenon
- Outdated rewards and recognition
  — Reward old behaviors
  — Penalize innovators
- Lack of "proof" that the change will result in positive outcomes

managers were circumventing a new, centralized product-sourcing approach. At first, executives thought that managers were resisting the change. However, once they investigated, they found that the new process lacked adequate resources to provide the branches with a turnaround time that met customer needs. Rather than lose business, the managers had returned to the old model of branch sourcing.

There is little doubt that some employees are threatened by change. There are those who feel that they cannot change in the ways demanded or who perceive that their personal status and authority will be undermined by the proposed changes. If unions directly oppose organizational change, which they do for a variety of reasons, it usually stems from a genuine desire to protect the interests of their members. There are also those who do not feel personally threatened but genuinely prefer the old way of doing things. These are the employees who should be listened to because they may see elements of the past that can be incorporated in, and strengthen, future approaches.

We have come to understand that much of what executives characterize as resistance is, in fact, a simple lack of awareness and understanding that has its roots in inadequate communication. If employees don't know what's expected of them, they are unlikely to perform appropriately. We were continually surprised in the course of our research by the continuing failure of leadership teams to communicate change to supervisors and wage-roll employees.

Some executives find that resistance can be significantly reduced by emphasizing their personal commitment and determination to make change happen and their unwillingness to tolerate opposition. At Acklands-Grainger, CEO Harrison ended every session in the same way: with a promise to keep the lines of communication open and with a clear and unambiguous message:

> We are embarking on a course of action to which many of us in the company are committed. However, we recognize that not everyone will be able to agree with this initiative, and if that is the case, I respect your decision. However, recognize that by taking such a decision, you have effectively decided to leave the company, and if that is the case, we will provide you with appropriate support. However, do not think that you can fight the direction to which we are now committed. We shall be relentless . . . and we need everyone's support in making it happen.

You could hear a pin drop at this time in the meetings, but the point had been made. This statement and the consistency of this closing message across multiple sessions spread quickly throughout the company. The fact that he backed up this message with several key "self-selected" resignations vaulted the phrase "we shall be relentless" to legendary status and caused it to reverberate throughout the company. With these words, Harrison was indicating his respect for individual decisions not to go along with this strategy but at the same time indicating his determination not to put up with opposition. In fact, in the weeks following this speech, several managers and supervisors voluntarily resigned or asked to return to salaried staff positions.

## 8. Identification and Management of Sources of Resistance

As important as it is to build a human flywheel to create momentum for change, it is just as important to address real resistance that creates drag on the process. The true resisters are, in fact, saboteurs who might constitute up to 10 percent of the employee population. Have you ever stopped to consider how much wasted effort is spent by those change-driven employees who try to convert the relatively small number who ardently oppose the change? At the limit, the ultimate outcome may be the failure of the overall change initiative. Effectively, every employee who resists change neutralizes the impact of one employee who promotes it. Therefore, for every resistant employee that can be dealt with, an additional person is freed up to move the process forward.

It is not always apparent at the beginning of a new initiative which employees are opposed to the change. Many of them will not declare themselves openly. And it is usually not appropriate to conduct a witch-hunt to ferret out these potential problem individuals. So what's left? What's left is to provide ample opportunity for employees to engage and believe in the change that's being undertaken.

Of course, there are many different ways to sabotage organizational change, ranging from a passive, wait-it-out approach to deliberate action. Vocal opposition is the easiest to address because the sources can be easily identified. The most difficult and most debilitating is passive noncompliance: employees voice their agreement to change, but then nothing actually happens. Communications don't get passed on to employees. Initiatives languish and lose momentum. Some changes do get implemented, but poorly, so as to create expressions of discontent.

Organizations must purposefully encourage employees to fully engage in the new reality. At the same time, tough decisions have to be made regarding those who don't or won't engage. At some point, one is either for or against a change. If you're not on board the train, you can't continue to hold up its departure and progress. Failure to deal adequately with opposition has derailed more than a few major change efforts.

## 9. Follow-through on Changing Organizational Enablers

There are many existing systems, processes, and structures that pose potential barriers to the change process because they are aligned with the past, not the future. On a more positive note, changes in these factors can facilitate new business approaches and create the required alignment and cooperation within the organization for successful implementation. These organizational changes are often overlooked altogether in the change process or else are made too late to undo the harm done by not addressing them early enough.

As an example of this. When firms were making initial forays into the world of e-business, these initiatives were often housed in the wrong part of the organization. As a case in point, there's a good reason why Amazon.com got such a jump on the established booksellers such as Barnes & Noble. Leaving the e-business group inside the existing operation meant that there was much to lose with respect to changes in the existing and proven business model and customary ways of doing things. At Barnes and Noble, e-business languished for so long before the unit was spun outside the company that it was too late to recapture lost ground; Amazon had already re-created itself to catch the next wave.

The key organizational enablers that facilitate change are as follows:

- *Organization structure*, which influences how different parts of the organization cooperate and communicate, how resources are allocated, and how work is accomplished.
- *Policies*, which directly influence the behavior of people in specific situations, how resources are made available, and the degree of risk employees are willing to take in specific situations.
- *Information dissemination and communication*, which are critical determinants of how awareness and understanding of the need for change are disseminated.
- *Training and development*, which determine the degree of understanding people have of what's expected of them and how effectively they can respond.
- *Performance evaluation, recognition, and reward*, both formal and informal, which directly influence the behavior of individuals and teams.

It may take some time to address these organizational enablers; however, there are two items that can be addressed immediately to change behavior: performance measures and the corresponding recognition and rewards. One of the classic articles in the management literature is "On the Folly of Rewarding A while Hoping for B."[18] The title says it all. There's no doubt that many change initiatives fail because recognition and rewards are misaligned with the new direction. In fact, they are so badly misaligned in some organizations that employees who are early to embrace the new direction may be penalized by the old systems, formal and informal. Consequently, if opponents to a new direction have the opportunity to do so, they will use an existing reward system to penalize the innovators.

Thus, it is imperative early on in a new change initiative to realign performance measures, as well as recognition and rewards, with the new direction. Initially, it's likely that informal recognition and rewards will be put in place to reinforce and reward the innovators. Then, as quickly as possible, the formal systems should be realigned as well. Chapter 5 provides numerous examples of how creative some companies have been in these respects.

## 10. Demonstrated Leadership Commitment

Appropriate leadership styles are required for successful change. Executives who fail in this regard often do so because they neither recognize what leadership approach is appropriate nor understand the key tasks involved in each. Daniel Goleman, the author of *Emotional Intelligence*, has identified six leadership styles, several of which are appropriate for different change situations.[19] Goleman considers *coercive* leadership ("do what I tell you") to be appropriate for a crisis or for launching a turnaround. He perceives *authoritative* leadership ("come with me") to be appropriate for mobilizing people toward a new vision. *Pacesetting* ("do as I do now") is the right style to get quick results from a highly motivated and competent team, and a *democratic* style ("what do you think?") is recommended to obtain consensus from employees.

A pacesetting or democratic style of leadership appears to be most appropriate for anticipatory change that requires a determined effort to build awareness and understanding of the need for change, create a sense of urgency and momentum, and secure some quick wins to demonstrate real progress. Although, even in this type of situation, there will be times when the leader needs to be authoritative if inertia or lack of commitment is a problem, particularly at the outset.

We disagree with Goleman with respect to the leadership style for crisis or turnaround. In our experience, coercive leaders never implement sustainable change. They may get short-term results, but at what cost to human capital? The longer-term consequences are frequently disastrous. Rather, we believe an authoritative style is more appropriate in the early stages of crisis-driven change when there is a need for rapid development of a highly focused game plan, some fast, tough decisions, and effective communication about the real state of the organization. However, once the immediate crisis is past, a pacesetting style might be more appropriate. Whatever the nature of the change, it is imperative that the executive team demonstrates relentless commitment to new behaviors and values appropriate to the future direction, particularly if change is at the cultural or paradigm level.

In a similar vein, Michael Beer has identified a number of the key attributes of change leaders, most recently in his book coauthored with Nitin Nohria, *Breaking the Code of Change*. Beer and Nohria propose a blended theory of change leadership that indicates a need for executives to have insight into when to be more directive and when it's appropriate to be more consultative. They characterize *Theory E* as a top-down, programmatic change approach adopted with the intent to maximize economic value. They contrast this with *Theory O*, which is participative and emergent, intended to develop organization capabilities. Their conclusion is that successful change initiatives require both approaches, sometimes in combination and occasionally sequentially, usually with E followed by O.[20]

What is also required is continuing reinforcement of the importance of the required change. It's relatively easy to understand the change challenge and commit to it at the beginning of the change process. And then reality hits: today's customers still need to be served and served well while the change is happening. The organization must continue to operate throughout the change process. In addition, change initiatives don't always go right. CEO Harrison of Acklands-Grainger commented:

> At the start of the process, I was amazed because everyone said that they wanted change. But when the depth and breadth of what was required became apparent,

many employees drew back. At that time, they weren't prepared to make the personal changes in behavior that were demanded of us.

The best of intentions and the "warm and fuzzy" feelings related to embarking on the change challenge can quickly dissipate in the face of the day-to-day reality. Thus, the reinforcement challenge is twofold. The first aspect is maintaining "top of mind" awareness of the change challenge and what is required to make it happen. The second is reinforcing senior management's commitment to making change happen.

"Top of mind" awareness means that the messages regarding change must stand out among the glut of information that pervades organizations. E-mail messages just don't cut it. The question for organizations is how to create messages that stand out—the medium is as important as the message and has tremendous signaling implications. This is where personal leadership and creativity come in. Larry Weinbach, CEO of Unisys, commented:

> On my first day on the job I went on syndicated business television and publicly committed to us paying back within twelve months $1 billion of the $2.8 billion in debt that we had outstanding. I then gave out the same message on our own internal television. After that, I toured the country, and personally delivered the message to over 20,000 employees during the next month.

Personal leadership from the top is essential. However, change does not always start at the top. Executives and managers in the middle and upper-middle echelons of the organization can often be the stimulus for change, with or without the direct support of the CEO. And the broader reality is that for deep change to be successful, leadership must ultimately be found at all levels of the organization. It's only when rank-and-file employees start to take ownership of change, and provide leadership in their own work environments, that it really starts to happen.

## Creating, Optimizing, and Consolidating the Winning Conditions

Each of these ten Winning Conditions is central to success in driving organizational change. Some create guidance, others generate speed, while still others build critical mass. Some are accomplished over finite periods, and others must be nurtured and refined throughout the change initiative. Although each condition is straightforward in and of itself, the correct combination creates unstoppable and self-perpetuating momentum for the change effort. So the next question is, How do these Winning Conditions need to be combined? What needs to happen and when? The answers to these questions are the focus of the next two chapters, which discuss the processes and levers through which the Winning Conditions are created and managed.

# 3

## Translating Change into Action

There is general agreement among successful change leaders and scholars that a process is required to make everyone recognize the need for change and that this process must be tightly linked to one in which the plan to drive that change can be mapped out and managed. Organizations that are successful in driving change fast have such a process—strategic planning. It is not the traditional, long-term, financially driven process to which far too many organizations continue to be wedded. In these companies, strategic planning is a creative process, covers the entire future time spectrum, focuses on what's critical, and ultimately results in a game plan for change.

For the last thirty years, the predominant mechanism for defining an organization's future has been strategic planning. Initially hailed as being essential for charting an organization's direction, the strategic planning theme now has many variations, not all of which have been, or are even capable of, delivering on the original promise. In particular, most strategic planning processes are simply too slow to function effectively in today's rapidly changing business environment. Taking up to twelve months, or even longer, to carry out, by the time the plan is complete, it's out of date! Contrast this, though, with a comment by Gregory J. Owens, CEO of Manugistics, the world leader in supplying logistics software:

> The first thing we did in the first thirty days I was here, we wrote a strategic plan for the company. And the strategic plan was not for me, it was for the company because this was an organization that was confused about their place and where they stood in the market and their strategy of going forward.

Owens's statement poses a fundamental question for all organizations. How can a process be created that is capable of serving the goals of the organization by *rapidly* defining new directions and, at the same time, establishing the winning conditions to get there? Thank heavens for Canada that Lucien Bouchard never met Gregory J. Owens!

In our research, and for the companies we work with, we asked CEOs and their executive teams how they determine whether or not strategic planning delivers value to the organization. Value in this case is defined two ways: first, as a reasonable return on the time and energy invested in the activity; and second, as delivering some form of desired organizational outcomes—financial and market performance, customer and employee satisfaction, and most important, change. Sam Hayes, CEO of Canada Steamships Lines, one of the world's most successful shipping companies, commented on the value of strategic planning to his corporation:

> The strategic planning process takes time and effort to do; however, its value is high . . . as team development of strategy builds consensus and support for the strategy and increases the chances of success in its execution . . . and boiling down strategic alternatives as a group creates peer pressure to focus on that which is most important and not waste time at the low-value fringes . . . the resulting strategic plan is more intelligent because of the group dynamics.

Many of the CEOs we've worked with and interviewed draw much the same conclusions as Hayes does when discussing strategic planning. Their views are that it creates value for their organizations by:

- *Creating focus* through developing shared understanding of the critical, make-or-break issues and opportunities for the organization and enabling tough choices and decisions to be made about future direction.
- *Creating stretch* through the establishment of challenging, yet attainable, objectives and goals.
- *Obtaining leverage* from the effective utilization of resources, both internal and external.
- *Establishing differentiation*, the basis for a sustainable competitive advantage, by developing a unique positioning for the firm, as well as its products and services.
- *Creating alignment* (a shared sense of purpose) among different organizational units and executives to eliminate silos or chimneys, which tend to increase as the organization grows.
- *Building momentum*, as committed employees and other key stakeholders take action and move forward.

These points must sound familiar by now, because they use terms and concepts similar to those reflected in the Winning Conditions. "Valuable" strategic planning is not only about making choices and putting into motion activities that ensure effective and efficient efforts for executing on those choices, it is, in fact, the leadership process in organizations that enables executives to spearhead and manage organizational changes. But it must be used properly, and failure to do this is the source of much criticism. Good, valuable strategic planning is not a one-time event; rather, it is a continuous process. The organization and its environment should be under continuing review to enable fine-tuning and adaptation of the small number of carefully selected strategic initiatives under way at any particular time.

Extracting this value from the strategic planning processes is challenging for many organizations. This is partly because neither the purpose of strategic planning nor the elements that are critical to its timely and effective execution are well understood. These elements are the subject of this chapter. Before launching into our discussion of just what a value-adding strategic planning process looks like, it is instructive to sift through and examine some of the most common approaches to strategic planning that have been put forth by both scholars and practitioners. There is a plethora of strategic planning approaches and schools of thought, and our intent here is to highlight their major contributions to the understanding of effective strategic planning.

## A Brief History of Strategic Planning

Over the last seventy years, the "planning" school of business leadership has become increasingly influential. With organizations becoming larger and more complex, and the environment becoming more uncertain, business leaders have sought new tools and techniques to aid them in developing winning strategies for the future. The heart of this process has always been strategic planning. Differentiated from operational planning, this process been used in various ways to invent the future of an organization. Some approaches have been predominantly financial in nature, some highly quantitative, and others have offered a more balanced approach, taking into account both qualitative and quantitative aspects of strategy. However, two problems have arisen. First, many executives do not have a sound understanding of what strategy involves resulting in processes that are often about everything, rather than what's strategic. Second, along the way, the process has become increasingly elaborate and time consuming, resulting in strategy making that is slow and ponderous rather than nimble and responsive.

Many different approaches to strategy making have recently been proposed. In fact, "guru" status has been accorded to the authors of some of the more well known and highly promoted approaches. The classical school of thought, which include authorities such as Igor Ansoff and Peter Lorange, put heavy emphasis on the analytical process.[1] The central tenet of their approach was a rigorously analytical process, and if it was followed carefully and to the letter, then the answers that managers required would become self-evident. Henry Mintzberg, a perennial thorn in the side of these classic strategic planning devotees, has roundly criticized this approach because of its fatal flaw—the failure to recognize that analysis is not synthesis.[2] Mintzberg points out that synthesis is at the heart of strategy; it is the ability to creatively pull together a variety of diverse sets of information and draw insightful conclusions to guide decision making and resource allocation. In-depth analysis alone cannot provide "the" answers and has rarely resulted in outstanding strategies. In his opinion, since the 1980s, despite the resources devoted to it, strategic planning has lost its way and failed to live up to the promises of the "gurus."

More recently, Michael Porter has viewed the strategy process as being driven by an understanding of competitive forces, and he has developed a framework that creates strategy through detailed industry and competitive analysis.[3] By contrast, Gary Hamel and C. K. Prahalad have proposed a competency-based approach to strategy formulation in which the core competencies of the organization are central to determining its future direction and growth.[4] These and other similar approaches have contributed to our understanding of the issues to be discussed in the context of strategic thinking. However, all have focused primarily on the analytical aspect of strategy making and in some cases require substantial amounts of data collection and analysis over an extended period of time.

Other writers have focused on the nature of the process itself. Arie De Geus has proposed that the essence of strategy making is learning[5] and that the value of planning lies not so much in the output as in the process itself and the shared understanding created among participants. If a dialogue can be generated and sustained among executives with different experiences and perspectives, then a powerful sense of shared understanding can emerge. This theme has been taken up by Peter Senge, who views dialogue as the vehicle for a leadership team to learn and think creatively together without reverting to a sterile debate based upon established positions, beliefs, and assumptions.[6]

More recently, Hamel has proposed that strategy is a revolutionary process for periodically and fundamentally rethinking the corporation and its businesses.[7] In our view, strategy is all about action, and the process is really about providing a framework and a context for actions that change the organization.[8]

All of these approaches contain valuable insights, but how can practitioners faced with the challenge of implementing change make good use of them? It is clear that analysis is necessary because without analytical frameworks, there is limited opportunity to make sense of the vast amount of information available to organizations—market, competitive, financial, organizational, and operational. Of course, these frameworks don't provide the answers; rather, they are a starting point for synthesis, action, and further discussion.

This is Mintzberg's point. He maintains, and we agree wholeheartedly, that exhaustive analysis is not a formula for making strategy. He goes so far as to say that even the term "strategic planning" is an oxymoron, because analysis is not synthesis and the term "planning" implies only analysis. On this point, we differ. "Planning" can be a balanced blend of analysis and synthesis, and we have worked with many organizations that view "strategic planning" in this way.

The fact remains that, in many organizations, strategic planning continues to be carried out, but it has lost its way. There is no doubt that the return on investment in strategic planning is often dismal. Even without the large planning staffs that characterized the process in the 1970s and 1980s, the activity is viewed by many participants as a financially driven bureaucratic exercise that returns disproportionately little value for the effort expended. At the heart of the issue is the fact that most so-called strategic plans are not strategic at all. They may be a mixture of operational and strategic content and either overly concerned with detail and lacking a real focus on what's critical or too abstract, high-level, and generic and consequently incapable of driving change and action.[9] We have identified several specific modes of failure that may not be well understood by many executives but that can be easily remedied:

- When strategy is owned by consultants or the corporate planning group, there is no ownership for execution among line and field managers. An effective approach is to have the process led by a high-level executive, aided by a small staff and, planned by line executives and managers. Task forces can be created to carry out specific assignments.
- Long, complex, and detailed plans are never read. Rather, it is more appropriate to produce short documents that focus on critical issues, objectives, and actions.
- An extended planning process usually turns into a year-round burden on executives. A more useful process is one that is largely completed in a maximum of six or eight weeks with continuing updates and reviews throughout the remainder of the year.
- When critical issues are kept off the agenda, perhaps because senior executives perceive them as too sensitive for discussion, the credibility of the process will be undermined. Strategic planning has to identify and address the tough issues, even the "undiscussables."
- Many strategic planning processes either do not address or do not leave enough time for action planning. All plans should be firmly grounded in short-term specific actions for which employees are held accountable.

There has also been considerable discussion about the value of planning with respect to deep organizational change. Among academics, there are two distinct schools of thought. One views change as essentially a process in which *emergent* strategies are critically important because of the inherent flexibility and responsiveness provided by this approach. Wanda Orlikowski defines emergent change as the realization of new patterns of organizing in the absence of explicit prior intentions.[10] Supporters argue that this approach leads to a dynamic, rather than a static, mind-set among executives, a critical ingredient for successful change.

Planned change is the alternative approach advocated by a number of scholars, and almost universally applied by consultants in this field. Sumantra Ghoshal and Christopher Bartlett examined more than a dozen companies over a five-year period and concluded that the distinctions between success and failure were accounted for by two major factors. First, successful firms adopted a phased approach to change that focused on developing organizational capabilities in a particular sequence. Second, successful firms recognized that deep change is as much a function of individual behavior as it is of strategies, structures, and systems introduced by executives.[11]

There is little doubt that change has to allow for emergent strategies, but without some kind of initial planning that focuses and sequences activities, the process is likely to take far longer than necessary and is also likely to be a haphazard affair. In certain types of change, such as a turnaround or the integration of a new acquisition, this is almost certainly a recipe for disaster. Appropriate leadership styles are also an issue in this respect. Planned approaches are often a product of authoritative leadership, whereas emergent strategy is associated with a democratic or participative style. Remember, though, that approaches can be blended. Michael Beer and Nitin Nohria describe the best model of change leadership as one in which *Theory E* (economic, value-driven leadership), a more planned approach, is combined with *Theory O* (behavioral), a more emergent style, to produce a blended result.[12]

In summary, strategic planning cannot be a once-a-year event. It must not be solely focused on analysis, and the end goal must not be simply synthesis. The product must not be static; instead, it must be capable of adapting to environmental shifts and incorporating emergent strategies. Hence, it must be an ongoing process within an organization. It must include sufficient analysis but then push through to synthesis. But it cannot stop there because only when that synthesis is translated into concrete actions does the strategy process begin to add value to the organization. What is abundantly clear is that, to be effective, strategic planning has to result in action, action that will drive the necessary change.

## Fundamentals of Effective Strategic Planning for Change

What, then, makes for good strategic planning that can drive deep change in organizations? What is the nature of the process that can create an appropriate blend of a planned approach and emergent strategies? In the remainder of this chapter, we describe a planning approach for change that can initially be undertaken with great rapidity and that is flexible enough, through continuing review and updating, to allow for a considerable degree of emergent strategy content.

In reviewing the value parameters identified earlier, it is clear that both the process for creating the strategic plan and the content of the eventual plan itself are important, and neither one more so than the other. The *process* is important in that it provides the vehicle by which the following can be accomplished:

- Learning about the business environment, corporate capabilities, positioning, and how the firm can compete and win; exposure to new ways of thinking about old problems.
- Creating and sustaining a dialogue among stakeholders about major issues and opportunities.
- Negotiating the allocation of major resource pools among various competing interests in the organization.
- Creating an action-oriented agenda for change.

One CEO of a major public investment fund expressed his dismay that a proposed strategic planning agenda allocated so much time to discussion. Over the years, he had been frustrated with strategic planning because no real buy-in for the proposed activities was ever achieved. It eventually came out that the executive team, having had little opportunity to debate issues, paid lip service to the plan and often never believed in the choices that were made in the planning sessions. Once sufficient time was allocated for debate, however, this escape avenue was effectively closed. This example demonstrates how these aspects of the activity related to the development of shared understanding among the participants in the process. Dialogue and learning are the key components in enriching and deepening the team's understanding and commitment—not just intellectual commitment, but operational commitment as well.

The *plan* itself is important because it provides:

- An articulated sense of direction and focus, not just vague "we want to be the best" statements and laundry lists of "things" to do.
- Specific actions on major issues and opportunities and decisions on who is going to do what.
- A sense of priority and timing that can instill a feeling of urgency.
- Significant resource reallocations because the wherewithal to accomplish tasks is everyone's main concern.

A successful strategic planning approach can achieve benefits from both the process and the plan, and neither to the exclusion of the other. A wonderful plan is useless if there is no understanding and commitment to make it a reality. Conversely, all the understanding and commitment in the world won't get you very far without some idea of the specifics of who is accountable for doing what and when.

Many consultants still promote strategic planning as a long-term process. One question frequently asked by all participants in strategic planning is how far ahead the process should plan for. To this question, there is only one right answer—as far ahead as the dynamics of your industry and organization permit. For some corporations in rapidly changing environments, this may be as short as one or two years. For others with longer business cycles, the horizon may be five or even ten years. What's important is that in both cases, these long-term horizons must be brought back to short-term action time frames of 60 or 90 days. These points describe strategic planning as the process for creating the *game plan for change.*

## The Strategic Plan: The Key Role of Vision, Mission, and Objectives

Strategic planning results in a plan of some sort, one that articulates the choices that have been made, why they were made, and how they are going to become reality. It is the blueprint for taking the organization forward. It should not, however, be considered a blueprint for a brand-new building unless the organization is starting from scratch. It does not need to be redrawn every time changes are made. Rather, it is more useful to regard it as a blueprint for a renovation project. Anyone who has renovated a house, especially an older one, knows full well that the original blueprint is often modified as drywall is stripped, load-bearing walls are identified, original fireplaces are uncovered, etc. Likewise,

**Table 3.1** Generic Outline of a Strategic Plan

- Statement of vision/mission and objectives (½ page)
- Identification of major clients and markets (1 page)
- Positioning statement (½ page)
- Specific key performance indicators (½ page)
- Review of major environmental factors/trends (1 page)
- Major strategic issues, external and internal
  Strengths and weaknesses (1 page)
  Opportunities and threats (1 page)
- Strategies and action plans to achieve objectives/address strategic
  issues (1 page per issue)
- Requirements from other business units/functions (1 page)
- Summary of major programs/projects (1 page)
- Summary of anticipated human resources requirements (1 page)
- Summary of financial implications of the strategy (1 page)

a strategic plan must be flexible enough to allow adaptation and fine-tuning as new facts come to light or something new develops.

The plan itself is not usually a long document, possibly ten or twelve double-spaced pages. It may, in fact, be possible to capture it on fifteen to twenty PowerPoint slides. A typical outline is shown in table 3.1.

An extensive lexicon of strategic planning terminology has developed over the years: vision, mission, objectives, strategies, goals, tactics, etc. To a certain extent, loose use of this terminology has obscured the original intent of these terms. In articulating the choices made in a strategic planning exercise, the key is to ensure that, regardless of the terminology, the vision for some future state is broken down logically into a map of how to get from point A, where we are now, to point B, where we need to be (as we see it today) at some point in the future. At its most basic level, strategic plans need to clearly articulate this map, with vision, mission, and objectives being the destinations and strategies and action plans being the travel arrangements. What's most important is that within a particular organization, all participants in the process share a common understanding of the purpose and the meaning of the terms being used.

How, then, does one articulate this map and thus define strategic direction? The relationships among the key map elements are shown in figure 3.1. It is essential in strategic management to understand the importance of well-articulated vision and mission statements and of focused, concise objectives. Defining these statements is one of the tasks of senior executives, although all stakeholders may contribute input during the formulation process. Many executives do not understand the nature of these concepts, why they are so important, and how they should be used. Consequently, they complain that their plans are ineffective and do not provide the necessary direction for decision making.

**Figure 3.1** From Vision to Action Plans

### Reaching for the Future: Vision and a New Sense of Mission

The strategy process should define vision, mission, and objectives. These are the directional elements of strategy—future states to be achieved and specific, measurable outcomes that the strategy aims to attain. These directional statements provide a reference and criteria that enable tough choices to be made among major investment opportunities (does the opportunity fit with our vision and our current mission?). They should stretch the organization to achieve a level of performance that, in their absence, many employees would not seek to attain.

A vision statement provides key stakeholders with a word picture of what the corporation ultimately intends to become, which may be five, ten, or fifteen years in the future. As such, it is an important element of any change agenda. This statement should not be abstract. It should contain as concrete a picture of the desired state as possible to enable strong identification and association to be developed among stakeholders and to provide the basis for formulating a mission and objectives. Some executives confuse a slogan—such as "Quality is Job 1," "We Try Harder," or "A Minerals Company Striving to Be Best"—with vision and mission statements. Although it is good to have a short, catchy phrase that captures the essence of a corporation's strategy, this in no way should be viewed as a substitute for a well-articulated mission statement.

Typical elements in a vision statement include the desired scope of business activities, how the corporation will be viewed by its stakeholders, areas of leadership or distinctive competence, and strongly held values. In 1984, auto manufacturer Ford formulated the following vision statement: "Ford Motor Company is a worldwide leader in automotive and automotive-related products and services as well as in newer industries such as aerospace, communications and financial services."

The past decade has seen an overemphasis on strategic vision, which is an important element in establishing direction but not really useful without a complementary sense of mission, and the requirement for clear objectives.[13] In Ford's case, the vision statement provided the unique identity, and the mission statement read: "Our mission is to improve continually our products and services to meet our customers' needs, allowing us to prosper as a business and to provide a reasonable return for our stockholders, the owners of our business."

The value of articulating and disseminating such statements has been the subject of considerable debate. One view is that a shared vision, one that is "lived" by all the employees of a corporation or business unit, provides a strong motivational force. In a situation in which most employees can identify strongly with this ambition, the statement may, indeed, be very useful. However, an opposing view holds that vision statements can be dysfunctional. They can be wrong, which would create substantial momentum toward the wrong future and be very difficult to change. If the vision appears to be either too abstract or out of touch with current reality, most employees will view it with cynicism and question the competence of the executives who created it.

Timing is clearly an issue. Ford did not articulate its vision until four years into a deep strategic change initiative. In fact, many deep change initiatives can be set in motion without a compelling long-term vision that defines the desired end state as long as the initial activities have a clear sense of purpose defined through a shorter-term set of missions and objectives.

Except for minor changes, vision statements should remain valid for periods of up to five or ten years if they are to provide constancy of purpose, although the specific time frame for such a statement has to be defined in terms of industry and corporate strategic horizons. For some companies in fast-changing industries, such as software, it may be impossible to define a vision much further out than two or three years. However, for some major government organizations or corporations with long strategic lead times, such as mining and oil and gas, ten- or twenty-year visions may be appropriate.

Should a mission statement be for the same period as the vision statement? Companies are increasingly using mission statements not to directly complement the vision, but to define a series of major strategic platforms that drive changes for a definable time period and that have to be achieved if the vision is to become a reality. Thus, a five-year vision may be achieved through a series of three twenty-month missions or a three-year vision through a series of three one-year missions. We have found that using these concepts in this way—by introducing a much shorter-term strategic horizon—makes the huge time span in such statements more manageable for many employees. In addition, each mission can be clearly seen to comprise a limited number of change initiatives (perhaps three or four). This notion of introducing a clearly defined sense of prioritization and sequencing helps deal with the problem of attempting to do too much at once.

The key reason to have a well-defined mission statement is to have a yardstick for tough, strategic decisions. When major alternative initiatives are being evaluated, one of the key questions that should be asked is how they fit with the mission. If the fit is sound, then the initiative is valid. However, if there is no fit, then either the initiative should be scrapped or, infrequently, the mission should be reconsidered. Obviously, a second reason for a mission statement is to provide key stakeholders with a clear, unambiguous sense of corporate identity and purpose for a specific time period. A typical mission statement usually contains the following elements:

- Purpose—for example, "we intend to be the world's best integrated minerals corporation."
- Unique identity—for example, "through outstanding exploration and the development and deployment of innovative technologies."
- Key values—for example, "trust, highest standards of health and safety, environmental responsibility, having fun, and innovation."
- Stakeholder benefits—for example, "the highest financial returns in our industry."

In a military context, the vision that drove the allies in the Gulf War was a liberated Kuwait and an Iraq with significantly diminished regional power. However, two short, sequential missions were necessary to achieve the vision: Desert Shield, which provided an initial defense for Saudi Arabia and stabilized the situation; and Desert Storm, which liberated Kuwait and limited the capabilities of the Iraqi army. Using a similar approach, the executive team of Collahuasi, a $1.8 billion mining development high in the Chilean Andes, defined and executed three missions through which they would achieve their vision of becoming one of the world's great copper mines:

- An initial two-year mission to build the mine successfully—safely, on time and on budget, capable of world-class operations.
- A second eighteen-month mission to optimize the mine, achieve target outputs and costs, and gain safety, environmental, and quality accreditations.
- A third three-year mission to expand the mine output to ensure sustained copper production levels well into the future.

At Acklands-Grainger, Doug Harrison and his strategy team quickly developed a five-year vision statement early in February 2000, which reads as follows:

With revenues in excess of $1 billion, and corresponding profitability, AGI will be Canada's leading MRO supplier, recognized for our ability to anticipate and satisfy the needs of our customers, through:

- customer-focused delivery channels supported by superior service, processes and technologies
- becoming known as a great place to work, by creating a winning atmosphere that attracts, retains and rewards employees who contribute to our success

- leveraging our strong relationships with WW Grainger and our key partners
- being recognized as a valued member of all communities in which we do business

This vision statement has been the focal point of Ackland-Grainger's strategy since then and has been communicated broadly, including being posted on the company's Web site.

Harrison and his team recognized that the achievement of this vision would require several strategic campaigns aimed at deep cultural change. Hence, they developed a corresponding eighteen-month mission statement:

We will create an e-enabled, customer-focused company, capable of delivering sustained, rapid, profitable growth by:

- refocusing our branch network to provide outstanding value for small and medium customers
- creating a business unit dedicated to serving the needs of our large business customers
- achieving operational savings, and investing in appropriate technologies, processes and people
- enabling our employees to provide outstanding service and recognizing them for their achievements

Along with supporting objectives, strategies, and action plans, this mission was communicated to all of the company's employees and its key suppliers, and it became the focal point for action into late 2001. By that time, however, the key initiatives in this mission had been largely accomplished, and a second mission, providing direction through 2003, was developed by the strategy team. The vision, however, remained constant.

## Raising the Bar: Strategic Objectives

Strategic objectives relate directly to the mission statement. For example, if a key element in the mission is to be the market leader then an objective for market share or position is appropriate. If cost leadership is part of the mission, then an objective relating to costs should be stated. Acklands-Grainger's objectives corresponding to its vision and mission included five-year targets for profit and revenue, shorter-term targets for cost reduction, and specific objectives relating to e-business and large-account customers.

Objectives, sometimes referred to as stretch targets, are not scientifically derived forecasts. They are statements of what the strategy team believes needs to be achieved in specific areas by a specified date. They can be related to either substantive targets, such as return on investment, market share, or the launch of a new business or product, or enablers, such as the launch of a new compensation plan, level of employee involvement, or the implementation of a new information system. They provide a yardstick against which progress can be measured. They are there to challenge the corporation and provide measures of strategic achievement. They define *what* needs to be achieved over a specific time frame. Hence, they should be specific, measurable, and actionable. Every strategic objective should have some quantifiable measure for evaluation purposes. Objectives should also be mutually compatible; in other words, it is not realistic to have, at the same time, objectives to reduce the workforce by 50 percent and to ensure security of employment.

## Making It Happen: Strategies and Action Plans

So, how do you map out the change journey? That is the role of strategies and action plans: the means, how-tos, and to-do lists of the process. Strategies are the major initiatives that embody decisions and major resource allocations that together ensure the achievement of objectives. In most industries, they typically have a duration of months, rather than years. Recently, we have come to understand that strategies do not work well individually but work powerfully when bundled to achieve one or two focused objectives. Thus, for example, a teamwork strategy by itself is unlikely to achieve the objective of a high-performance workplace, and a focus on securing new customers is unlikely to achieve outstanding revenue growth on its own. In the former case, several strategies including teamwork, continuous improvement, and employee investment strategies may produce a high-performance workplace. In the latter case, customer loyalty and product improvement strategies are likely to be required as well.

Strategies are embodied in concrete actions. Whereas vision, mission, and objectives—and possibly strategies—may stretch out a number of years into the future, action plans cover the immediate time period ahead. In essence, these are the statements and commitments that make strategic plans real and tangible. In our research, we have found that the existence of specific action plans covering a varying period, depending on firm and industry, from 90 to 120 days is a critical determinant of implementation success.

Action plans are tactical statements that define the who, what, how, when, and with what elements of strategy. A typical action plan statement, linking actions in the next 60 days back to corporate objectives, is shown in table 3.2. Not all action plans are real, however. We distinguish between action plans that either study or validate decisions and those that actually either communicate the strategy or move it forward. Too many strategy workshops conclude with action plans that only refine the understanding reached in the meeting, rather than delineate real steps to move the strategy forward rapidly. In fact, one experienced executive commented: "Studies and validations are a great delaying or procrastination tactic used by people who aren't really committed. They can delay real implementation by six months or longer. When I walk out of these sessions, I want 80 percent of our actions to be decisive."

The importance of action plans lies in the shared understanding that they create of the key steps that will be taken to move the strategy forward during the next tactical time period. This is the essence of operational commitment. Moreover, action plans are not needed for everything, just the key steps that will

**Table 3.2** Action Plan Structure

| | | |
|---|---|---|
| Objective: | | Increase market share five points |
| Strategic Thrust: | | Develop brand extension |
| Action: | *Who*: | Product Manager |
| | *What*: | Market research—characteristics |
| | *How*: | Focus groups, in-store surveys |
| | *When*: | Within 90 days |
| | *How much*: | $50,000 |
| Action: | *Who*: | Product Development Director |
| | *What*: | Develop new brand concepts |
| | *How*: | Build on market research/project team |
| | *When*: | Within 60 days |
| | How much: | $150,000 |

most likely initiate further actions. (In fact, inexperienced teams often develop action plans that are far too ambitious for a given time period.) In addition, these statements create accountability by defining the lead individual responsible for implementation. This process is most effective when each individual has to report at the start of update workshops (typically held every 60 or 90 days) on what he or she has accomplished. Of course, these responsibilities can also be incorporated into individual accountability accords that many organizations now use to evaluate the performance of executives and managers.

## Measurement

An important element of the planning process is the establishment of measures that can be used as a yardstick of achievement and milestones along the way. For strategic purposes, these measures, sometimes called key performance indicators but now more commonly referred to as a scorecard, need to be focused, not merely historic, and indicative to some degree of the need for corrective action, or even changes in strategy.

The simplest way of deriving a scorecard is through identification of specific measures of success associated with vision, mission, and objectives. If properly stated, objectives are by themselves key elements of the scorecard because they are made up of specific and measurable ends that must be attained—for example, reducing costs by 20 percent over the next two years, increasing market share by 10 percent over the next three years, or reducing turnover among key employees to 10 percent annually. Other measures can be derived from statements in the vision and mission that are not reflected in specific objectives but that can be translated into measurable outcomes. For example, if being a great place to work is a statement in the vision, then corresponding measures, for example of employee satisfaction, can be included in the scorecard. Goals, or milestones, can be derived from these objectives to provide periodic measures of progress along the way.

Recently, the notion of a balanced scorecard of measures for evaluating corporate performance has been put forward by Robert Kaplan and David Norton.[14] This approach advocates four key dimensions to performance evaluation—customer, financial, internal, and learning and growth—and proposes that corporations track measures along all four dimensions. Corporations that have adopted this approach have had mixed experiences, with some reporting considerable success and others abandoning it. For example, a number have ended up with a plethora of measures, up to 160 in one reported case, that are confusing and often contradictory.

How valid is the use of a balanced scorecard for driving change initiatives? Executives that we have interviewed have stated categorically that what is needed to drive deep organizational change is an *unbalanced* scorecard. When asked to explain, they state that for deep change to succeed, the organization has to focus around a limited set of performance measures that reflect the priorities of the organization. An extreme example is turnaround, in which knowledgeable executives focus on a few key measures such as cash flow, unit cost, breakeven, and perhaps customer satisfaction or loyalty. They most certainly do not use a balanced scorecard. Similarly, in the early days of an entrepreneurial start-up, a balanced scorecard is inappropriate.

Change does require a scorecard, but one that is tailored to each unique strategy and that does not necessarily have balance. As well as the key milestone measures, the scorecard also needs to contain a few leading indicators that can provide the executive team with early warning of the need for additional changes to the strategy or corrective action.

## The Planning Process

As discussed, the process of developing the plan is as important as the plan itself. One of the most important considerations of the process is that it must provide a platform for dialogue.[15] Why is continuing dialogue so important? It has only recently been widely acknowledged that a prime purpose of strategic planning is to stimulate and sustain a dialogue about strategy throughout the corporation. In fact, leading strategic thinkers are suggesting that the strategic planning process be thought of as the design and facilitation of multilevel strategic conversations.[16] Planning may be far more effective in a corporation that has no formal process but has key executives who meet once a week over lunch or dinner to discuss the key issues, than in corporations that have plans prepared by dedicated staffs with minimal input from line managers and employees.

As corporations grow larger, executives tend to meet less frequently, especially in geographically dispersed corporations in which much time is spent traveling. As a result, they tend to develop individual views of the firm, its environment, and its challenges, which they have little time to share with their colleagues. In addition, their views on these matters are influenced by the particular aspect of the business for which they are responsible and the people with whom they have the most contact.

Moreover, the informal channels of communication—which in smaller companies are capable of providing most employees with reasonably accurate information about the firm's future intentions—break down, particularly at the first line of supervision. The result is that many employees first hear of significant developments in the press or on radio or television or, worse still, through gossip and rumors that may be totally without foundation.

A sound strategic management process provides the framework for a continuing dialogue within the corporation on major concerns and issues. The dialogue also has to be creative. Strategic planning provides the corporation with a chance to periodically rethink the business and to challenge prevailing assumptions and conventional wisdom. It also provides a vehicle for a continuing exchange of information among executives and managers, which is necessary for the alignment of views and activities. In addition, a judicious sharing of strategic information with all employees strengthens the sense of commitment and purpose throughout the organization.

A variety of vehicles are available to stimulate this dialogue, both formal and informal. Periodic strategy reviews, cascaded down throughout all levels of the organization, are the most important of the formal sessions. Depending on the rate of change, these can be monthly, quarterly, or even annually. For example, during periods of rapid change, senior executives may meet to review strategic developments on a monthly basis and communicate developments to the workforce on a quarterly basis.

The value of informal dialogue should be recognized as well. Much of the creativity in strategic management comes out of short, informal meetings among small groups of employees, sometimes with customers, suppliers, or other key stakeholders. All employees should have some time to participate in such activities. In strategy workshops, these informal dialogues always occur between formal sessions and after hours. For example, one executive team we know developed the framework for a whole new organizational structure in a bar between 10 P.M. and 2 A.M.

## A Streamlined Process

Strategic planning is an ongoing, iterative process that can embody a number of specific techniques, such as portfolio analysis and shareholder value analysis. The challenge for executives is to strike the right balance between formal processes, such as strategy reviews and the preparation of plans; informal processes, such as casual discussions among executives; and ad hoc approaches, such as studies of specific opportunities.

Some corporations have reduced the strategic planning process to a rigid bureaucratic exercise that kills creativity. In others, the process is so loose that it never gets as far as implementation. It is vital to maintain the focus of the activity at an appropriately high level while dealing with specific issues, and not generalities. A sound strategic planning activity addressing "how we will *change* the business" needs to be complemented and followed by a more detailed operational planning and budgeting process describing "how we will *run* the business."

In today's rapidly changing business environment, this process must be completed in a relatively short time frame. Taking nine months or a year to develop a vision and mission just is not realistic. In fact, the entire initial strategy definition process should be capable of being undertaken in three months or less, from start to finish, for the entire corporation. This means a streamlined approach that produces an 80 percent solution, with subsequent refinement in the field as the strategy is deployed.

At each level of strategy (corporate, business unit, and service unit/integrative), there are five major segments to an effective strategic planning process:

- *Size-up:* aimed at identifying major strategic issues and opportunities through an assessment of the corporate environment (competitive and market at the macro level) and an examination of corporate capabilities.
- *Analysis:* intended to secure greater insight into specific strategic areas (e.g., competitors, customers, cost structures, etc.) required for strategy formulation.
- *Synthesis and positioning:* aimed at determining the overall strategic posture of the corporation and its business units.
- *Strategy formulation:* establishing the specific direction and enabling elements of the strategy.
- *Implementation:* a process of execution, follow-up, and review of the strategic plan.

These are best carried out in a series of activities organized around two distinct strategy workshops, as shown in figure 3.2. The first workshop is utilized to carry out a size-up and assessment of future strategy requirements. The second

**Figure 3.2** Streamlined Strategic Planning Process

establishes direction and develops initial action plans. In between the two, it is appropriate to reserve a period for additional analysis of strategic issues and opportunities, together with reflection and insight.

The first of these workshops—the size-up—is intended to create a shared view among the key participants on the organization's future business environment, its current strategy and capabilities, and the major issues and opportunities that it faces. This meeting should be preceded by a variety of prework tasks, including environment and market scans, informal discussions among employees, and specific assignments for individuals and task forces, such as benchmarking competitive strategies.

During the size-up meeting, a variety of activities can be undertaken by the planning group, in both plenary and small-group formats. These include:

- *Scans of the business environment*: sharing information, identifying future trends and major areas of uncertainty, and reviewing key external stakeholders.
- *Industry analysis*: identifying changes in key value drivers and assessing their impact on competition.
- *Competitive analysis*: examining competitors' strategies, simulating possible competitive initiatives, and determining what responses might be appropriate.
- *Organizational assessment*: assessing the corporation's current strategy, capabilities, opportunities, and threats.

In addition, a series of stretch or challenge questions should be brainstormed in this initial workshop as a way of stimulating creative thinking. As Hank Mc-Kinnell, CEO of Pfizer, commented: "The old model was doing what you currently do faster, better, cheaper . . . the new model is thinking of things you weren't able to do. So it's thinking of things, that, well, what would I do if?"

Typical questions to promote this kind of thinking, preferably discussed initially in small groups, include the following:

- What must our organization be able to do in the future (perhaps two or three years from now) that is impossible to do today?
- How will changes in technology affect our industry and our organization?
- What conventional wisdom, from our industry and within the organization, constrains our ability to change?
- If we were to build our organization from scratch today, how would it be different, and what would we do differently?

On occasion, it is also useful in this first workshop to identify the specific tough decisions that have to be made, which lie at the heart of any future strategy. At the end of the process, the planning team can return to these and determine whether they were, in fact, addressed in the process.

The most important outcome of this initial workshop is agreement on the three or four (certainly no more than five) significant make-or-break challenges and opportunities facing the organization over the next strategic time period. In between the first and second workshops, these *critical few* strategic issues are the focus of studies and review using a variety of analytical techniques and approaches by a series of task forces established expressly for this purpose.

In the second workshop, which takes place about four to six weeks after the first, the strategic plan is actually formulated following the outline shown in table 3.1. The major objectives of this meeting are to establish future direction and formulate specific plans to initiate action. If the activity is being undertaken for only the first or second occasion, considerable time should be allocated to formulating vision and/or mission statements. On the other hand, if statements of vision and mission already exist, they normally will have been reviewed in the first session, and it may not be necessary to modify these statements if they adequately express the future intentions of the organization.

The first morning of the second workshop is used to deliver and discuss the reports of the task forces on the various strategic issues and opportunities facing the corporation. Out of this discussion emerge the elements of mission and key objectives, stated in specific terms. The second and, if required, third days of the session can be used to move from strategies to detailed 90- to 120-day action plans for the initial deployment steps that specifically address these questions: What's to be done? How? By when? And who is accountable? In order to maintain momentum, action plans should be as economical as possible and commence as soon as practical following the workshop.

Toward the end of this workshop, when action plans are being prepared, the identification of strategic "moose" issues, or "undiscussables," can be useful. These are issues that are known to everyone, but individual participants may not wish to place them on the table for discussion. However, they can derail implementation if not identified and addressed. In addition, participants should discuss the risks associated with the strategy and how they can be managed.

The workshop should not end without developing a short action plan for the communication and initial deployment of the plan. This should include who will draft the plan, how a final version will be prepared (fine-tuning and necessary changes to dates, but no significant content revisions), when it will be distributed, and how it will be communicated to stakeholders. A date should be established for an initial progress review.

## Planning Tools—Analytical Frameworks

Inherent in the dialogue during strategic planning is the use of appropriate analytical tools. If the best results are to be obtained, strategy formulation and positioning require a rigorous analysis of the business and questioning of assumptions, together with sound creative thinking. Planning tools and techniques don't provide answers, but they can provide insight.

A variety of tools and techniques have been developed since the 1980s, although many of them are financial analysis and modeling tools that can be applied to certain aspects of strategic planning. The major techniques are as follows:

- *The Political-Economic-Social-Technical (PEST) framework:* for analysis of the macroenvironment for business; a sound framework for size-up and scanning purposes.[17]
- *Scenario analysis:* a multidimensional technique developed initially by Shell for developing a variety of alternative views of the future to be used as the basis for evaluating alternative strategic options and, hence, robust strategies in uncertain and complex environments.[18]
- *Electronic brainstorming:* a PC-based technology that permits executive teams to anonymously brainstorm the various elements of a strategic analysis; research findings suggest that creativity is enhanced, especially in teams in which open face-to-face discussion is difficult.[19]
- *Porter's five forces industry analysis framework:* which views the forces among customers, rivals, new entrants, substitutes, and suppliers as determining industry and corporate performance; now seen as the most important tool for competitive analysis, it avoids the potential for taking a "blinkered" view of competition.[20]
- *Portfolio or matrix analysis:* the best known being the Boston Consulting Group's market share–growth matrix and General Electric's industry attractiveness–relative share matrix; initially, these tools were used as *normative* indicators for strategic direction and positioning, but their limitations in these respects are now understood, and they are more widely used for providing *prescriptive* guidance during strategy formulation.[21]
- *Experience curve analysis:* based on learning curve theory as a way of relating competitiveness, pricing, and costs to accumulated experience and output; the technique has proven useful in some industries, such as aerospace and electronics, but has limited applicability in others.[22]
- *Profit impact of market share analysis (PIMS):* developed at the Harvard Business School and based on the premise that profitability is correlated to market share, it incorporates an extremely large database of corporations from almost every sector (including minerals) to establish empirical policies and performance measures for individual client corporations; it has been found to be more relevant to some sectors, such as services and packaged goods, than others.[23]
- *Benchmarking:* a comparative approach to evaluating best practice, which can be used for strategic purposes.[24]
- *Strategic modeling:* a number of computer-based systems are now available that generate models that will provide real-time analysis of strategic options, such as divestment, acquisition, expansion, etc.; the better packages, such as STRATEX, developed by the Finnish firm Nokkia, permit this analysis to be carried out in real time during a two- or three-day strategy review, providing virtually instantaneous analysis of options under discussion.
- *Core competence analysis:* can be used to provide insight into critical skill gaps and to identify possible activities that might be outsourced in the future.[25]

These tools and techniques are useful in providing additional insight and different perspectives on strategic issues and opportunities, but none of them, in isolation, provides *the answer*.

## Moving to Action—Suggested First Steps

We will discuss the deployment of a new strategic plan at length in chapter 5. But first must stress the importance of *quickly* moving to action when any new strategic plan has been developed—even before formal approval has been given, if at all possible.

If one of the processes that we have described is followed, a powerful sense of energy is often created within the strategy team and among those associated with the activity. There's excitement in the air. There is an expectation that things are going to change. The worst thing possible is to ask people at the end of the exercise to go home, sit tight, and wait for the go-ahead following the next board meeting, which may not be for several months, or to wait until the corporate executive team gives its blessing.

We have heard about so many strategic plans that fail at this stage. Nothing happens for a month, or perhaps three months. This frequently occurs in public-sector organizations and in large private-sector corporations. The sense of urgency dissipates. People actually start to forget what it was that they agreed to. If you want to succeed, this cannot be allowed to happen. Maintaining a sense of urgency is essential if speed and momentum are to build.

So, how does one proceed, especially if formal approval has to be sought? Usually, it's possible to move ahead on a number of initiatives that fall within the authority level of the strategy team, even without higher-level approval. Possibilities include a communications activity, perhaps including workshops for management, supervisory, and professional employees to review the proposed plan, to build commitment, and to develop more detailed implementation approaches. Informal "selling" discussions can begin with other key stakeholders such as unions and suppliers. In addition, changes that are aligned with the strategy but do not require major funding or formal approval can be taken. At the very least, these provide tangible indicators that things are changing.

The approach also depends on how much personal risk the senior executive team is willing to take. In our work, we see a significant difference in outcomes between corporations with executives who are willing to take some initiative, even if it means some personal risk, and those with executives who will not act before they have formal approval. This may be a time, perhaps, to be bold and to make use of the change-agent motto, "It's better to ask forgiveness than permission," if you want to succeed.

## Laying the Foundation for Implementation Success

Much of the success achieved in any change initiative is determined by the activities undertaken during the period when the plan is still being developed.

In fact, awareness and commitment can be developed, even as the strategic plan is being created, by involving a broad cross section of employees in enabling activities. In addition, it is not at all unusual to initiate some actions that will certainly form part of the strategic plan that do not require its finalization before they can proceed.

Typical activities that build awareness and understanding before and during the planning process include:

- Surveying employee views on strategy-related issues.
- Involving employees in task forces to analyze specific issues and opportunities.
- Creating informal "buzz groups" in which executives seek out employee views on possible strategic options and plant ideas of their own in the minds of influential employees.
- Identifying and reinforcing current actions and behaviors that are in line with the new direction.
- Getting work underway on any long lead-time activities or processes that will be an integral part of the new strategy.
- Consulting and preparing stakeholders, such as key customers and vendors.
- Identifying resources that are likely to be limiting on the rate of progress.

Actions such as these can ensure that the best possible conditions exist for building speed during the first 100 days.

During this period, it is also possible to develop the timetable and key elements of the communications initiative. Meetings can be scheduled in executive calendars. Slide presentation decks can be prepared. Supporting media, including logos, posters, videos, and employee handbooks, can be prepared. Later in this period, as initiatives are starting to formalize, the release process can be designed

If limiting resources have been identified, actions can be put in place, even before the first 100 days, to ensure that adequate resources are available when required. For example, as noted earlier, information technology capabilities are often limiting on the rate of deployment of systems supporting a new strategic plan. With this in mind, the CIO can plan and budget for additional staff, perhaps on a contract or outsourced basis, to be available to support strategy deployment.

## The Outcome: Power Performance from Aligning Leadership, Strategy, and Culture

An effective strategic planning process will have both resulted in a great strategic plan—a *game plan* for change—and encouraged and created buy-in and commitment throughout its development. It should have also, if executed properly, aligned three elements critical to ongoing organizational success:

- Leadership to provide vision, direction, and reinforcement of appropriate behaviors.

**Table 3.3** Southwest Airlines Business Model

- *Leadership*—focused, disciplined, people-oriented, un-conventional
- *Target market*—value-oriented customers who might otherwise drive or take the bus: short-haul flights
- *Value proposition*—frequency, convenience, timeliness, friendliness at a low price
- *Key strategies*—cheap, economic facilities, standardized fleet, minimal systems infrastructure, high asset productivity
- *Culture*—highly involved workforce, route ownership, 'luv culture,' multitasking, low unit-cost operations

- Strategy focused around realistic plans, providing focus and supporting resource deployment.
- Organization culture—the values, beliefs, and appropriate behaviors that will ensure that the strategy can be implemented.

For outstanding corporate performance, these three elements must be strongly aligned, as they are in corporations such as Hewlett-Packard, 3M, and General Electric that have demonstrated sustained business success over several decades. Southwest Airline's success can, in part, be attributed to this alignment, as shown in table 3.3 The personal leadership style of CEO Herb Kelleher, as reflected throughout the company, was strongly aligned with the strategy of being the low-price, no-frills leader in the short-haul market. Implementation of this strategy was then creatively enabled through the implementation of the corporation's "luv" culture, in which teams of highly motivated employees provided levels of service and input for cost improvement that underpinned the corporation's continuing success.

In recent years, leadership has emerged as a key determinant of successful strategies. Corporate leadership is critical in establishing vision, mission, and direction for the corporation, and without it, any strategy will fail. That being said, there are many different ways of leading, but it is generally believed that executives must demonstrate appropriate behaviors and recognize outstanding performance if any strategy is to be credible. For example, strategic plans are credible only if senior executives are *seen* to be committed to the process and the outcomes.

Sound strategies underpin outstanding leadership by focusing activities, decisions, and resources on the critical, make-or-break issues and opportunities facing the business. In a complex, uncertain, and fast-changing business environment, corporations have to be nimble and responsive; strategy has to be formulated and deployed in a manner that allows the corporation to react to changing circumstances and new opportunities. Strategy making is one of the prime responsibilities of executives at all levels in a corporation.

Culture is critical in the determination of successful strategic outcomes because, to a great extent, strategy deployment is dependent on the values and beliefs of the organization. For example, are executives willing to make hard choices? Are they willing to focus resources on a few key initiatives? Is a propensity for action a characteristic of the management style? In the next chapter, we examine one of the critical cultural enablers for rapid change—the ability of leaders to make major decisions fast.

# 4

## Building Rapid Decision-Making Capabilities

A strategic planning process is effective only if it helps or allows an organization to make major decisions quickly. Executives in many companies are seriously concerned about the speed at which they make, resource, and implement major decisions. One executive in a large telecommunications firm commented, "We still think in periods of months and years to implement strategic decisions. Typically, we still take nearly a year to shift funds behind some major initiatives. In today's world this just doesn't work. Our decision making is glacially slow in comparison to many of our smaller competitors."

The pace of change is accelerating in all industries, and the ability to implement major decisions rapidly is becoming a major determinant of success in both the public and the private sectors.[1] However, many organizations still take up to a year to complete strategic plans, with similar time frames for the deployment of major initiatives.

As with space missions, there is typically a window of opportunity for a favorable launch of any change initiative. Delays reduce the available options and the likelihood of a successful outcome. For example, marketing studies have shown that being late to market with a new product can cost market share.[2] Consequently, it is important to be able to move rapidly from awareness to action. Gerald Schwartz, CEO of Canada's highly successful Onex Corporation, observed, "One of the things we always try to inculcate in people has to do with speed. Don't take forever. Normandy was designed, created and executed in a year. So don't tell me that it takes two years to do something. We try and get people to move with speed."

Traditional, linear decision-making processes are inadequate to meet this need for speed for a number of reasons. First, by their very nature, they are more time consuming than processes that proceed via a set of parallel paths. Second, our analysis of these processes reveals that much of the elapsed time is actually taken up by "white space" periods in which nothing is happening. The decision is waiting for the next element of the process—an executive team meeting, budget approval, or the like. Third, linear processes are similar to American football, in which one fumble can bring the whole game to a halt. Contrast this with rugby, a game so fluid that fumbles can be quickly recovered and the game plan continues to move ahead.

Executives are realizing the need for new management processes, ones that emphasize parallel deployment and that are strongly integrated and aligned, to achieve desired implementation rates. The most publicized example of this kind of process is concurrent engineering, used by companies as diverse as Honda and Hewlett-Packard to dramatically accelerate the pace of new product introduction.[3] It is not as well known that leading-edge companies are using accelerated approaches for activities as diverse as acquisition integration, plant construction, and strategy deployment.

Although this type of procedure is important for all companies in a world of accelerating rates of change, it is particularly so for companies moving into the world of the Internet and e-commerce. Companies that are accustomed to taking six months to make decisions and then implementing them over the following twenty-four months are finding themselves outmaneuvered by companies that can decide, deploy, and achieve outcomes within weeks, not months. Large companies must develop reaction times that rival those of smaller, traditionally more nimble, competitors.

As part of developing appropriate capabilities to enable this kind of performance, executives are more conscious than ever of the need to measure and benchmark the speed at which their organizations take action on strategy. As academics, we are often faced with such questions as:

- How long should it take to implement a deep, cultural, and strategic change in our organization?
- How quickly can we expect to achieve outcomes from the launch of our new strategic plan?
- How fast should we be able to take a new product or service from concept to market?
- How long should it take us to deploy a specific major initiative; for instance, a quality accreditation process?
- How rapidly should we be able to successfully integrate an acquisition into our corporate organization?

The contemporary strategy literature contains relatively little by way of either frameworks or processes to help executives find answers to questions like these, although the concept of *strategy as hustle* is not new.[4]

The purpose of this chapter is to take an initial step in remedying this deficiency and provide a way to analyze and improve the effectiveness of decision-making processes. First, we outline a six-step model of the strategic process—from concept through decision making, deployment of resources, and achievement of outcomes—that can be applied either to a broad corporate or business-unit strategic plan or to the development and implementation of a specific strategic initiative. By defining the process in this way, we establish a framework that is amenable to measurement. We then suggest a set of parameters that can be developed to measure the speed of this process. In this respect, we argue that your organization requires measures that are approximate and robust, rather than precise and situation specific. We close the chapter by describing six approaches that corporations are successfully adopting in order to accelerate strategy formulation and implementation by means of short-cycle planning and decision-making models, parallel-deployment initiatives, and accelerated communication programs.

## A Six-Step Model

Our framework for strategy development and implementation contains six steps, as illustrated in figure 4.1. These steps are shown as overlapping because our model makes it unnecessary to complete one step before starting on others. Thus, for example, even as they are creating awareness of the need for strategic action, executives can move ahead on building shared understanding of the nature of the action required. This contrasts sharply with the traditional linear models for strategic decision making, such as the new product "gating" process, employed by many corporations, in which one stage does not commence until the preceding one is complete.

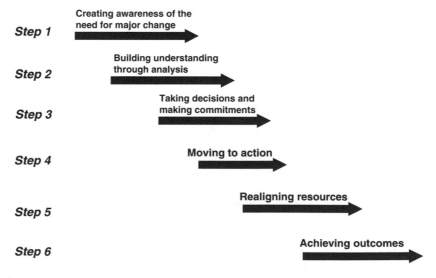

**Figure 4.1** Model of the Strategy Development and Deployment Process

## Step 1: Creating Awareness

A typical comment from executives in large organizations is: "We often do not know that we have a major issue or opportunity, but our smaller competitors are already taking action."

This is when the entire strategy process begins, and the first step is to make decision makers aware that there is a need for major decisions and action. Creating this awareness can be problematic for larger companies, in particular, for several reasons. First, it may take a considerable amount of time for intelligence gathered by frontline employees to percolate through to strategic decision makers. Second, organizational silos can lead to the fragmentation of information that, taken as a whole, might indicate the need for change. Third, on the broad strategic front, we have found that most executive teams lack an agreed-upon set of leading-indicator measures that will signal the need for some form of change. Fourth, the pace of events and organizational grind that are realities in many large organizations often make it difficult for executives to meet frequently enough to identify major threats and opportunities.

Consequently, even when a company has a continuing strategic planning activity, it is not unusual for some time to elapse before there is sufficient awareness at the executive level of the need for change to drive, for example, a major strategic repositioning. Thus, a first measure for executives to track is the length of time it takes for them to become aware of the need for significant change. The signals for change can arrive from a variety of places. This means that a key task for executives is to ensure a rapid flow of information and a quick translation of this information into knowledge and understanding.

## Step 2: Building Understanding

How long does it take your organization to factor in available information, analyze a situation, identify alternative courses of action, and evaluate options? This is part of the process of creating shared understanding among the executive team of the nature of the decisions required. Executives in slow-moving firms look at their more nimble competitors and comment wistfully, "In our company, we suffer from analysis paralysis. Every strategic decision we take must be examined from multiple perspectives, pored over by the bean counters, and even then we hesitate."

In some industries, this process of creating understanding can be accomplished in days, but in others, it takes years. In a large, mature industrial corporation, the analysis and development of plans for new initiatives may take a year or more. In the mineral industries, the prefeasibility and feasibility studies and detailed engineering for a major new mine may take three or four years before firm decision can be recommended to the board of directors. In some packaged goods companies, the new product development process has become so elaborate that it can take a similar length of time to develop and launch a new line. However, in fast-moving, responsive companies, the decision to develop a new product or service to meet a newly identified market opportunity can be made in a matter of two or three days. These companies have come to understand the need to eliminate the white space.

E-business is a case in point. Once corporations have decided that they require an e-business strategy, they have to determine the nature of this strategy, its scope, and how it will affect the current business. In large companies, most executives have little understanding of e-business, so gaining this understanding usually requires the executive team to educate themselves about alternative e-business models and approaches. Frequently, consultants are retained to facilitate and accelerate the analysis process and assist with the development of possible business models and options. All of this can take several months, maybe even a year or more. During this period, even as analysis is under way, e-business models are evolving, and faster, more alert rivals may already be taking advantage of the next wave.

Executives need to develop a measure that lets them understand how long it takes them, on average, to be in a position to make decisions that commit them to a definite course of action. In most companies, strategic analysis is carried out on an ad hoc basis, when time is available. We have observed that much of the time taken to study strategic options is simply waiting time. People assigned to such projects often carry these responsibilities in addition to their regular duties, so completing the analysis may take weeks or even months. Process studies can help determine how much of the analysis period is "active" time, actually working on the analysis, as opposed to "down" time, waiting for people or information to become available—yet another example of the counterproductive white space.

### Step 3: Making Decisions

A critical third step is making decisions and committing resources to the strategy. In many large corporations, there is often a fixed periodicity to strategic decision making that is aligned with either the budgeting process or committee meetings. In this respect, a typical executive comment is: "We have a great opportunity to take the lead in a particular area of our business, and everyone is ready to roll, but then we hear that there's no money in the budget this year, and we'll have to wait, maybe for six months. . . . Then we have to go through the entire approvals process again."

Delays such as these put companies at a significant disadvantage to those competitors that have a continuous strategic decision process in which funds are allocated to major initiatives as they are approved. In some entrepreneurial corporations, the CEO will make a major strategic decision within ten minutes of being presented with the options. By contrast, in many mature corporations, it can take a year or more to gain approval for a major strategic decision once the preferred option has been identified. In the world today, such delays are unacceptable.

A major contributor to delays during this stage of the process is the nature of decision making itself. Who can commit the organization to a major change initiative? Many executives cannot commit their organization to any significant initiative or expenditure without checking with their CEO or an executive committee of the board, leading to delays of weeks or even months. If the authority is delegated to individuals, decisions can be made expediently. If the executive team as a whole has to approve these decisions, they usually take longer, particularly if the CEO utilizes consensus for major decisions. In such cases, one individual can hold back the entire corporation. A more expedient approach is one described to us by a senior executive as the "you may not love it, but can you live with it?" approach.

It is important to understand how long it takes to move from an understanding of the preferred option to a firm commitment to proceed. Defining the strategic decision-making process and developing measures of the time to actually make decisions constitute the important third step in measuring the speed of deploying change.

## Step 4: Moving to Action

Once a strategic decision has been made, the first implementation step is to mobilize the organization. In many corporations, this stage can take a significant period of time. It is not unusual to hear an executive complain, "Even when we made the decision, senior executives insisted that we validate several key aspects, which delayed implementation by several months. Our senior team has real difficulty taking a well-calculated risk, and we are continually being beaten to the market by our competitors."

Members of the executive team may insist on studies to validate certain aspects of strategic decisions, and some may even second-guess the original decision. Full-scale implementation may not occur until trials and pilots have been implemented. These activities are seen by many as a way to reduce risk, although the opposite may be the outcome because delay often increases the risk of failure. In addition, executives may delay the implementation of a change initiative until support has been built among different constituencies.

Executive teams need to develop an understanding of how much certainty is required prior to making a decision. The price of certainty is prohibitive in this respect. Unisys CEO Larry Weinbach takes this view: "If you wait to get a hundred percent of the information so you know you're making the right decision, it's too late. What you need to do is you need to be comfortable at around sixty, seventy percent of the information."

The frequently expressed need for validation can be viewed as a major enemy of timely strategic decision making. In some organizations, it is not unusual for up to 80 percent of the "actions" that result from a strategic planning activity to be related to creating teams or asking consultants to study or validate initiatives and report back in a period of weeks or, more often, months. In these situations, nothing is really happening during this time.

This deferment contrasts starkly with the approach used by Doug Harrison at Acklands-Grainger. Toward the end of every sixty-day review of the company's strategy, Harrison asks the team to commit to between three and five tangible deliverables from the strategy that all employees would be able to identify by the end of the next sixty-day period. This focus ensures that the strategy remains grounded in outcomes rather than in the process.

If validation is required, then it has to occur expeditiously within days or, at most, a few weeks. It should be apparent whether the call for validation is merely a stalling tactic used by one or two members of the strategy team who are uncomfortable with a particular proposal.

Another major element in this stage of mobilization is the communication of strategic intent to those involved and affected. Measuring the time taken to mobilize the organization around a new initiative involves measurement from the point when the decision is made to the point when employees involved in implementation are aware, educated, and committed to action.

In larger organizations, it may take many months, or longer, before all employees are generally informed about a new strategic plan or initiative. In addition, several months may elapse by the time the communication has been developed and presentations have been scheduled and delivered. For example, by the time a plan has been formally approved and the communications department has worked on the "message" and possibly a video, the communication of a new strategic plan, even to lower levels of management and supervision, may take six months for rollout. The more steps involved, the more white space usually present. In the interim, not much change is being accomplished. Smaller, more alert rivals who know about eliminating white space are likely to be able to move overnight to create a communications package and teams around new full-scale initiatives. In fact, all strategic planning sessions should end with agreement on an immediate, interim communication from the leadership team to the rest of the organization; then, a complete communications package, with white space eliminated, should take no longer than five or ten working days to approve and develop.

### Step 5: Realigning Resources

Step five is redeployment, or the shifting of resources to align with the new strategic direction. Although a new initiative may be approved, it may take a long time to make the necessary resources available. We interviewed one frustrated executive who complained, "Everything has been approved—the project, the budget, the manpower levels—but it's taking Human Resources an age to hire the people I need, and it's going to take sixty days for our procurement group to place orders for some critical equipment."

As noted earlier, in most corporations, resource allocation is aligned with budgeting. Even if an employee has developed a blockbuster new product proposal, it may be impossible to initiate it until funds are allocated in the next round of budgeting. In contrast, entrepreneurial firms often maintain uncommitted pools of funding to permit the rapid deployment of new growth initiatives.

Other problems that delay effective deployment are often related to the availability of resources. It is not unusual for the start of key projects to be deferred until key members of the team complete projects and tasks to which they are already assigned. A particular example of this situation, given the pervasiveness of systems development in change initiatives, is the availability of information technology resources. Many information technology groups are overwhelmed by projects and change requests and, increasingly, the launch of change initiatives can be delayed by months because of the inability of this function to respond in a timely fashion.

During this resource deployment phase, organizations have to measure the time taken from making a decision to actually having resources in place and *substantive* activities under way. In this respect, studies and pilots do not count, unless a pilot is on a major commercial scale. Process analysis can reveal consistent patterns that indicate when delays are occurring. For example, one corporation involved in our research discovered that 70 percent of all delays in change initiatives were due to bottlenecks created by a shortage of information technology people and resources. In the Canadian government, it can take up to a year for a human resources group to reclassify employees for new responsibilities. Once the cause is understood, measures can be taken to eliminate the delays and frustrations. These can be as simple as hiring temporary employees or contractors to provide additional capacity or reducing the level of approval required to reallocate resources.

### Step 6: Achieving Outcomes

The final step in the process is achieving outcomes. Executives have to ask how long it takes to obtain tangible results from strategic initiatives. All too often, the message heard from lower levels of an organization is along the following lines: "We heard that there's been a new strategy put in place, but that's nine months ago now, and we've seen nothing happen. In fact, things are worse today than they were nine months ago!"

Even when a major change initiative is agreed upon and resourced, why does it often take so long before anything tangible is achieved? Even though it is generally recognized that achieving "quick wins" can be important in building credibility and momentum for a new initiative, frontline employees in many organizations frequently report seeing little tangible change in results or outcomes for several years while the enabling business processes are laboriously constructed.

A number of factors contribute to this situation. In particular, concern with following "due process" may get in the way of achieving results. For example, even though a decision may have been made to proceed with a change initiative, those responsible for implementation may feel that they need to undertake further study beforehand. In our research, we were frequently told about Human Resource groups that felt that a lengthy "needs assessment" had to be done prior to undertaking any major training initiative. This approach contrasted starkly with that of more action-oriented groups that rapidly implemented a pilot program, which was then modified and rolled out across the organization. In the former case, no actual training had taken place after six months, but in the latter situation, the initiative was completed within that time frame. This situation can be particularly problematic in public-sector organizations that can delay major change initiatives for months or years by these actions.

Another issue standing in the way of achieving outcomes is the nature of the implementation approach adopted. In many cases, an "all or nothing" approach means that nothing substantive is delivered for a considerable period of time. The implementation group may refuse to deliver a product that is anything less than 100 percent fully functional. Of course, there are some compelling arguments behind this approach, such as the belief that customers and users may be unhappy with anything less than a fully functional outcome. However, our experience indicates that many lead users and customers prefer to receive something that works early on and then build functionality incrementally through subsequent process improvements and upgrades.

In this stage, executives have to measure the time taken to achieve significant initial outcomes from the strategy as defined by objectives or interim goals (milestones). For example, with respect to a new product, the measure may be the time to achieve initial sales of the product or to attain a minimum significant revenue target. For a new process operation, such as a call center, the measure could be the time to achieve full-rated output capacity.

## Measurement

When measuring strategy deployment time frames in today's business environment, we believe that elapsed weeks are more appropriate measures than either months or years. Strategic initiatives and strategic plans need to be developed and deployed within a period of weeks rather than the months consumed in many corporations. In industries in which the pace of change is extremely rapid, days may even be a more appropriate measure than weeks.

Measurement processes should be designed to allow an executive team to address four key questions with respect to strategy deployment:

1. In the future, how fast do we need to deploy major strategic decisions in our industry and our market in order to be successful?
2. At present, how fast can we take action and achieve outcomes with respect to these decisions?
3. What are the major contributing factors in each stage of the process to the time it takes us to act?
4. How can we dramatically speed up our strategy development and deployment process?

These questions can be addressed through the use of any of a number of process analysis methodologies, including reengineering.[5] Executives we have worked with have found that their strategic decision-making and deployment processes are no different from other organizational processes in this respect. As a first step, process mapping can be undertaken for several types of strategic decisions. This analysis usually reveals where the major delays occur; these are often white spaces during which nothing is happening. Basic reengineering can

**Table 4.1** Comparison of Strategic Plan Development and Deployment Times

|  | Packco | Finco | Softco |
|---|---|---|---|
| Creating awareness | 90[a] | 90 | 30 |
| Building understanding | 180 | 150 | 60 |
| Making decisions | 240 | 180 | 60 |
| Moving to action | 330 | 210 | 90 |
| Realigning resources | 390 | 250 | 90 |
| Achieving significant outcomes | 600 | 300 | 120 |

[a]All times in cumulative days

then improve performance dramatically. For example, one telecommunications corporation reduced the cycle time for a major new product or service from eighteen months to four months. In addition, strategic decisions can be differentiated through this process so that those requiring fast decisions and implementation can move along a "fast track."

We suggested earlier that the best measures are robust and approximate rather than precise. Deployment times are also likely to be variable, given the nature and magnitude of the specific initiative. Companies may find that they are quite fast at making and deploying certain types of major decisions but much slower in other areas. As one might expect, our case studies indicate that executive teams make and implement major decisions relatively quickly on familiar subjects in which there is a high level of shared understanding among the group. However, decision making and the move to action are much slower in new, unfamiliar areas, such as e-business, in which shared understanding is low and perceived risk is significant. Consequently, when measuring the speed of strategy development and deployment, it is first necessary for the executive team to agree on the key elements of strategic decisions to be measured.

Table 4.1 compares times for the development and deployment of strategic plans among a company in the packaged goods industry, one in the financial services industry, and one in software development. The table presents a study in contrasts. By using a rapid strategy development and deployment process similar to the one described in chapter 3, Softco was able to develop its strategic plan within sixty days from the inception of its planning activity, move to action within the next thirty days, and show significant initial outcomes by the end of the fourth month. Softco experienced rapid growth as a result of this strategic plan, but changes in its markets were occurring so rapidly that within nine months, a new strategy had to be formulated to keep the company positioned as a leader within its industry segment.

At Packco, the situation was entirely different. It took almost three months for the executive team to agree on the need for a major review of the strategic plan. Initial assessment and analysis activities took another three months, and it was not until eight months after the commencement of the activity that the executive team agreed on a new future direction for the company. However, at that point, several key executives believed that validation of several key elements

**Table 4.2** Comparison of e-Business Development and Deployment Times

|                                  | Telco | Newco | Callco |
|----------------------------------|-------|-------|--------|
| Creating awareness               | 30[a] | 0     | 30     |
| Building understanding           | 150   | 30    | 90     |
| Making decisions                 | 270   | 60    | 100    |
| Moving to action                 | 360   | 75    | 120    |
| Realigning resources             | 450   | 100   | 180    |
| Achieving significant outcomes   | 540   | 150   | 210    |

[a]All times in cumulative days

of the strategy was required, so significant resource redeployment did not begin until over a year after the commencement of the activity. Because of the time subsequently taken to roll out the strategic initiatives, Packco did not begin to benefit from its change in strategy until almost two years after its planning activity commenced. The consequence of these delays was that Packco experienced a sharp decline in both market share and profitability because it failed to respond in a timely manner to changes in its industry and markets.

Finco presents a more common picture. It took the executive team and the board of directors some time to agree upon the need for a major strategy realignment. However, once that agreement was reached, the actual process of strategy development moved ahead rapidly, and a new plan was approved by the board within sixty days of initiating a strategic planning activity. In this case, board approval also included approval for major investment programs, so the strategy was substantially deployed after an additional sixty days. As a result, Finco experienced substantial gains from its new strategy within ten months of initiating its strategic planning activity. On the basis of the understanding gained from studying the time involved in the various phases of its activities, Finco significantly streamlined its planning and decision-making processes, making it one of the most responsive firms in its particular marketplace.

Table 4.2 shows a comparison of times for the deployment of major e-business initiatives among three corporations in the telecommunications industry. Telco is a major, established telephone company; Newco is a well-financed start-up company; Callco is a relatively young, entrepreneurial corporation.

Newco was able to have its e-business model operational in the time that it took Telco to analyze its requirements and review alternative business models. Acting with the traditional utility mindset, it took Telco a full year to actually take action on the new approach. Callco, a rapidly growing corporation, took almost twice as long as Newco to make a decision about its e-business model, but once the decision was made, the company was able to bring its resources to bear to ensure a rapid deployment of its e-business initiative, achieving significant initial outcomes only two months after Newco and almost a full year ahead of Telco. As a result of Telco's poor performance, its senior executives undertook a major review of the company's strategy process aimed at reducing strategic decision-making time by 80 percent. They recognized that such an improvement was a basic requirement for the corporation's long-term survival.

## Rapid Deployment Approaches

So what are the characteristics of corporations that develop and deploy strategies rapidly? In our research, we observed six key attributes:

- Rapid, short-cycle strategic planning processes.
- Timely, strategic decision making.
- Continuous funding of strategic initiatives.
- Concurrent, or parallel, deployment activities.
- Pursuit of near-term results and outcomes.
- Proactive, pervasive communication protocols.

### *Rapid, Short-Cycle Strategic Planning Processes*

As we have argued, in a fast-paced world, strategic planning cannot be an annual event, nor can it take nine months to complete; it has to be transformed into a continuing process, updated as required by the rate of change in the corporation's business environment. Corporations that move quickly from concept to action use strategic planning as a process to enable continuous, strategic decision making. As we described in chapter 3, what is required is a short-cycle planning process, lasting no more than six to eight weeks and updated at least quarterly. This process creates and maintains shared understanding within the executive team[6] and a highly focused strategic agenda of a limited number of initiatives, say three or four, that can be deployed simultaneously. This approach greatly enhances the likelihood of successful rapid deployment.

### *Timely, Strategic Decision Making*

An effective strategic planning process is worth nothing if strategic decisions are not made on a timely basis. Responsive organizations use strategic planning to enable the implementation of tough strategic decisions, but they also exhibit other characteristics that ensure timely decision making. They are willing to make decisions on emergent strategies as required. Once the need for a major decision is evident, they do not wait to make it. And they minimize the time spent studying the decision, knowing that on balance they are more often right than wrong.

Timely decisions require a number of enablers. The most important of these include an orientation to action, a clear understanding of who is accountable for making particular decisions, and systems that can provide relevant information fast.

## Continuous Funding of Strategic Initiatives

Many executives are realizing that in a fast-paced business environment, the funding of strategic priorities cannot wait until the next budget cycle. Companies that outpace their competitors often employ budget processes that enable them to fund major initiatives as they arise, rather than wait for the next budget cycle. This approach can dramatically shorten the time between making a decision and moving to action from months to weeks or, in some cases, days.

## Concurrent or Parallel Deployment Activities

As described in chapter 2, we have observed that corporations that achieve significant initial outcomes increasingly focus on a limited set of initiatives at any one time. For each initiative, they employ a parallel-deployment approach that dramatically shortens the time needed to achieve results.

As we will discuss in chapter 7, in the case of concurrent product development, corporations carry out market, product, and process development in parallel.[7] In the case of new facility construction, buildings are likely to be erected even as detailed engineering of the processes that they will house is being completed. There are strong parallels to these approaches in the deployment of a corporate or business-unit strategic plan, as was shown in figure 2.3.

Ford's transformation in the early 1980s[8] is a striking example of this type of approach. Even during the initial major downsizing activity that was undertaken to reduce costs and lower break-even volumes, Ford was piloting new approaches to automobile design in the Taurus project and conducting initial experiments with employee involvement. Thereafter, major changes in Ford's substantive business practices were paralleled by the redesign of its organizational processes, continuing communications initiatives, and numerous symbolic initiatives that demonstrated commitment to a new strategy and culture. Consequently, Ford was able to complete a radical strategic and cultural transformation in less than five years, whereas the more publicized efforts simultaneously under way at General Electric took over a decade.

## Pursuit of Near-Term Results and Outcomes

Organizations that deploy strategies rapidly appear to recognize the importance of achieving near-term results and outcomes from their plans and initiatives. When action plans for deployment are being developed, they specifically address the requirement for demonstrable results. For example, Softco's deployment plan included five specific deliverables within a sixty-day time frame. These included the launch of a new service line, improvements in customer service, and an employee involvement initiative. All of these deliverables were in line with the company's four major long-term strategic initiatives.

Executives report that the pursuit of near-term results has several benefits for the strategy process. Most important, it enhances the credibility of the entire process, demonstrating to employees and customers alike that strategy is really about action. Second, this focus maintains the sense of momentum and energy that is often created in successful strategic planning activities. Third, the results provide an early indication of the likely success of the entire strategy.

## Proactive, Pervasive Communication Protocols

To enable rapid strategy deployment, a correspondingly fast network is required to communicate strategic decisions to key stakeholder groups that, in addition to employees, may include key customers, suppliers, and investors. Given the nature of these communications, direct face-to-face interaction is preferable, especially for manager, supervisory, and professional groups, because it provides an opportunity for questions and discussion that can lead to significantly deeper understanding and greater buy-in. If this is not possible, live simulcast video-conference presentations are increasingly feasible for many large organizations. These face-to-face presentations can be supplemented by use of the Internet, videos, and other electronic media.

## In Summary

If organizations want to learn to move faster, then it is imperative that they measure and understand the speed at which they develop and implement strategic decisions as a basis for improved strategic effectiveness. Their executives need to learn to act on strategic issues and opportunities within weeks, rather than months or years. As a first step in this process, executive teams should develop a shared understanding of why strategic decision making takes so long in their organization and how out of touch they are with leading companies.

To initiate this change in thinking and culture, a first step is to measure representative times for each of the six stages in the strategy development and implementation process. Benchmarking and process analysis can then indicate the possibilities for achieving significant improvements. This analysis, in combination with the adoption of the characteristics exhibited by fast-moving corporations, can lead to radical reductions in the time required to achieve significant strategic outcomes for any organization.

# 5

## Launching the New Strategic Plan

The new strategy, your game plan for change, has been developed. Through the strategic planning process, you've laid the foundations for implementation success and established the initial Winning Conditions:

- Correct diagnosis of the change challenge.
- Creation of initial shared understanding and a sense of urgency among the executive team and other key stakeholders.
- A limited and focused agenda for change, broken down into campaigns.

Now it is time to launch the plan and ensure that other critical Winning Conditions are established, namely:

- Diffusion and enrichment of shared understanding.
- Establishment of a sense of urgency throughout the organization.
- Rapid decision making and deployment of initiatives.
- A human flywheel of commitment.
- Identification and management of the sources of resistance.
- Follow-through on changing organization enablers.
- Demonstrated leadership for the change.

These Winning Conditions rarely get established without proper consideration of critical organizational issues; for example, eliminating silos, replacing outdated policies, and enhancing communications. In addition, basic characteristics of organizations, such as degree of decentralization and levels of hierarchy, influence the outcome of change initiatives. Taken together, they have clear implications for the success of implementation: address key organizational issues or risk failure. As a case in point, one frustrated vice-president of technology told us that she could never build real momentum around new product initiatives because her colleagues were unwilling to help her break down the silos between Marketing, Operations, and the Research and Development group.

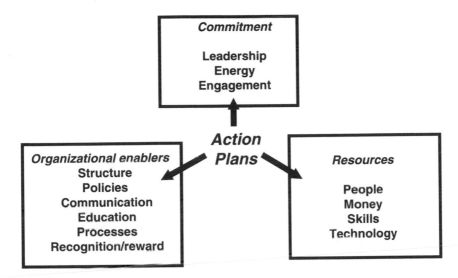

**Figure 5.1** Strategy Implementation

Without addressing organizational, resource, and commitment issues, it will be impossible to establish the rest of the Winning Conditions. As figure 5.1 shows, these three major factors are at work with respect to deployment. Specific action plans, with clearly defined accountabilities, provide the "glue" that holds these elements together. By rapidly aligning all three with the new direction, a sufficient level of acceptance can be gained so that change can proceed rapidly, even if most employees have not yet internalized the new strategy. Nevertheless, there are differences among organizations that affect implementation activities. These are the focus of the next section.

## The Impact of Organization Characteristics

Organizations vary along any number of dimensions. As these dimensions relate to strategy deployment, the difficulties encountered appear to be associated with:

- The size and extent of decentralization of the organization.
- The complexity of the strategic initiatives undertaken.
- The cultural orientation toward change.
- The extent to which new skills, capabilities, and behaviors are required.
- The credibility of strategic intent, which is determined largely by the corporate track record in previous cycles.

Strategy deployment becomes more difficult as firms increase in size, particularly if all employees are affected. Sheer size makes it much harder to gain broad commitment to a strategic direction. Communication is difficult: there are barriers horizontally, between units, and vertically, between levels in the organization; it is hard to build an informed consensus. Moreover, once a commitment has been made, it is hard to change direction should the strategy need to be significantly revised.

In addition, the more decentralized an organization is, the more difficult it becomes to create alignment among divisions, departments, and functions. In decentralized firms, executives value their autonomy to the extent that subunit objectives and strategies can take precedence over the primary interests of the entire corporation. In this situation, strategy deployment depends heavily on political influence and negotiation.

Complexity of initiatives adds a considerable degree of difficulty to strategy deployment. Strategies that require significant levels of involvement from different groups within the corporation, and also from external resources, are extremely difficult to execute well, particularly if they involve a multitude of tasks. Successful execution in this situation requires an extremely high order of project management capability to manage the risks. The deployment of a major, new information technology system, with links to customers and suppliers, is an example of this type of initiative, for which failure rates are very high.

The further change strategies are from the thrust of existing strategies and from the current culture of the organization, the more challenging they are to deploy, especially in organizations that consider themselves successful. In these organizations, in which executives with a degree of foresight may be trying to implement anticipatory changes to strategy, it is extremely difficult to convince employees—even at relatively senior levels—to abandon traditional practices and attitudes that have worked very well for them.

In organizations that employees perceive to be failing, there is a large degree of openness to change, in the interest of survival. However, once survival has been achieved, there is a risk that attitudes and behaviors will revert to precrisis norms unless some follow-up activities are implemented to entrench the shifts that have been made.

Many strategic initiatives are doomed to failure from the outset because executives responsible for implementation are unable to see a need for new skills and capabilities that are not present in the corporation. A typical mistake in this respect is making executives accountable for strategies in areas in which they lack a basic level of competence or comprehension, rather than recruiting the appropriate skills from outside the corporation. A customer-focus initiative in a nonmarketing corporation is much more likely to be successful if headed by an experienced outsider than if led by an inexperienced executive from within.

Ultimately, the success of strategy deployment comes down to the effectiveness of the process itself.[1] In many corporations, the whole process is undermined by lack of success with previous efforts due to failure to deal with opposition, absence of a collective approach, failure to resource initiatives adequately, and lack of accountability. In these circumstances, each new initiative is met with a high degree of skepticism, particularly in corporations in which employees perceive executives to be heavily influenced by current management fads and trends; "this, too, will pass" is a typical attitude in these instances.

There is no doubt that organizational culture is a principal determinant of the effectiveness and efficiency of strategy implementation. Launching a strategic plan is easiest when the culture supports the direction of change from the outset. As we have seen, however, the toughest type of change to implement is one in which culture, as well as strategy, has to change. This situation would not seem to bode well for implementation. But we found it interesting that many organizations managed to launch their new plan successfully even when the culture appeared inappropriate at the outset. How can this be? In this chapter, we will demonstrate that as long as employee behavior can be changed rapidly, then implementation can proceed, even if the fundamental values of the organization have not yet been realigned with the new direction.

For example, one corporation that we studied wanted a rapid acceptance of employee involvement, one aspect of which was a high and sustained level of implemented proposals for cost and quality improvement. At the outset, few supervisors and employees appeared interested enough to actively support the initiative. One executive described the response as "widespread apathy, in fact, dynamic apathy." However, the executive team set a challenging target of an average of five proposals per employee in the first year of the activity. Managers demonstrated their interest in the proposals that were submitted, provided rapid feedback and encouragement, and supported fast implementation for good proposals. As supervisors and employees experienced the resulting personal and work-related benefits, support for the activity grew quickly. By the end of the first year, proposals were running at an average rate of one per employee per month, with a 70 percent implementation rate. Quality was up, costs were down, and there were tangible signs of a positive culture change as values shifted to catch up with behaviors.

## Launching the Plan—The First 100 Days

What are the key challenges in the first 100 days? If this period is truly about creating speed, then the challenges relate to moving forward purposefully and generating acceleration. Frequently, however, speed is not achieved within the first 100 days. The strategy may be snarled up in validation and approval activities. Key executives may still be withholding support. Communication may be fragmented and ineffective. The old rules may continue to apply. Even worse, if the strategy is launched at the wrong time of year, perhaps in the early summer months or around a major holiday such as Christmas, everyone could be away!

If the first 100 days in the life of a new strategic plan concern building speed in its deployment and bringing it to life, then typical objectives must include:

- Gaining required approvals for the plan.
- Implementing two or three tangible initial deliverables.
- Champions and coalitions active around each key initiative.
- Completion of any validation activities.

In many ways, the primary concern in the first 100 days is winning the hearts and minds of the initial 20 percent of employees who will actively support the new plan. It is also about building broad awareness and understanding of the need for change. Some initial tangible deliverables should also be secured. Key enablers required in this period include:

- Developing awareness and understanding of the plan among employees and key stakeholders.
- Gaining direct involvement of the initial 20 percent of employees to generate the human flywheel.
- Dealing with any identified sources of resistance.
- Aligning of short-term recognition and rewards.
- Symbolic executive actions demonstrating leadership with respect to behaviors appropriate for the new direction, particularly if culture change is an issue.

## What *Not* To Do in the First 100 Days

The first and most important thing to avoid during the first 100 days of rolling out the new strategic plan is another reorganization. Unless the organization is truly "broken," it should not need to be reorganized during this period. Employees in many organizations, in public and private sectors alike, are highly cynical about reorganizations. They have endured this action so many times, and yet nothing *really* changes as a result. Moreover, reorganization may take the focus and energy away from more important, substantive activities that need to be implemented. In the first days of launching a new strategic plan, the focus should be on tangible actions that support a change in direction, not on another rearrangement of the deck chairs. Only if reorganization can be tied directly to a key substantive element of the strategy should it be a priority.

What about recognition and rewards during the first 100 days of the new strategic plan? Unless these have been worked on in parallel with the development of the new strategy, it's unlikely that a revised formal system of performance evaluations and rewards can be developed quickly. In fact, it is probably not realistic to attempt a complete overhaul or redevelopment of the current system at this stage.

Within this period of time, it's frequently more appropriate to put in place a temporary and relatively informal recognition and reward process that celebrates individual and team achievements with respect to the new direction. For example, milestones can be established that, if attained, trigger token awards and celebrations. These awards can be lighthearted. For example, one organization established the "giraffe" award for people who were willing to stick their necks out and take a risk and the "flying pig" award for people who implemented ideas that seemed impossible at first.

Above all, don't starve the key strategic initiatives of resources. The resources required for implementation have to be secured and put in place quickly if speed and momentum are to be built rapidly. During the action planning stages of developing the plan, it is vital to identify the key human resources required, particularly those that will be dedicated on a full-time basis, and to prepare initial budget estimates.

## The Second 100 Days

The challenge of the second 100 days of deploying the new strategic plan is to ensure that momentum builds to the point that it cannot be reversed. Typical objectives for this period include:

- Achieving of initial major objectives and outcomes.
- Gaining active commitment from up to 50 percent of the human flywheel.
- Eliminating of active resistance to the strategy.

Key enablers include:

- Key organizational processes and systems in place.
- Realignment of resources and priorities around the new strategy.
- Budget and human resource commitments to key initiatives.

What are the key challenges in the second 100 days, when the aim is to build momentum? Building momentum requires both mass and speed. Speed should have been building through the first 100 days, so now mass is required to drive the strategic plan forward. When new strategies are starved of key resources, implementation is often still a part-time activity. Key employees have not been deployed to work full-time on the new strategy. Priorities have not been re-aligned. If communication is poor, most of the organization is still operating under the old rules. If budgeting is inflexible, necessary financial resources have yet to be committed.

Hence, the primary task for the second 100 days is realigning resources to build momentum. It's also about increasing the size of the human flywheel that drives the process. Key actions that build on the speed generated in the first 100 days and that now will build momentum include:

- Increasing the size of the human flywheel core to over 40 percent.
- Realigning key human resources behind the critical strategic initiatives.
- Ensuring budget allocations to major strategic initiatives.
- Realigning organizational priorities with those of the new strategy.
- Having initial key deliverables embodied in success stories.
- Reinforcing the initial strategic communications with key stakeholders through newsletters, success stories, and updates.

## Establishing the Remaining Winning Conditions

### Diffusion and Enrichment of Shared Understanding

Communication is clearly one of the major organizational enablers for launching a new strategic plan, one that executives frequently deal with inadequately. The breadth, depth, and speed of communication throughout the organization profoundly influence the diffusion and creation of shared understanding and, hence, the pace of implementation. If it takes six months or a year for frontline people to receive effective communication about strategic initiatives, then the organization is in trouble. However, this is frequently the case. Major decisions, even those with frontline implications, frequently take months to filter down. When they do, the impact is often fragmented and disjointed, reaching some areas but not others. Of course, control of communication channels is also important from the perspective that if it is in the hands of people who are opposed to change, then only the information that they wish to be communicated will be passed on.

Successful CEOs know that they have to communicate the key elements of their plan to all employees within the first 100 days if speed is to be secured. Although there are no hard-and-fast rules in this respect, successful executives tend to agree that the more information that can be provided, the more accepting employees are of the new strategy, especially if it is being carried out in a proactive manner, without a crisis. They also concur that the faster it is achieved, the better.

How much can you tell people about a new strategy? If you don't communicate fast, then it's inevitable that the rumor mill will do the job for you, usually with corresponding negative side effects. In fact, an organization can be paralyzed by stories of impending divestitures, closures, or layoffs. Many successful executives, like Paul Tellier of CN, are known as straight shooters by the rank and file in their organizations. They present a truthful message, be the news good or bad.

Secrecy is frequently a factor that limits communications. If major business changes are involved, then disclosure requirements may limit what executives in public corporations can share with their employees. Of course, there's always the fear that the competition will find out about your intentions. But if you act fast, this is less of a concern because by the time they can respond, you should already be well down the road.

If you don't communicate frequently enough, then the shared understanding that's required for implementation does not develop. High-level presentations fail to provide the needed level of understanding for employees to understand how the new strategy affects how they should behave. A one-time communication simply isn't sufficient.

Few companies execute strategic communication very well. Typically, it's too little, too late, and unidirectional. Even the good change leaders frequently give themselves poor marks in this respect. Employees certainly do, and they demonstrate their dissatisfaction in a variety of ways, from apathy to outright resistance. CEOs we have interviewed generally identify this aspect of the task as the one that the executive team underestimates far too often. Increasingly, the reality seems to be that if the strategy is not well communicated after 100 days, it is destined to fail.

This problem is not atypical. Managers and supervisors are asked to communicate the new strategy to their subordinates, but rarely does it happen as planned. Many simply do not do it. Others pass on the message, but either they fail to capture the essence, leaving employees somewhat confused, or they cannot answer the questions and allay the concerns raised in the presentations.

In one government department that launched a major change initiative, the executive team met to finalize a new strategy and left the meeting with a ninety-day action plan and a commitment to share the game plan with their subordinates within two weeks. Three months later, when the management council met for their twice-yearly meeting, over 80 percent of the second-tier managers still had not heard directly about the new game plan. Although the chief executive in the department was shocked by this disclosure, there were no consequences for those who had failed to communicate the plan. This was a complete failure in leadership; six months after the first meeting, the plan still had to be communicated to the department's workforce. Needless to say, strategy implementation stalled.

Strategic communication is far too important to be left to chance. In its own way, this vital component of organizational change needs its own strategy just as much as other components. Phases should be designed to build awareness, create and enrich understanding, as well as to communicate progress and successes. In fact, many organizations we have worked with have a communications specialist who works with executives on these matters.

So who needs to know what, when, and how? Does everyone in the corporation need to know at the same time, or can communications be phased in over a period of time? Those directly engaged in driving change and those who will be affected need to know as soon as possible. One question remains: Is it better to leave others relatively in the dark so that they can remain focused on what they have to do, or is it better to provide some information to everyone to reduce uncertainty and the likelihood of ill feelings that arise from people who feel that they have been left in the dark?

There are advantages to rolling out the communications in a rapid, phased manner. Sessions with managers can be held prior to those with supervisors so managers are informed and supportive when their subordinates have questions and concerns. Similarly, supervisors and key professionals need to be informed before wage-roll employees. This is particularly important because, as we have noted previously, supervisors can make or break a strategy, depending on their attitudes. If they express confidence in the new direction, you are well on the way to building a human flywheel. If they are uninformed and skeptical, the task of creating momentum will be more difficult.

While working on change with corporations, we have come to talk of the "strategy release" process, using an analogy to software releases in high-technology firms. Some companies that are successful in quickly moving change have developed a disciplined process of simultaneous release of strategic information, tailored to each audience, throughout their organization. In fact, some go so far as to have simultaneous meetings each month, attended by every employee, that are devoted to a specific strategic initiative "release" synchronized across the company.

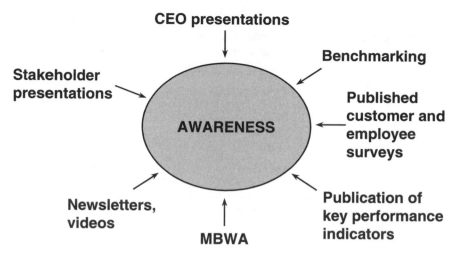

**Figure 5.2** Building Awareness and a Sense of Urgency

## Establishment of a Sense of Urgency Throughout the Organization

Deployment of a new strategic plan proceeds best if awareness of the plan can be created rapidly and a sense of urgency can be built around deployment of the early initiatives. Hopefully, involvement of a broad cross section of employees in the planning process itself will have started to create this dynamic. More will need to be done, however. Figure 5.2 summarizes a number of the tools that executives have at their disposal to create both awareness and a sense of urgency during the first 100 and 200 days.

CEO presentations are a good place to start. These can stress commitment and the need to move fast. They should be accompanied by an opportunity for employees to discuss the plan among themselves immediately after the presentation, followed by a question period. Employees also need to be able to discuss the implications of the strategy for their own department and behaviors, either in the same session or shortly afterward. This initial presentation should be followed, within a few weeks, by a second presentation, this time by members of the executive team to all employees in their jurisdictions. This second presentation reinforces the initial message and is also an opportunity for further discussion of how the plan will affect particular units. These presentations can be complemented by articles in the company newsletter, videos, a Web site, and other vehicles. Of course, the message will be all the more powerful if these presentations are reinforced by informal MBWA (management by walking around) activities.

There should also be presentations to other key stakeholders within the first 200 or, depending on criticality, even the first 100 days from launch. Because the plan may have important implications for customers and vendors, presentations of relevant parts should be made to at least the largest and most important of these. Again, the message should be clear: "Be ready—we're on the move." In addition, the plan may have to be presented to the board for approval during this period. As we have noted, though, the launching of some activities can probably proceed without formal board approval. Finally, a summary of the plan may be communicated to the business media.

These presentations can be structured in such a way as to communicate a sense of urgency. In addition, either as part of the content or separately, messages can be conveyed about the competitive reality or the customer requirements that make speed imperative. Hard, cold facts from benchmarking activities are a useful tool in this respect. Facts on the emerging competitive challenge were a key ingredient in the messages that Doug Harrison conveyed to his employees and the parent company at the launch of Acklands-Grainger's strategic plan.

Of course, the 100-day and 200-day action plans, with associated goals and accountabilities, in themselves provide a sense of urgency at this stage, particularly if those responsible for implementation know that there will be follow-up. This feeling can only be heightened if executives and managers know that part of their performance assessment will be based on how well they execute these initial tasks.[2] Also heightening the sense of urgency, but to be used with discretion, are short-term "big hairy audacious goals." Setting challenging targets for the first 100 and 200 days can inject urgency into the process. However, if employees are not shown how these can be achieved, or if they believe that they are ridiculous, then these can demotivate, rather than inspire.

### Rapid Decision Making and Deployment of Initiatives

The major reason that many executives believe that they do not receive full value from their strategic planning activities is that deployment is weak. In part, barriers arise because many organizations view change as a part-time activity, something to be done on top of everyone's usual job. Few organizations dedicate resources to change activities. Instead, the process is regarded and treated as something to be worked on once normal work is completed.

Access to the appropriate resources is critical for building and sustaining momentum. However, in our research and consulting, we have been told time and again by managers, "We are strategic until budget time, and then strategy goes out of the window." In other words, despite the best of intentions, needed resources are not made available.

Why does this happen? If you designed a house and told the builder that you had only half the money you needed, he would build you a much smaller house. When engineers are told that the available capital budget for the new plant is smaller than originally estimated, they take out the frills and reduce the capacity. Yet, managers are always attempting to deploy strategies with considerably smaller budgets and fewer resources than they expected to have. Then they wonder why they finish late or fail completely.

The first issue for many organizations is their approach to establishing and processing their capital and operating budgets. The traditional budgeting model treats a number of key investments in support of strategic initiatives as period expenses. Far too often, budgeting is a negotiation game: an initial level is proposed, then one or two rounds of reductions are demanded. What is often sacrificed in this process are the budgets for employee training and development, infrastructure spending, and product and market development—items that can be perceived as "discretionary" in a given period. Faced with demands for additional cuts in their "operating" budgets, these are the items that managers reduce or defer, rather than actual period operating expenses. The result? Inadequate levels of support for key strategic initiatives.

A complementary problem is that most managers do not want to tell their superiors that they can deliver only so much with a given budget and level of resources. Strategic plan commitments are based on the assumption that the required resources will be forthcoming in the budget. During the budgeting process, if the level of resources available is sharply reduced or a promised increase does not materialize, then the full scope of the strategy, in the time frame contemplated, is probably unattainable. In this situation, a reappraisal of the plan is needed to reduce its scope, extend time frames, or creatively rethink the overall approach. However, managers feel that either they do not have time or they would be seen as failures if they asked for a reappraisal.

Implementation of the new plan is made possible by ensuring that the right resources are available in the necessary form. We have already seen how traditional budgeting approaches often lead to an insufficiency of resources to support rapid change. Recognizing this problem, an increasing number of corporations, such as General Electric, no longer talk about capital and operating budgets in a traditional accounting sense, but about *program* and operating budgets in a management accounting context. Within this new framework, program budgets to support strategic initiatives are established separately from the operating budget. Business development, employee training and development, and infrastructure investment are included as part of the program budget. When the time comes to fine-tune the operating budget, the required reductions cannot be obtained from the program budget, which is not allowed to be cut at this point.

Successful deployment of a new strategic plan has as much to do with the tactics as with the context. In this respect, there are a number of critical success factors that must be observed:

- Each initiative should be embodied in a limited set of concise action plans.
- Action plans should not be overly detailed; initial actions should be planned and subsequent decisions left to managers in the field.
- Each member of the planning team must state his or her agreement to these plans.
- An employee should be assigned full-time to champion each major strategic initiative.
- Periodic reviews should be held to evaluate progress and create continuing action plans.

- Achievements of significant goals and milestones should be acknowledged and celebrated.

As noted earlier, the first requirement for effective deployment is to ensure that specific action plans for each key initiative are developed. These plans have a maximum time horizon of three to six months, with specific accountabilities detailed within this horizon. In most corporations, detailed action planning beyond this horizon is not realistic due to the uncertainties inherent in any business.

Although these action plans need to be fairly detailed, they need not be exhaustive. If the overall objectives and goals are clear, and managers understand the initial thrusts that are planned, they can sustain momentum by making sound decisions in the field and by being aware that they will be held accountable for their actions at periodic review sessions during which strategies and action plans will be broadly reviewed, aligned, and updated.

Each major strategic initiative should have an employee with appropriate qualifications, experience, and seniority acting as a full-time champion to drive implementation. Evidence accrued from a variety of unsuccessful quality, involvement, and customer service initiatives indicates that collective commitment to an initiative within an executive team is not sufficient to create and maintain momentum. The cost of a full-time champion, even a senior executive assigned for one or two years, is likely to be small in any firm when compared to the costs of a failed make-or-break initiative.

Reinforcing and maintaining momentum require a sense of accomplishment and accountability that can be achieved only through periodic reviews and updates. A typical format is to hold a quarterly strategy review session (either face-to-face or by tele/videoconference) in which progress is reviewed and action plans outlined for the period ahead. Some corporations also hold brief assessments of individual initiatives on a rotating monthly basis so that each initiative is thoroughly reviewed at least three or four times per year. In addition, some chief executive officers periodically hold individual performance reviews with individuals accountable for successful implementation.

Finally, it is important to recognize achievement and celebrate successes when they occur. Newsletters are a useful vehicle by which to report progress and provide recognition. Significant milestones can be marked by lunches, dinners, and small token awards involving either the team directly involved with an initiative or the whole organization unit. Whatever means is employed, progress will be reinforced and maintained only through delivery of appropriate recognition to the individuals who are making it happen.

### A Human Flywheel of Commitment

Engagement is the key to building a human flywheel during the launch of a new strategic plan.[3] This can be secured through communication, as long as it is two-way, but more important, through involvement in action. During the first

**Table 5.1** Symbolic Indicators of Change

- Hire/fire employees
- Change the slogan
- Drop products and close facilities—fast!
- Experiment with new approaches
- Visible executive actions
- Informal recognition schemes
- Physical workplace changes
- Visible targets and performance measures

100 and 200 days of the launch, this can come through either symbolic activities or involvement in substantive initiatives that can be launched quickly.

What are the symbolic actions that can reinforce the launch of a new strategic plan? As illustrated by table 5.1, there are many alternatives to choose from. The only limits here are imposed by the imaginations of the leadership team members. These actions must be tailored to the nature of the strategy. When there is no crisis, symbolic actions take on additional meaning when launching a new strategic plan. For example, if innovation is required, rapid implementation of an informal system of recognizing successful innovators can be a powerful symbol. In customer service, everyday reminders for employees about their attitudes, such as buttons, computer screens, and posters, can provide powerful visual reinforcement in the first 100 days.

Whatever the situation, the rate of change is likely to be accelerated if the executive team takes some immediate steps to address sources of resistance and barriers to progress. These may be substantive, but if taken early, they can also be highly symbolic of management's determination to succeed. One of the most obvious of these is dealing effectively with one or two employees who are seen as the focal points for resistance. Whether the action taken is removal, demotion, or sidelining, dealing with resistance quickly sends out a powerful message that it will not be tolerated. Usually, the only response to such moves from the majority of employees is "What took you so long?"

Changing logos and slogans is another way of demonstrating intent symbolically. We all know how powerful and enduring "Quality is Job 1" was in Ford's turnaround in the 1980s. One Canadian organization adopted "Bravo" as its rallying cry for recognition because the word has powerful positive connotations in both English and French. It became the title of the organization's newsletter, which was used for communicating strategy and success stories. Bravo awards were developed to recognize outstanding efforts in the organization. However, care has to be taken with changing symbols. The intent that they embody has to be backed up by actions that ensure that these are not empty promises.

Not changing symbols that have become sources of cynicism can inhibit deep change by delaying employee buy-in. For many employees, particular symbols can be flags to indicate change. In interviews with wage-roll employees and supervisors, we have often heard the phrase, "I'll only believe that things are really changing around here when. . . ." The subject matter may be something as trivial as reserved parking spaces, the executive dining room, or the free coffee for executives and managers. Finding out what these symbols are and addressing them within the first 100 days can send out small, yet powerful signals of commitment and intent that help bring the fence-sitters on board and give those driving change something tangible to point to.

What about substantive actions? Quick wins have long been identified as a major ingredient of successful change, but these wins need to be real and not just cosmetic. In the first 100 days of strategic plan deployment, every attempt should be made to achieve some key deliverables that will convince employees that the organization is serious about its change initiative. One of the key elements of the action planning phase of strategy development is to identify actions that can be taken rapidly and that will produce tangible benefits for frontline employees. That's when change really starts to have meaning.

So what kind of actions are these? We refer to them as "no-brainers," whereas others may call them the "low-hanging fruit." Typically, these are actions in line with the new strategy that require little study, planning, or piloting before they can be implemented. There are a number of ways of identifying what these might be. Often, members of the planning group are able to suggest them. They may even be actions that have been advocated for a considerable period of time but have never been implemented. During the planning process, one CEO we interviewed makes a point of finding out from his frontline managers and employees what actions could improve the effectiveness of what they do. Then, during the action planning stage of the strategy development process, she finds a way to incorporate some of these items into the 100-day deployment process. Not only do these actions often have real meaning for employees, but they are also symbolic of a new direction.

Another concept that is relevant in the first 100 and 200 days is the strategy release, one of the key enablers of building shared understanding. One of the major challenges in the deployment of a new strategy is how to phase in the change. Typically, too much is introduced at one time and implementation is uneven across the organization, particularly if there is substantial decentralization. In some areas, one aspect of change becomes the focus, while in others, the emphasis is different. As a result, momentum fails to develop. When strategy deployment is phased in across the organization in a series of coordinated "releases" in which managers and supervisors inform and educate employees about the initiative, the results are a sense of coherence in moving forward, the creation of momentum, and greater consistency. In addition, employees gain the feeling that the organization is being thoughtful about change.

Strategy releases are organized around the staged deployment of a new strategic plan. As a part of the planning process, specific dates and milestones are targeted for implementing the next initiative. For example, the first of January is an opportune time in many organizations for the release of new employee compensation plans. New products, processes, and programs can all be introduced in this manner. A release has a specific set of activities associated with it, including a design and preparation stage, a communication and rollout stage, and a follow-up activity. It is important that each organization unit involved moves through the process in a simultaneous time frame; this contrasts with the relatively ad hoc process employed by most organizations, which results in patchwork implementation.

## Identification and Management of the Sources of Resistance

There is always resistance of some form to the launch of a new strategic plan. Much apparent resistance, as we have already noted, stems from lack of awareness and understanding, which can be substantially alleviated by effective communication of the plan. However, there will still be perceived winners and losers. Executives and managers may feel that their priorities are not reflected in the plan. Others may be upset at the fact that resources have been reallocated away from their area. Major changes in human resource strategies and programs may cause supervisors to offer resistance because they feel threatened.

A possible resistance issue is a lack of commitment demonstrated by members of the leadership to others in the organization.[4] At the launching of a new strategic plan, the 20-70-10 rule may be operational within the leadership team. A typical observation in this respect is that when the change plan is being developed, everyone in the team appears to be in agreement and committed. No dissenting voices are heard. However, as one insightful executive noted, "We wink as we leave the room." In other words, there is no deep commitment to elements of the strategy, particularly those on which tough decisions have to be made. Although, in principle, everyone is in agreement with the strategy, there are certain elements that individuals do not agree with. Once out of the room, they vocalize their dissent or, even worse, may be heard disparaging the strategy to coworkers. The best remedy for this is for the CEO to go around the table when key decisions are being taken and ask the following: "Are you in support of this decision? Can you at least live with it? Don't leave the room and complain outside if you haven't voiced your concerns here."[5]

More generally, the challenge in dealing with opposition is to first find out where it is coming from. One-on-one conversations are then appropriate. Another solution is to have the leadership team assign responsibilities for actions to individuals whom they suspect of being against the intent of the plan. This assignment is an opportunity for these individuals to visibly demonstrate their commitment, or lack of it, to the new direction. If they deliver, that's great! However, if they intentionally fail to deliver, then, as one executive told us, "It's three strikes and you're out. I've given you an opportunity to perform, the message was clear, and you chose not to accept the challenge."

## Effective Follow-through on Changing Organizational Enablers

The launch of a new strategic plan can be either facilitated or hindered by a number of organizational characteristics, including structure, policies, processes, communications, and knowledge, as well as rewards and recognition. We have talked with many executives and managers who believe that they have either been defeated by these factors or succeeded in spite of them. Conversely, we have heard many accounts of how rapid changes in these elements, early in the change process, can make all the difference. For example, CEO Tellier told us about his five key "levers" that include changing the leadership team, compensation, training, new blood, and communicating successes. Talking of initiating deep change at Unisys, Larry Weinbach commented, "The first thing we did is we had to get competitive from an HR standpoint and that's why we put in pay for performance, Unisys University, flexible benefits."

Organization processes are also important factors in implementing change because these determine how the organization works.[6] Employees will sometimes state that they implemented change "despite" these processes. Once again, control of organization processes can be used to stifle and defeat change. For example, in a number of major corporations, it has been necessary to break the entrenched power of finance departments before real change could get under way. In the name of prudent financial control, an entrenched finance group can starve change initiatives of required funding. In other cases with which we are familiar, the Human Resources group has stalled change for months and even years by failing to cooperate with requests for the redesign of employee reclassification or reward systems.

Changes in processes are complementary to substantive organization change. If employee empowerment is on the agenda, then it is highly likely that the organization will have to completely redesign the processes by which employee ideas and proposals can be submitted, evaluated, and implemented. If innovation is the focus, then it is quite likely that both funding and development processes will have to change.

Education and employee development are also powerful enablers of effective implementation.[7] Until they are shown and instructed in the new behaviors that are required, employees at all levels find it hard to implement change. Education should be part of the early stage of any change initiative because it can play a critical role in building awareness of the need for change and understanding of the new behaviors and task structures that are necessary for success.

Another major organizational issue is lack of alignment among corporate functional groups. Part of our research looked at the role of such groups as Human Resources, Information Technology, Logistics, Purchasing, and Finance and Accounting in facilitating change. Too often, we heard that these groups were not aligned with the process or that well-intentioned initiatives had the opposite outcome to that originally intended. For example, in many cases, poorly executed programs aimed at taking low-value-added work out of field processes actually ended up creating more work for line managers and supervisors. Interviews with leaders of functional groups provided the following reasons that they often fail in their role as change agents:

- Failure to understand the real issues.
- Ivory-tower "arrogance," losing sight of day-to-day operations, lack of understanding of business needs.

- Distance from internal and external customers or failure to understand their expectations.
- Conflicting priorities/measurements or lack of alignment.
- Lack of communication.
- Unrealistic expectations or poor planning.
- Lack of buy-in by customers, functional groups, and management.
- Poor testing and piloting of new initiatives.
- Lack of standardized processes across the organization.
- Ineffective/intermittent leadership or lack of ownership.

Several organizations that we have worked with have held joint, functional strategy workshops among different departments that last up to three or four days. There are a number of benefits that flow from this kind of event. First, there is information sharing as each group presents its strategy, demonstrates its alignment with the overall organization strategy. Second, there is usually a significant opportunity to look at priorities, alignment, and synergies among the different group strategies. Finally, there is a substantial team-building component because this usually is the, first time that the participants have all been together in the same room at the same time.

The launch of a new strategic plan is either enabled or impeded by components embedded in the organization. Six of these are key factors, as shown in table 5.2.

The most critical of these factors, without a doubt, are reward and recognition systems, both formal and informal. Almost all of the executives we interviewed cited changes in these systems, early in the process, as key to success. Steele Alphin of Bank of America put it most succinctly: "I think that you set a huge goal, get the right people, and reward the hell out of them."

If reward and recognition systems are aligned with the new direction, change is facilitated. If they remain aligned with the past, they can stifle any change initiative. We could cite many examples of this, but a typical concern for many corporations involves sales productivity and performance. A number of corporations we have dealt with reported very low productivity from their sales forces. Upon closer inspection, a relatively small proportion of the salespeople's time was spent with customers and an almost insignificant proportion with new or potential customers. In almost every case, the reward system was primarily based on total territory sales revenues, rather than growth in sales. Employees with

**Table 5.2** Strategy Implementation Mechanisms (The Executive "Levers")

- Recognition and reward systems
- Organization structures
- Communication networks
- Information systems
- Employee education and development
- Policies and procedures

**Table 5.3** Recognition and Reward Framework

|  | Individual | Group |
|---|---|---|
| Recognition | — Commendation letters<br>— Articles, photographs, and publicity<br>— Senior executive visits<br>— Pats on the back | — Recognition dinners<br>— Articles and publicity<br>— Token gifts (jackets, T-shirts, etc.)<br>— Charitable donations<br>— Social events |
| Financial Reward | — Idea/suggestion plans<br>— Pay for performance<br>— Dinner awards<br>— Monthly drawings<br>— Vouchers or gift certificates | — Profit sharing<br>— Options<br>— Facilities or benefits<br>— Group discounts<br>— Pay for performance |

new territories were rarely able to earn a bonus, but those with a more established account base earned high bonuses just from maintenance activities.

Companies that realigned the sales compensation scheme with the growth objectives of the corporation achieved sustained improvement in sales performance fairly quickly, although not without some initial challenges. Salespeople with newer territories were motivated by the new plans and worked harder to bring in new business. However, a number of previously high-bonus employees were unsuccessful at developing new accounts, even with additional training and encouragement, and suffered a reduction in bonus earnings. Some eventually quit, which opened their territories to newer and more ambitious employees. By contrast, companies that did not change compensation systems, but did restructure, add training programs, and exhort management, hardly improved at all.

In most cases, it may be impossible to change the formal reward system quickly. It may be a year or more before existing pay and variable compensation systems, usually managed by Human Resources staff, can be realigned. Does this mean that change has to wait? Not at all. Successful change leaders have found that in the short term, effective use of informal recognition and rewards can be powerful motivators for change. Table 5.3 shows a matrix of individual and group recognition and reward. It's clear that there are many options for informal recognition that can provide powerful change incentives. In the early stages of change, the informal, nonfinancial recognition elements can be equally as motivating as the traditional financial elements.

Organization structure is a major factor that determines the success of implementation activities. In fact, it may be impossible to introduce change without changing structure. Which aspects of structure impede change the most? The most commonly mentioned are organization "silos" or "chimneys." These are the barriers that develop between different units and functions over time and that can critically inhibit horizontal cooperation and communication. It is not unusual for a major restructuring to last a year or more and, in the process, absorb large quantities of effort that might be more productively employed elsewhere at this stage of a new strategic plan. In many cases, however, simple changes in reporting relationships can accomplish much of what a major reorganization could, with much less effort involved. For example, one high-technology firm that wanted to improve its rate of new product launch quickly created the position of vice-president of technology, to whom all involved in this process now reported, either directly or through a "dotted line" relationship. With one stroke, the company effectively eliminated a number of the organizational silos that had been standing in the path of a flow of innovative new products.

Early in any change initiative, leaders should review how organization policies are influencing implementation. Policies influence change in profound ways. Frequently, policies are symbolic, as well as substantive, issues in change. Failure to address them can send out conflicting messages to employees and can reinforce inertia, not momentum. For example, executive perquisites, such as first-class travel, preferred parking, and club memberships, send out powerful signals about status. Faced with demands for change, employees will often state, "When they give up their perks, then I'll change my behavior."

Banks have found it necessary to change many policies in their efforts to become more responsive to customer needs. For example, in the past, most customer service representatives, or tellers, had to check with a supervisor or manager before they could make a financial adjustment to a customer account. Nowadays, some banks have limits as high as $1,000 under which these employees can take corrective action without approval from a supervisor. The result has been not only improved customer service, but also a far greater sense of empowerment by frontline staff.

### Demonstrated Leadership for the Change

Finally, even when the right organizational conditions for change are in place and the resources are available, personal factors still make the difference between success and failure. Although there is no single generic model for an effective change leader, a study of individuals who do a good job of implementation on a continuing basis suggests a number of personal traits that make a difference.

One of the major leadership issues in many large organizations is what we term "executive churn." The time frame for executive tenure in specific jobs has decreased markedly during 1990s in many organizations. We often hear of corporations and business units that have had three or four or five chief executives within five years. What is the strategy in these situations? All too often, a new executive wants to develop a whole new approach, so everything goes on hold while the new strategy is developed. What results is not that much different from what was in place before, but another six months or even a year has been added to the implementation timeline. Even worse is a new executive who arrives with "the shake-up formula," which often includes a token head-count reduction, a reorganization, and a reevaluation of all spending priorities. The uncertainty created by this type of approach in organizations that are already performing well can be extremely damaging.

*The Right Behaviors* What are the habits and characteristics of effective implementation leaders? Are they the same as those of successful senior executives and change agents? One aspect of our research has been to study the personal traits of individuals who have led the implementation of successful major change initiatives of different types. One conclusion that we have come to is that relatively few senior executives are effective implementers of change directly. Many of them have effective implementers working for them, but they don't actually do it themselves. For example, we have met a number of senior executives who are brilliant at making acquisitions, but they leave the integration and value capture to others. Likewise, we have had the opportunity to observe a number of multibillion-dollar capital projects in which the executive team leads the process, but skilled project and construction professionals lead implementation. CEO Alphin of Bank of America said the following about his COO:

> Ken Lewis's platform to lead is really based off of outstanding management skills—outstanding. He always makes his business plan. He always makes crisp decisions. He took his great management skills and then used them as a platform to become a great leader. . . . He talks about focus and discipline.

Rule number one for many executives, then, is to secure an effective implementer to lead change initiatives.

Although there is no one leadership style that appears to work, we found the following to be true of effective implementation leaders:

- Are unflappable.
- Have a high task focus.
- Are disciplined and logical about implementation.
- Are effective communicators.
- Work long hours.
- Energize teams.
- Get out to the "site."
- Demand results.

In our interviews, we also found that they appear to share seven habits (with due acknowledgment to Steven Covey)[8], which are shown in table 5.4. Most of these individuals have a normal operating mode that is delegative and participative, but they also appear to know how to be directive when their subordinates are unable to reach a decision. One senior executive told us, "Most of the

**Table 5.4** Seven Habits of Effective Implementers

- Never assume that *it's happening*—always follow up personally
- Develop an open relationship with people in the front line—obtain feedback
- Encourage people to express concerns
- Make surprise visits—socialize, observe, and learn
- Establish specific short-term deliverables with specific dates
- Establish clear expectations and accountabilities around key performance elements
- Don't tolerate lack of commitment

time, I'm willing to go with what the team decides—they usually know what's the right thing to do. However, when the team can't agree, then it's my job to listen and say, 'Here's what we'll do.' "

*Alternative Leadership Approaches* The approach to launching a new strategic plan may differ considerably according to the situation. In our experience, executives who fail at strategic change do so because they neither recognize which leadership approach is appropriate nor understand the key tasks involved in each. For example, failure to bring about change in a crisis situation often occurs because senior executives abdicate their responsibility for tough decisions on nonperforming employees, resource allocations, or "sacred cows" that are paralyzing the organization. By contrast, poor anticipatory strategic change frequently results from excessive secrecy about the new direction, failure to build awareness and understanding of the need for change, and failure to build a sense of urgency and momentum.

*The Crisis Approach: Top-down Management* Strategic change in the crisis or reactive mode is a top-down management process in which the willingness to exercise power is critical. Failure on the grounds that subordinates could not agree on a course of action is not an acceptable excuse. In the crisis mode, when results have to be forthcoming within days or weeks, change usually has to be led, at least initially, by direct executive intervention and decision making. Personal leadership, tough-mindedness, the willingness to ruthlessly abandon the familiar and the past, and the use of informal strategic "levers" are the hallmarks of sterling executive performance in such periods. Of his early days at Oracle, Ray Lane commented:

> When I first came on board I found myself in the middle of a political quagmire. The job that (CEO and founder) Larry Ellison brought me in for had not been fully communicated to everyone in the organization. So I had some senior people questioning if they worked for me or I worked for them, and what my actual role was. Fortunately, I was able to realign some of the senior management and in doing so clarified my role right away. . . . It allowed me to establish credibility and authority and have the whole organization recognize that I would be taking decisions, making them quickly, and that Larry would back me.

Pending insolvency or the rapid erosion of markets by competition leaves little time for the initial deployment steps that we have been describing. In these circumstances, strategic change has to be a process directed from the top down, often in the face of opposition from and disagreement among lower-level executives who have only a partial view of the complete strategic situation and who fear the loss of their own power.

Consensus management is practically impossible under these conditions, yet it is vital that dissension on substantive issues within top management not paralyze the corporation. One major Canadian consumer products manufacturer wasted a year and lost significant market share as executives fought over the "correct" strategic response to changed markets and declining corporate performance. An employee later commented, "Anything would have been better than the nothing that came out of the executive suite."

However, top-down leadership does not mean the imposition of a totalitarian state within the organization. Steele Alphin remarked, "I can find people to make really hard, tough decisions that have no people skills at all, and they'll make a decision one time because they'll have no one following them after that." So these individuals have to be prepared to make difficult decisions, but they also must possess the capability to work with and build a leadership team. Lack of commitment is not an option. Many chief executives faced with this situation ensure commitment to a major new direction through personal interviews with their executives in which they offer generous severance packages if the subordinates cannot completely support the proposed course of action. A fully committed executive team is the single most important success factor during periods of rapid strategic change.

The commitment of lower-level employees is best gained by direct communication between senior executives and the workforce. This is one time when "management by walking around" really pays off, even though there is a temptation during rapid change for executives to remain at the helm in the corporate office. Paul Tellier of CN continually visits the corporation's operating units as part of his communications strategy. He described his approach as follows:

> You have to be very straightforward with people, particularly when the news is tough. I remember visiting our facilities in Prince George [British Columbia] and being confronted by a woman in my audience who was concerned for the future of her family because both she and her husband worked for us, and job reductions were on the way. She broke down in tears. This is where your real test lies. You can't be false. You have to be direct, sincere, and compassionate. Your credibility rests on it.

Another executive we interviewed who has directed several corporate turnarounds said that his major policy in this period is "communicate, communicate, communicate," even though the temptation is to say as little as possible. Employees who are aware of the challenge facing them and who understand the need for quick, tough decisions are generally quick to accept reality and commit themselves to the new direction.

Long planning sessions are unproductive when rapid strategic change is necessary. Instead, having agreed on an overall strategy, successful executives prefer to hold frequent meetings throughout the organization. Progress is reviewed and a limited set of actions is agreed upon for the 90–120-day period immediately ahead.

In crisis change, there is little time to develop extensive plans, change the organization, or argue alternative courses of action in depth. It is a time for boldness in action and willingness to take on additional business risk for strategic advantage. Obstacles to change and "sacred cows" have to be identified and eliminated through direct top-management intervention. Some resource misallocations are likely in this period, and follow-up to ensure that the cows are really dead is usually necessary.

Existing strategy implementation mechanisms sometimes create major barriers to rapid change. The organization structure may be overly hierarchical, which imparts inflexibility and inertia to decision making. Resource allocation policies and reward systems often promote the status quo and discourage innovation. Recognition and reward policies, both formal and informal, may continue to encourage inappropriate behavior of the type that led to the need for change.

In such circumstances, executives know that radical moves may be necessary. Levels of management and supervision have to be eliminated, and long-established polices and procedures must be circumvented or abandoned. For the short term, at least, personal and informal procedures are most effective to deal with these issues until time can be found to institutionalize new structures and policies that support the changed strategy.

*Anticipatory Change: Mobilizing the Organization* When it is possible to anticipate and plan for change, the executive role becomes one of preparing the organization and creating a climate in which the driving force can be the commitment and involvement of many employees. The sponsoring of champions of the strategy and a willingness to persuade rather than order complement demonstrated personal commitment and are key factors in this type of strategic change. Executives can use changes in the implementation mechanisms or "levers" shown in figure 5.2 to create a corporate climate that builds employee commitment to the new direction, enables changes in behavior, and allows implementation to be led largely from the bottom up.

In well-prepared anticipatory change, it should also be possible to carry out many of the initiation activities already described in order to prepare the organization for full loyalty to the new strategy. Trials and pilots will have identified new strategic thrusts, which can now be followed up with major resource allocations. Changes to information systems, organization structure, rewards, and corporate culture can be planned for and implemented in a staged manner. Such was the case with the broadly based transformation strategy implemented by Ford in the early 1980s. Following an initial crisis, executives, outsiders, and supervisors worked together to develop a new strategy in which the driving force for improved quality and reduced costs would come through employee involvement.

The major threat to the success of this type of strategic change is usually passive resistance that emanates from employees in middle management who are unwilling to abandon old approaches or incur personal risks associated with moving in the new direction. To put it simply, nothing happens.

The success of initiatives taken by the strategy's champions usually encourages others to follow. In addition, middle managers are influenced by pressure to change from both above and below, so it is important for executives to mobilize the rank and file. To ensure success, however, executives must be prepared to deal with managers who, after a reasonable period for adjustment, demonstrate a total aversion to change.

During anticipatory change, executives may spend as much time in communication sessions listening to the views of employees as they do promoting the new direction. Feedback from throughout the organization can provide useful information on how well the new strategy is being accepted, as well as ideas for fine-tuning. Executive planning and review sessions, held at least quarterly, are important for keeping implementation on track.

Failure to provide sufficient support for strategic initiatives is a major cause tardy or failed implementation. Continuing top-management support can be demonstrated in a variety of ways. The most important is ensuring that strategic programs are adequately resourced. Executive sponsorships of major strategic thrusts, personal recognition of successful innovators, and occasional intervention to eliminate roadblocks are further tangible ways to provide leadership.

Building commitment to new initiatives is essential to successful deployment. In this respect, the total commitment of the planning team and the demonstrated leadership of the executive group are critical. One of the worst signs of poor strategic planning is completion of the planning phase with team members who either have no commitment to an initiative or are in outright opposition to it. The strategy review provides an opportunity to gain total commitment from the team through open discussion. Before leaving the session, participants should be asked to either state their unequivocal support for the strategy or state their reservations, which can then be addressed.

Preaching is not enough to build commitment to a new strategic plan. Executives have to demonstrate their support and take leadership through communications and actions. In this respect, actions do speak louder than words. Executives might want to consider the acronym PRIDE with respect to strategy deployment:

- *Promote* the new direction,
- *Recognize* appropriate employee behaviors.
- *Inform* employees about the new direction.
- *Demonstrate* personal commitment through action.
- *Expedite* implementation through timely decisions.

For example, executives who promote a "seamless society" in their corporation—one in which no distinction is made among different groups of employees—should be prepared to implement policies for travel, accommodation, and other benefits that reflect the appropriate value set, and then live by them themselves.

## In Summary

The challenge in successfully launching a new strategic plan is to sustain and build on the momentum that the planning process should have generated. Developing speed through the first 100 days of launch should be translated into momentum during the second 100 days as the flywheel steadily builds. Key elements of a successful launch include:

- A rapid, comprehensive communications blitz.
- Demanding that all executives demonstrate PRIDE with respect to the plan.

- Ensuring that the plan is well grounded in action plans with clear accountabilities and time frames.
- Arranging for short-term tangible deliverables that create "quick wins."
- Ensuring that key initiatives are well resourced from the outset.
- Providing for frequent, periodic follow-up and discussion of progress and accomplishments.

Too many good strategic plans endure a fate in which the vision ends up on the wall and the document ends up on the shelf. Other than that, not much happens. Real success, as we have described, occurs when the plan becomes a living document that drives a living company to sustained success.[9]

PART II

SIX PLAYS IN ONE ACT

# 6

## Rapid Value Creation from Acquisitions

What are the critical aspects of an acquisition? What differentiates the successful acquisitions from the failures? One veteran of many successful acquisitions explained his personal framework to us:

> Everyone knows that the vision in an acquisition is to make money for your shareholders, but how few of us actually do it! In fact, there are three campaigns to an acquisition, all of which need to be concluded successfully. The first is doing the deal. For this I have a couple of objectives—ensure it's friendly, and no more than my maximum price. The rest of it is very tactical. The second is integrating the acquisition successfully. This is all about culture and process, and we try to do it in less than 100 days. The third campaign, then, is to generate wealth for our shareholders, and that's very strategic.

Being acquired is a major change for any company, even if the degree of integration with the new parent is very limited. In fact, the change necessitated in both companies by an integration can be characterized by our framework that defines the depth of organization change (see figure 2.1). In a few acquisitions, the degree of change is shallow—the company continues to function much as it did prior to the acquisition and has only minimal operating changes. This may be the case in some unrelated acquisitions in which the business of the acquired company bears no market or technology commonalities with the businesses of its new parent. More typical, however, is change at the cultural level, in which the acquired organization is required to change both its strategy and its culture to align with those of the new parent. Eugene Pollistuck, the CEO of Celestica, one of the world's fastest growing high-technology contract manufacturers, made this comment about acquisitions:

> It's our first criterion. If we don't think we can integrate it well, it's not a cultural fit, we don't do it. . . . We look at the quality of management, the quality of

people, what kind of baggage they have. Can they adapt into this new environment? Do they have, or can they achieve a high trust level? Can they work with each other in a more informal environment? . . . So every acquisition we do, we have SWAT teams that go in and figure out where we're at from that direction.

The statistics on acquisition are decidedly bearish. Far too many create little, if any, value for the shareholders of the acquiring companies. Acquisitions are a means of supplementing internal growth in shareholder value through external dealings, usually through the purchase of corporations or selected assets. There has been a considerable amount of research into the value creation impact of this type of transaction, and the results can be generally summarized as follows: "About one-third of all acquisitions make money for the shareholders of the acquiree, about a third make money for the shareholders of the acquired business, and about one-third are a wash."[1]

There is general agreement that the true value from most acquisitions is realized only after the deal is consummated. The best analysis and most creative negotiations can be nullified by weak execution following conclusion of the deal. In addition, acquiring companies are realizing that an outstanding level of integration effectiveness can lead to the identification of additional benefits not previously considered.

Acquisitions essentially have three sequential phases:

- Determination of which company to acquire and preparation of a bid.
- Once the bid is accepted in principle, there is a period of due-diligence work and preacquisition planning.
- Once the deal is closed, there is a period of integration of the acquired company with the new parent.

Unless the second and particularly the third phases are carefully managed, integration can take many months or even a period of years. However, companies that have successful acquisitions are increasingly focusing on the 100 days before and after the acquisition to capture value and ensure successful integration. The first 100 days is spent developing strategies, policies, and even operating plans for the period immediately after the deal is finalized. The second 100 days is then spent locking in the value to be captured from the acquisition. In fact, companies that make many acquisitions, such as Celestica, GE Capital, and Cisco, have relatively standardized procedures for integrating acquisitions in the first 100 days after the deal closes.

Our research indicates that acquisitions can be led and managed like any other business activity. In certain important, fundamental respects, they are not unique, "one-shot" processes, but they have enough recognizable similarities that it is possible to develop a comprehensive framework for managing them with expediency. Flexible policies and procedures can be developed that build quality into the process, thus maximizing the likelihood of value capture and creation from any particular deal.

In this chapter, we propose a comprehensive framework for integrating acquisitions into corporate strategy (see figure 6.1). From an initial corporate def-

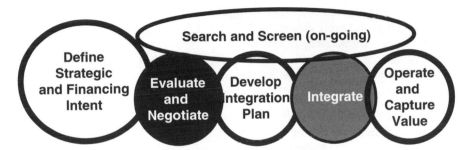

**Figure 6.1** The Acquisition Process: Schematic Overview

inition of strategic and financial intent, which links the acquisitions process into corporate strategy and establishes broad criteria for evaluation purposes, we propose that the process should move through the following stages:

- *Defining of strategic and financial intent*—linked into either corporate or business-unit strategy, which establishes the rationale for the acquisition strategy.
- *Searching and screening activities*—which we perceive to be a continuing process during which prospects are identified and broadly evaluated in terms of their fit with financial and strategic criteria.
- *Evaluation and negotiation*—including due diligence procedures—which sets up the terms of each specific deal and includes the actual go/no-go decision.
- *Pre-acquisition planning* (to the extent possible)—focused on whether and how the acquisition will be integrated into the organization and how it will be managed and led after the deal is finalized.
- *Integration*—to whatever degree is determined appropriate after the acquisition, leading to initial *value capture* for the acquiring company.
- *Ongoing operations*—during which most of the *value creation* will occur.

These phases are not discrete; they overlap with each other to form a continuous, evolving process over the life of the acquisition.

For corporations that perceive acquisitions to be a continuing element in their strategy, there is a considerable challenge in establishing a process that enables a stream of acquisitions prospects, deals, and integration activities to be handled in a manner that maximizes the likelihood of value capture and creation from each deal. If the process is too formalized and procedure-bound, flexibility and responsiveness will be sacrificed and good deals will be lost. On the other hand, if the process is too loose and roles are unclear, poor decisions may be made, value may be lost, and learning—critical to continuous improvement in managing the acquisition process—may not be captured effectively. Over the years, acquisitive corporations (such as Johnson & Johnson, Procter and Gamble, Textron, and General Electric) have recognized that acquisitions have specific characteristics:

- They are infrequent and typically unplanned,
- The process is highly opportunistic.
- Decisions must be made rapidly.
- A unified view must be developed among key decision makers.
- There is often limited access to relevant information.
- Most executives are not skilled in the process.

Accordingly, they have developed structures, policies, and procedures to manage the process, much like any other business activity, and to enable them to undertake the process expediently and efficiently. Some of the key elements in their successful approaches have been:

- A CEO who is willing to delegate responsibility for acquisitive initiatives (some CEOs either perceive acquisitions as their personal domain or are unwilling to actively support deals initiated by their subordinates).
- A small corporate capability to provide a center of expertise and support for acquisitions, including financial, legal, negotiation, and planning activities.
- Distinctions between corporate-level acquisitions—major new business units or deals that have a major impact on business units—and those that should be made by business-unit executives.
- External and in-house executive education in acquisition skills—to complement on-the-job experience—for corporate and business-unit executives.
- Development of guidelines and procedures for acquisition initiatives.
- Rigorous application of a postaudit procedure to evaluate each acquisition and retain the lessons that should be learned for future activities.

## Acquisitions Are Not All the Same

There are a number of different ways to categorize acquisitions.[2] Like any other form of financial dealing, acquisitions have risks associated with them and it is important for the deal maker to fully understand the nature of the risks associated with a particular type of decision.

One important basic distinction among acquisitions is whether or not they bring strategic value to the acquirer. Of the total number of acquisitions, only a small proportion are strategic; that is, of sufficient significance that they will dramatically reshape the entire corporation. Many have strategic significance at a business-unit level, but not at a corporate level. In fact, most acquisitions fit into this category—they are made to fill out a product line, acquire additional capacity, or provide an entry point into a new market segment.

Somewhere in between strategic and tactical acquisitions are a number that are made for either exploratory or learning purposes. These are transactions that provide the parent company with exposure to new areas of activity. They may possibly have strategic significance at some future time, but at the time of the transaction, they have tactical significance in terms of size and risk.

Building on theories of diversification,[3] another extremely useful way of characterizing acquisitions concerns the degree of relatedness to the acquiring company's own business. Four major classes of diversification—and degrees of relatedness—have been identified:

- *Single product*—same business as the acquiring firm; made to expand the core business of the acquiring firm (e.g., Boeing's acquisition of McDonnell Douglas)
- *Related product*—different business, but linked through common core skills in marketing, manufacturing or distribution; made to extend the corporation's scope of activities (e.g., Symantec's acquisition of Norton Anti-Virus Software).
- *Vertical integration*—forward or backward integration along the value chain; made to capture additional value or for logistical reasons (e.g., Sony's acquisition of Columbia Pictures).
- *Unrelated product*—no product or market relationship between the businesses; made to diversify the corporation into entirely new areas; which cannot be achieved through internal growth (e.g., General Electric's diversification into financial services).

Each of these types of acquisitions poses somewhat different problems at the analysis and integration stages, as well as an increasing degree of difficulty for the acquiring firm to manage. In many single product–type acquisitions, the acquiring firm will knowingly acquire a poorly managed or underperforming firm from which it can extract superior returns through better management practices. In unrelated product–type acquisitions, firms that lack turnaround or industry-specific skills prefer to acquire corporations that are not ranked either first or second in their industry but have a strong management team in place.

A quite different approach to categorizing acquisitions, based on integration requirements, has been suggested by Philippe Haspeslagh and David Jemison.[4] They argue that postmerger integration activities are the key to successful value creation from acquisitions, and they identify three distinct types of integration requirements based on the degree of strategic interdependence between the parent company and the acquired firm:

- *Absorption acquisitions*—a high need for strategic interdependence and a low need for organizational autonomy.
- *Preservation acquisitions*—a low need for strategic interdependence and a high need for organizational autonomy.
- *Symbiotic acquisitions*—a high need for strategic interdependence, but also a high need for organizational autonomy.

They believe that creating value from symbiotic acquisitions is the most difficult and complex because for real value creation, capabilities must be transferred between the acquirer and the acquired business, but the autonomy of the latter to operate effectively in a different business environment must be preserved. This may require the parent company to transfer capabilities and resources to and from its new subsidiary without impairing its ability to operate in an industry with different critical success factors.

Many corporations have developed policies on the characteristics of businesses that they will seek to acquire. For example, some unrelated conglomerate firms, such as Textron, will only make strategic acquisitions that exhibit the following characteristics:

- They are friendly; once negotiations become hostile, they are terminated.
- They are in specific industries that corporate executives generally understand.
- They involve companies that are, or have the potential to be, leaders in their markets.
- They do not constitute, say, more than 20 percent of the total corporate business portfolio in terms of assets and revenues.
- They are not in industries in which value and risks are intangible (such as high-technology and service firms, whose "assets leave the building at 5:00 P.M.").
- They have a strong management team in place.

These policies are in marked contrast to those of Johnson & Johnson and 3M, both of which are related product companies. Neither of these companies makes strategic acquisitions at the corporate level; instead, they generate growth from within. However, business units in both corporations frequently make acquisitions of small businesses that either provide exposure to emerging markets and technologies or possess products that complement the corporation's existing line and that can be rapidly grown and distributed through existing channels. Often, the value in these acquisitions lies in the people or the potential of a new product; these companies are rarely share leaders in an established market.

These quite different policies reflect the differing strategic intents of corporations with respect to acquisitions. These differences are ultimately reflected in how these corporations handle acquisitions both before and after the deal is signed.

## Acquisitions: The First 100 Days

Each 100-day action plan is in some ways unique to each acquisition. However, the overall purpose is the same—to build speed in ensuring the return of value to the shareholders of the acquiring company. With respect to the acquisition of Cap Gemini by Ernst & Young, Jeff Unwin commented:

> We did a lot of work pre- merger on planning it from an operational point of view . . . in terms of the structures, the services we would be selling, the clients we'd be focusing on, the sectors we would focus on and so on. So that. . . . three days after the shareholders approved the merger, we were then able to have a meeting with over five hundred of the top people in the new merged group. And quite frankly, I think we surprised them by the degree of direction and decisions

we were capable of . . . giving them within three days. Obviously we hadn't done that within three days but that was a result of very, very careful planning beforehand.

In the context of acquisition-related change, the first 100 days commences once a letter of intent or understanding has been signed or, if the acquisition is unfriendly, a bid for the target company has been made. The objectives for the first 100 days relate to the development and enrichment of shared understanding and planning for integration embodied in:

- The development of an initial strategic plan for the acquisition.
- The development of a 100-day integration plan.
- The identification of human resource requirements—the leadership team, organization structure, staff redeployment, and downsizing.
- The identification of operational and administrative integration requirements.
- The development of an incentive package for key employees in the acquisition.
- The development of a stakeholder communications package.

Planning for the second 100 days has to start even before the deal is finalized. Thus, a major objective for the first 100 days is to create a plan of action for the second 100 days. Depending on whether the acquisition is friendly or hostile, it may even be possible to make a number of key decisions and accomplish a substantial amount of work prior to the finalization of the deal.

A first challenge is to determine the degree of integration desired with the acquisition. This depends substantially on the purpose of the acquisition itself. For example, the continued identity of the acquired company may be a major concern affecting issues such as retention of brand names. Or, if the purpose of the acquisition is to acquire intellectual property or engineering talent, as in the case of the spate of high-tech acquisitions made by Nortel Networks and Cisco in the late 1990s, then the need for integration is very high.

If at all possible, this planning for the second 100 days should lead to a shared understanding between the executives of both companies of the future strategy for the acquired business. In line with our definition of shared understanding, this will include:

- A shared sense of vision for the acquired company—realistically with an initial time frame between twelve and twenty-four months, encompassing its relationship to the parent, how it will be integrated, and its future mission.
- A set of measures that will define success—such as increase in the acquirer's share price, return on investment, growth in market share, retention of key employees, and value created by the capabilities of the acquired business.
- Agreement on the key programs and projects that will be required to achieve these outcomes—including integration and rationalization tasks,

systems integration, human resource changes, and initial joint business initiatives.

- A process that enables these initiatives to be implemented—one that includes integration activities.

In a friendly acquisition, it should be possible to carry out this activity jointly with the leadership of the target company. In a hostile situation, it is likely that the planning will have to be undertaken by the executives of the acquiring company using the information at their disposal.

## Acquisitions: The Second 100 Days

There is general agreement that the postacquisition process of integration is critical in determining how effectively value will be either captured or created for the acquirer. This issue must be addressed during the evaluation and negotiation phase prior to signing a deal. Simply put, many deals have ended up as disasters for the acquirer because they were made with the thought that "we will work out the details of how we will work together later."

Without a framework for managing in the postacquisition period, the following scenarios are all possible:

- Conflict over verbal agreements and assurances made during the negotiation phase.
- Loss of key executives and technical specialists during the transition phase.
- A "clash of cultures" between the companies.
- Loss of business momentum if people lose focus on the day-to-day running of the business.
- Exploitation of the transition phase—such as market share increase—by alert rivals.[5]

There are many instances of each type of problem arising following what appears to have been successful acquisition negotiations. For example, Dart Corporation merged with Kraft only to find out too late that their businesses and culture were dramatically different. An amicable divorce was subsequently negotiated. In the two years following Black & Decker's acquisition of General Electric's small appliance business, Sunbeam was able to erode the market share of the combined entity quite significantly.

The second 100 days is all about speed of integration. After that, the focus has to be on regaining any business momentum that was lost in the ownership transition. At one extreme, little may change in the case of the acquisition of a successful company in an unrelated business. Minimal integration other than executive and financial systems may be required in the early stages. On the other hand, the acquisition of a failing company in the same product market may require a comprehensive turnaround plan to be executed within the second 100 days that encompasses rationalization, restructuring, and significant changes in leadership.

Objectives for the second 100 days relate to ensuring value capture from the acquisition and ensuring a smooth transition. Possible objectives for this period can include:

- Continued key customer loyalty by ensuring no disruption to customer service.
- Early achievement of value creation through rationalization of facilities, product lines, and resources.
- Completion of realignment of the leadership team for the acquired company.
- Loyalty transfer of key employees to the new parent.
- All acquired employees on the same compensation plan as those in the parent company.

The nature of these objectives is determined by the rationale for the acquisition and the degree of integration required. For example, Cisco's target in its acquisitions process is to have the products of the acquired company listed in Cisco's product catalog by the first working day after the deal is finalized.

As with any type of change, the objectives for the first 100 and 200 days are focused around establishing the Winning Conditions. The following sections discuss each of these as they relate to acquisition success.

## Establishing the Winning Conditions

### 1. Correct Diagnosis of the Change Challenge

To correctly diagnose the change challenge related to an acquisition, a series of questions must be considered:

- What type of acquisition is it?
- What is the purpose of the acquisition—how will value be achieved?
- What degree of integration is required?

Each acquisition is unique. Although there are broad similarities across acquisitions, the nature of each deal, the degree of integration required, and the way in which value will be created differ in each situation. A first requirement for success is for the acquirer's executives to diagnose the nature of the change challenge that the acquired entity will pose for its company.

A first step in carrying out this diagnosis is creating an understanding of how the acquisition will create value for its new owner; once this is determined, it should not be lost sight of throughout the entire process. Acquisitions are capable of creating shareholder value in a number of distinct ways, principally through:

- "One-shot," major acquisitions aimed at greatly enhancing the size and value of a corporation and possibly at entering new fields of activity (e.g., Westinghouse's acquisition of CBS for $5.4 billion or Disney's acquisition of Capital Cities/ABC for $19 billion).

- A series of acquisitions that either creates or expands a major business unit (e.g., GE Capital's strategy for growth that involved over one hundred acquisitions in one five-year period).
- An acquisitive strategy that restructures an industry (e.g., Boeing's acquisition of Lockheed Martin and subsequently McDonnnell Douglas).
- A series of smaller acquisitions that extends product lines or provides access to new markets or experience in new businesses, (e.g., Johnson & Johnson's succession of acquisitions that strengthen its divisions' product offerings.

It is also important to understand the type of acquisition being contemplated. There has been a considerable amount of effort invested in determining which type of acquisition is most successful. This research has taken two distinct directions—one dealing with substantive strategy, and the other dealing with the nature of the acquisitions process. The major findings from the substantive research are mixed, at best, and illustrate that it is not so much *what* you do, as *how* you do it:[6]

- Some studies indicate that related acquisitions are more successful than unrelated (conglomerate) acquisitions.
- Some studies indicate that greater shareholder wealth is created from unrelated (conglomerate) acquisitions.
- Studies have shown that for many acquisitions, the ultimate value and benefits are positive, but they are not those anticipated prior to the deal.

Whatever the school of thought, there is now a widely accepted view that related acquisitions do offer superior value creation potential. However, realizing these gains is not automatic. Postacquisition activities have a far more significant impact on the outcome than preacquisition analysis. In fact, although it appears that some kinds of acquisitions are more difficult to capture value from, there are instances of success among all types. Therefore, we are led to believe that it is the process, as much or more than the activity, that determines the value capture and, hence, the ultimate success of acquisitive activities.

The executive challenge for any of these acquisitions is to determine how they can create shareholder wealth through superior value capture and creation. Contemporary corporate views on acquisition distinguish between these two types of wealth creation—value capture and value creation—in part because the task of creating wealth may be different in each case.

Value capture benefits are those resulting from one-time gains that accrue to the acquirer from the target, such as tax write-offs available in the acquired firm that can be utilized by the new owner. Other examples of value capture are the activities of individuals like Lord Hanson and Oliver Goldsmith, whose strategy was to identify undervalued corporations, acquire control, and then restructure them to realize the underlying value for their own shareholders. For example, Hanson acquired the conglomerate SCM in 1985 for $930 million, sold various subsidiaries over the next two years for $1.25 billion, and still owned three core, highly profitable businesses from the group.

Value creation, on the other hand, is derived from the ability of the acquiring firm to manage the acquired assets to obtain financial performance in excess of that obtained under the former ownership regime. An overused synonym for value creation is synergy. Synergy arises when assets and activities are combined in ways that generate superior value to that obtained when they were independent. A number of different sources of value creation can be identified, most of which involve the transfer of capabilities from one firm to another:

- Resource synergies, in which economies of scale and scope can be obtained through, for example, sharing financial resources, production facilities, distribution channels, etc. In mining, the acquisition of a junior company with good property by a larger company with cash is a typical example. In consumer industries, the acquisition of a small company with a high-potential product that can be sold through the acquirer's distribution channels is fairly common.
- Skill transfer, in which the performance of either firm can be improved through the transfer of technical and managerial skills from one organization to another. For example, some companies are skilled at acquiring failing businesses and turning them around through application of their own management practices.

These examples of value creation are quite distinct from those that arise simply from the combination of the two enterprises—increased market share, a diversified risk profile, and greater financial strength and purchasing power. In practice, value creation through deriving real synergy from an acquisition has proved to be very elusive for many acquiring companies.

Given these different wealth creation approaches, the process-oriented stream of acquisitions research has developed a logical and prescriptive methodology for acquisitions analysis.[7] This has most recently produced an integrated process for acquisitions management in which postacquisition activities, such as integration and value creation, are perceived to be equally, if not more, influential on the ultimate value of the acquisition, as initial negotiations over the price.[8]

Corporations are now belatedly starting to realize that an acquisition is not complete once the deal is inked and that deal signing is merely one step in a process that can extend over many months. As a consequence, a significant shift in emphasis in evaluation and diagnosis—from largely financial to a balanced strategic-financial perspective—has occurred during the 1990s. Several new components have been added to this evaluation, including:

- Strategic fit—a precise statement of how the acquisition will create value through complementing the acquirer's corporate strategy.
- Cultural fit—a thorough review of how compatible the two cultures are.
- Integration requirements—the outline of a framework for how the acquisition will fit into its new owner's strategy and structure and how it will be managed.
- An assessment of the major business and financial risks associated with the deal—useful in creating a focus for due-diligence activities.

Harsh reality has driven corporations to incorporate these topics into their acquisition assessments. Many acquisitions that appeared to be attractive from a financial perspective came apart when the lack of strategic fit became apparent after the acquisition; for example, the multibillion-dollar acquisition of Utah Mining by General Electric in 1985. There is substantial anecdotal evidence that many deals entered into on the basis of working out the details of integration after the transaction have been extremely difficult to implement successfully. To avoid these unfavorable situations, successful acquirers recognize that diagnosis of the true acquisition change challenge relies on the following:

- The type of acquisition.
- The purpose of the acquisition—how value will be achieved.
- The degree of integration required.


## 2. Early Development of Shared Understanding

Part of the process of understanding the nature of the challenge posed by an acquisition is for the acquirer's executive team to develop a shared understanding of the financial and strategic intent of the acquisition. In addition, there is usually a need to create shared understanding with the executive team of the acquired business about the future strategy, operating mode, and leadership of their business under its new ownership. This is particularly important if the current executive team is to remain in place after the deal closes.

This shared understanding includes some sense of vision—what the acquired firm will ultimately contribute; measures of success—what value creation criteria are appropriate; key strategies and programs required to ensure that the process results in a successful outcome; and enabling processes—communications, recognition and rewards, and business and organization processes that make the deal work.

Given the nature of acquisitions, there are many potential pitfalls in the decision-making process:

- Excessive opportunism—failure to relate acquisitions to strategic aims.
- Fragmented perspectives—failure to bring together strategic, legal, financial, technical, and other perspectives in an integrated picture.
- Lack of foresight—failure to think ahead to post-acquisition requirements.
- Inherent momentum—once a deal is close at hand, there is often an internal dynamic pushing toward consummation, regardless of logic, particularly if there are career benefits that may accrue to the individual responsible for negotiations upon successful completion of a deal.
- Outside advisers—such as investment bankers, often have a financial stake in the deal and may create conditions in which management is rushed into a deal.
- Information asymmetry—the decision is made on the basis of incomplete information—which increases the risks.

- Secrecy and stress—the process is undertaken in a concentrated time period, which can result in rushed, poor quality evaluations.

To offset the worst effects of these characteristics of the process, corporations are increasingly developing a shared understanding among their executives through vehicles for justifying acquisitions, including screening processes, evaluation techniques, acquisition team membership, and postacquisition integration requirements. Although the time frames for these activities will vary enormously from deal to deal, depending on the degree of urgency, the process is followed closely in every case. For example, some deals may require a team of two or three working continuously for several months, whereas others, which must be transacted in a matter of days, may require a team of twenty or thirty working intensively for one or two weeks.

The acquisition evaluation process is of particular importance in terms of reaching a decision—not only because of the insights it can provide, but also because an effective process will identify areas in which information is lacking and uncertainty is present. In addition, an effective assessment process can overcome the problem of fragmented perspectives by providing a focus for communications among different specialist groups and interests.

### 3. Enrichment of Shared Understanding

A key task of the first 100 days is to acquire information that ensures that unpleasant surprises are minimized. Many acquisitions come undone because of unforeseen problems that were only discovered after the deal was finalized. Due diligence, joint working groups, and planning for postmerger operations are all activities that enrich shared understanding.

A key part of the first 100 days is the enrichment of shared understanding about the acquisition. The initial assessment work, prepared for making a bid, is unlikely to have been either comprehensive or accurate. During the first 100 days, a second assessment, frequently referred to as due diligence, is required. In some companies, this activity is limited in scope, covering only the evaluation of tangible and intangible assets. In reality, a more comprehensive assessment should be undertaken, one that includes these major elements:

- *Reaffirming the acquisition rationale*—how the acquisition will create value for the acquirer's shareholders and its potential strategic fit, together with specific criteria against which to assess postacquisition performance.
- *Market/industry attractiveness*—an evaluation of the target industry and markets in terms of growth, profitability, structure, and competition that includes the present and future positioning of the target company.
- *Corporate/business evaluation*—a financial and strategic assessment of the target company in terms of performance, positioning, and future prospects.
- *Specific value created by the acquisition*—an objective assessment of the opportunities for, and sources of, value capture and creation.

- *Integration requirements*—requirements for strategic interdependencies and organizational autonomy following a successful acquisition.
- *Organizational adjustments*—based on integration requirements, how the acquisition will report to the parent, cultural issues, reorganization options, leadership requirements, etc.
- *Financial scenarios*—the bases for optimistic, typical, and pessimistic financial evaluations.
- *Financial evaluation*—what price/terms are acceptable, including a walk-away upper valuation and nonnegotiable terms; and risk assessment, a sizing up of the critical business, financial, and technical risks involved.

Once the deal closes, there should always be a third, confirmatory strategic assessment immediately afterward, even if there has been considerable prior integration work. In fact, one of the first tasks of the integration team should be to conduct a definitive strategic and financial audit to ensure complete disclosure of all relevant information. Inevitably, this review turns up some surprises, such as hidden costs and declining market positions, that have a significant impact on future strategy. This type of information is crucial to enriching shared understanding, which, in turn, contributes greatly to integration success.

## 4. Establishment of a Sense of Urgency

Speed and momentum are an important part of the acquisitions process, particularly after the deal is closed. There is rarely a lack of urgency prior to the deal signing. Prior to the closing of the deal, however, certain aspects of the timeline may be beyond the ability of the executive teams to control; for example, the deal may have to be reviewed by regulators. More often, the period to watch for follows the deal signing, when alert rivals exploit the period of uncertainty and confusion after an acquisition to improve their market position and grab an increased share. The faster the deal is closed and normal operations can be established, the less likely it is that rivals will be able to take advantage of the situation. In addition, a sense of urgency ensures that the period of uncertainty for employees and customers is minimized, leading to greater retention of both. The principal vehicles for creating this sense of urgency are the 100- and 200-day plans, which drive the deal and the subsequent integration period. Additional vehicles may include media coverage of the acquisition and stock market activities for both companies. Alert executives use both the media and stock market analysts to drive a sense of urgency through both companies with respect to realizing benefits from the deal.

## 5. Creation of a Limited and Focused Strategic Agenda

The first 100 days of the process should be used to create a limited, focused strategic agenda for the acquisition. It is extremely damaging to change everything at once immediately after the deal closes. The reality is that there is usually enough uncertainty without throwing fuel on the flames. A focused strategic

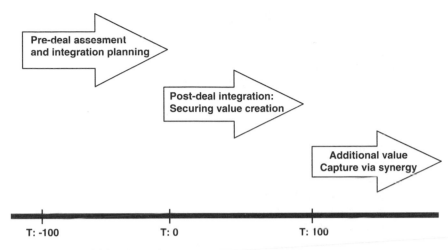

**Figure 6.2** Acquisition Campaigns

game plan for the 100 days after the acquisition is important, particularly if tough decisions have to be made about downsizing, facility closings, and the like. We view acquisition integration as a series of campaigns, the substance of which is presented in figure 6.2.

A practical discussion of GE Capital's integration approach is presented by Ronald Ashkenas, et al.[9] They suggest that the integration process is critical to value creation and list several key attributes of an effective process:

- Planning for integration should begin during the due-diligence phase of a deal.
- In corporations that are active acquirers, the integration manager's role is full-time.
- Major decisions should be made and announced as soon after the deal as possible.
- Integration has to deal with organization culture, as well as technical issues.

The integration practices that they describe are similar to those that we have found to be most effective in other situations that we have studied. However, many of GE Capital's acquisitions were successful businesses that, according to Haspeslagh and Jemison's taxonomy, were of a preservation or symbiotic nature and therefore required less integration effort.[10]

Regardless of the state of the acquired business, if the acquired firm is to be integrated into the operations of the acquirer, we have concluded that the following approaches are critically important:

- Identify the integration phase as a project, and run it as such with a project manager (usually dedicated), task forces consisting of employees from both companies, and stated time frames for completion of specified tasks.

- Rapidly initiate communications with employees of the acquired business, partly to familiarize them with their new owners and partly to mitigate the adverse effects of the rumor mill or grapevine, which will certainly be present.
- Carry out a rapid evaluation of the strategic and operational health of the acquired business; preacquisition information may be either incomplete or overly optimistic—find out the bad news fast.
- Work to convince customers of the acquired business that it is indeed "business as usual."
- Hold meetings to establish how the needs of these customers are presently being met by the acquired firm and aim to continue to meet these needs in order to mitigate defections to competition.
- Assess the magnitude of the *culture challenge*—what's going to be required for the two organizations to work together effectively.
- Assess the competence and value set of the executive team in the acquired firm and replace those whose performance is unsatisfactory or whose values are incompatible with those required in the future.

## 6. Rapid, Strategic Decision Making and Deployment

Moving as quickly as possible to eliminate uncertainty following an acquisition can contribute to the maintenance of considerable value. Acquisitions are always accompanied by a sizable amount of uncertainty, even if the deal is friendly, and it is important to communicate effectively to ensure that all employees of both firms, are clear as to their future status. Communication with customers and other stakeholders is also important to ensure that they believe that it will be "business as usual" in the future.

All of the evidence that we have acquired in our research on acquisitions indicates that the faster key decisions are made and deployed, the more successful the process is likely to be. Corporations with the best track record of successful acquisitions have a game plan ready to go and the key decisions made by the time the deal closes. For example, in many cases, Cisco is able to incorporate an acquired company's products in its own catalog the first business day after closing. What are the key strategic decisions that need to be made within the first 100 days and implemented during the second 100 days following an acquisition?

- The relationship of the acquired company to the parent, and the residual identity of the acquired company.
- Identification of business areas, products, processes, and facilities that will no longer be necessary, and how they will be disposed of.
- How customer service levels will be maintained.
- Initial cash flow and cost improvement initiatives.
- Facility and logistics rationalization.

- Workforce restructuring and realignment.
- Strategic communications activities with customers, vendors, employees, and other key stakeholders.
- Integration timetable and schedule.

Clearly, if an acquired business is well managed and is producing excellent results, there may be no perceived urgency for integration, even if it operates in the same business as the acquirer, except as dictated by the potential for initial value capture through cost benefits and synergies resulting from the merger of the two businesses. In fact, if management in the acquired business is truly superior, units of the acquirer's own business may be integrated into the acquired business unit. However, if the acquired business is in need of a turnaround (see chapter 9) and its management team is perceived as weak, then a "Monday-morning" strategy may need to be in place, even before the deal is closed. In this situation, experienced acquirers usually adopt the following process:

- Install a new interim management team—a blend of the old and the new—usually with a leader from the acquirer.
- Size up the business and establish control rapidly.
- Clean house—people, products, facilities—where appropriate.
- Put operations on an even keel.
- Strengthen the acquired organization with permanent appointments.
- Strategically reposition the business.

It may be difficult to implement all of the desired substantive changes within the second 100 days, but symbolic acts can be important in signaling future intent to all stakeholder groups. These acts come in a variety of different forms, from how people are dealt with, through the nature of communications, to the initial substantive actions taken by the new owners. For example, it is important to ensure that the executive team of the acquired company doesn't refer to the new parent as "our new owners." They should immediately use "we" when referring to the consolidation. It will be important to retain some sense of identity for the acquired company, but a sense of belonging to the larger whole is more important.

## 7. A Human Flywheel of Commitment

Most successful acquirers have realized that people largely determine the outcome of acquisitions. It is important to ensure that the energies of employees, particularly in the acquired firm, are rapidly harnessed to make the acquisition a success. Otherwise, valuable time could be spent worrying about the future or, even worse, playing games to preserve autonomy from the new parent. Usually, 20 percent of employees are willing to become the fulcrum of the human flywheel. As in any change situation, the challenge is finding them and mobilizing them.

As we have noted, initial employee communications should take place even before the acquisition is complete, if possible, in order to minimize uncertainty and reduce the possibility of losing key employees. Nevertheless, a Monday-morning communication on the first day after the deal is complete is critical. The content of this communication should include a review of the rationale for the deal, how it will be successful, and the going-forward strategy for the acquired company.

Some organizations place so much importance on this activity that they will arrange for all employees to participate in a full-day reinduction workshop within the first week. The content of this workshop is structured to introduce the employees to the new parent and present the initial game plan for the acquired organization. If possible, specific changes that will be implemented over the second 100 days should be identified. Employees then need to be allowed to discuss these changes in groups and consider the implications for their own roles. A subsequent question-and-answer session can dispel much of the uncertainty and latent concerns of participating employees.

What else do employees want to know? Their own personal situation is usually a major concern, including everything from whether they will still be employed, through their future role and responsibilities, to their terms and conditions of employment. Some acquirers find it useful to move acquired employees to their own compensation plans as soon as possible, particularly if they are better than those of the acquired firm. Severance terms for those employees who will be terminated are often included as part of the acquisition agreement and should be communicated as early as possible.

What do customers and vendors want to know and see? First, they want to know that they will continue to receive the same quality of products and services. They look for continuity in product line, ordering processes, and customer service. It is important to reassure key customers through either sales force contacts or direct executive communication. However, words alone are not enough. A critical step is the maintenance of existing relationships, assuming that they are satisfactory or better. Sales force and customer service restructurings need to be undertaken with an eye to maintaining customer relationships, particularly for the most profitable customers.

## 8. Identification and Management of Sources of Resistance

There will always be employees in any acquisition who resent the takeover and the perceived loss of independence. For many, communication and education will solve the problem. However, there are always likely to be those who will actively seek to sabotage the deal both before and after it is finalized. A major step in ensuring success is to identify the saboteurs and deal with them, one way or another. Unfortunately, the period after the deal closes is often so poorly planned that this opportunity passes with little being done, leaving a festering situation that has to be dealt with later, at greater pain and expense.

The first 100 days after the deal closes is a period of transition when the problem of resistance can be dealt with effectively. First, there needs to be an effective communications blitz. Awareness and understanding of the future and how the new owner will run the business can reduce resistance significantly or encourage potential saboteurs to self-select out of the organization. Aligning compensation plans and addressing perceived inequities also help to reduce resistance. For those who will not change, however, this first 100-day period can serve to identify these individuals and offer them an attractive exit opportunity. In the worst case, some form of employee compensation and job security guarantee has been included in the deal, and severance compensation is relatively high. However, executives tell us that the long-term gain from dealing expediently with these individuals is often worth the short-term cost.

## 9. Follow-through on Changing Organizational Enablers

Acquisitions are always accompanied by uncertainty. Employees are now working for a new owner, and they have basic concerns about job security, pay, benefits, and their future roles. In any acquisition, it's important in the first 100 and 200 days to address these concerns. Organization structure, roles and responsibilities, and compensation and benefits are all key issues that have to be addressed.

There is general agreement that whenever possible, especially if the acquisition is friendly, considerable thought should be given to how the acquisition will be led and managed once the deal is finalized. Of course, this is difficult to accomplish if the acquisition is hostile or if confidentiality is an issue. The following aspects of postacquisition operations may be included in an initial assessment:

- How the acquisition will report to the parent and the extent of integration.
- The composition and structure of the executive team for the acquired company.
- Which employees will be required and which employees will be surplus, and how surplus employees will be dealt with.
- How key employees will be retained.
- How compensation plans have to be adjusted.
- How culture, values, and morale will be developed in the acquisition.
- How the transition process will be managed, and the duration of this process.
- Critical systems integrations requirements including financial and information systems.

One of the most important challenges during the second 100 days is the degree of integration of financial, information, and other systems that can be achieved. In these respects, the systems both companies must be considered. Customer-facing systems are particularly important in this respect, especially if the acquisition creates a period in which key customers feel that their interests are being neglected or that it has become difficult to do business with the company. For example, in a major airline acquisition, elite customers of the acquired airline were forced to either endure a period without their usual privileges or change their allegiance to another carrier. This period can also be extremely stressful for customer service employees who have to endure the wrath of a continuing stream of irate customers. The challenge in these respects is to identify a transition period for systems that enables the acquirer to gain control quickly, yet appears seamless to customers and other external stakeholders.

## 10. Demonstrated Leadership Commitment

Should there be a permanent acquisitions team to lead the process? The debate over the value of a corporate acquisition function parallels the debate over strategic planning staffs. One view is that these groups reduce the authority of line executives and increase the rigidity of the process by introducing rules and procedures. An opposing view is that a small corporate group can serve at least five useful functions:

- Provide support for corporate executives on major deals.
- Stimulate a proactive approach to acquisitions throughout the firm.
- Act as a clearing house for ideas and proposals.
- Provide a source of expertise and professional help.
- Ensure that lessons learned are captured and communicated.

In performing these roles, corporate acquisition staffs are often asked to carry out the following tasks:

- Develop profiles of potential acquisition targets.
- Assemble and lead acquisition evaluation and integration teams.
- Establish relationships and networks for intelligence gathering.
- Develop procedures for acquisition evaluation and negotiation.
- Carry out postaudits of specific acquisitions.
- Provide advice on external training programs and sponsor in-house educational activities.

The effectiveness of a corporate acquisitions group depends on a number of factors, including the credibility and experience of the staff, their relationship to line executives, and where they report in the organization. Line executives cannot be expected to take the group seriously if they are ignored by corporate executives. Some corporations, such as Cisco and GE Capital, which make acquisitions on a continuing basis, have created an acquisitions team specifically dedicated to the integration phase.[11]

During the uncertainty generated by an acquisition, it is very easy for the acquired company to lose a sense of leadership. Executives are likely to be spending much of their time focused on the acquisition itself and may even be preparing exit strategies for themselves. Accordingly, it is important to have a leadership team in place the day after the deal is finalized. We have found that most successful firms insist on a blended leadership team, at least for the period immediately after the acquisition. Some, like Cisco, attempt to place an executive from the acquired firm as the senior member of this team, and others prefer to have their own nominee in charge. However, this decision is very much situational. What is important is to have the leadership team in place, with a plan, and empowered to act.

If the second 100 days must be run as a project, with a dedicated integration team spearheading the process, who should be on this team? A number of companies usually place an executive of the acquired company in charge of this team, but if the acquisition is made in a turnaround mode, it is more likely that an executive from the acquiring company, with an objective perspective, may be more effective.

Two kinds of errors are made by new owners with respect to the executive teams of acquired companies. The first is the destruction of a successful executive team by the new owners or the departure of several key executives from the acquired organization; it is a negative sign for employees and customers alike. The second is the failure of new owners to deal with a weak or ineffective executive team in the acquired company; it may be viewed as a sign of weakness by customers, competitors, and employees hoping for change. On the other hand, ensuring that the senior executive of the acquired company is viewed as being influential in the hierarchy of the parent can be extremely positive. Whatever the approach selected, the acquired company cannot be left to flounder, in limbo, with no effective leadership.

## In Summary

As noted at the outset of this chapter, many acquisitions create little value for the acquiring company. In fact, not only do some not succeed, but they can also distract management's attention from running the core business. The following are critical success factors for an acquisitive strategy:

- Have a well-defined assessment procedure and due-diligence methodology.
- Ensure that people involved in the process are experienced and knowledgeable.
- Be opportunistic, but within the framework of a sound strategy.
- For each potential acquisition, determine a walk-away price.
- Develop an integration plan prior to the deal, but be prepared to be flexible when additional information becomes available once the deal is closed.
- Be prepared to divest acquisitions that aren't working out and ensure that you know at the time of the deal what you will be able to realize in this eventuality.
- Postaudit all deals, then capture and retain the learning.

Most important, executives should remember that in most cases, the value from an acquisition is secured or lost within 100 days on either side of a deal.

# 7

## Rapid New Venture Creation and Introduction

Growth is a major objective for most corporations, and it can be achieved in any number of ways, from organic growth to growth through acquisitions. Success in the quest for organic growth lies in an organization's ability to consistently and successfully launch new products and services. These new ventures can take many forms, from simple product line extensions to completely new businesses. A few firms, such as 3M, Hewlett-Packard, and Johnson & Johnson, have been able to sustain a continuing stream of new ventures over a period of decades. Not only have they been able to do this, but they have also been able to get these innovations to market rapidly. For example, if necessary, Hewlett-Packard can develop and launch a new product within ninety days.

Other companies have been unable to achieve similar results. In fact, employees in some corporations become so frustrated that they leave and establish their own companies. Many organizations stumble in the launch of new products and services for any number of reasons, including:

- Failure to address well-defined customer needs. This is the classic "better mousetrap" scenario in which something is created without any or enough market input. It hits the market, and no one cares.
- Poor product definition. There is a market need, but the features and benefits built into the product are not completely aligned with what the market is looking for.
- Production economics. The new product or service may be a great idea, but it can't be produced economically.
- Inability to hit the market window. Definition, development, and launch take too long and a more nimble competitor obtains the much-coveted first-mover advantage.
- Lack of competitiveness. More aggressive competitors create a better value proposition for their new products and services.

**Table 7.1** New Ventures Are Risky

| Individual event | Probability |
| --- | --- |
| Venture has enough capital (two or more rounds) | 75% |
| Key personnel are available, competent, focused | 75% |
| Research is successful | 75% |
| Patents are granted, enforceable, and broad | 75% |
| Regulatory approval | 75% |
| Early clinical trials are successful | 75% |
| Competitors act as expected | 75% |
| Combined probability | 13% |
| If one variable drops to 50% | 9% |

What makes the difference between success and failure? Research has pointed to the people, the culture of the organization, the process itself, and, of course, luck.[1] New venture success is complex and usually depends on a number of activities happening and happening as planned. Table 7.1 summarizes the activities involved in launching a biotechnology venture.[2] It is evident that if any one of the activities doesn't work out as planned, the probability of success for the entire venture drops precipitously.

In the world of new ventures, you must assume that if you have the idea, then so do at least ten other people. Thus, speed of execution is one of the most critical determinants of success. In turn, speed relies on the establishment of our ten Winning Conditions. The rest of this chapter describes how these Winning Conditions can be applied in the specific context of creating and launching new ventures.

## Managing New Ventures—The Introduction Process

At its core, new venture introduction is a simple process of taking ideas, determining which ones are most promising, and applying required resources against the chosen few. For the sake of simplicity, we will refer to new products, recognizing that the discussion also applies to new services and new ventures in general. Champions of these initiatives have to be able to answer four basic questions:

- Is there a market?
- Can we be competitive?
- Can we deliver against customer expectations?
- Can we make a financial return?

Many organizations have, however, taken these four simple questions and embedded them in a complex decision-making process that gets executed poorly. Others have kept the process simple and have reaped the rewards.

As we discussed in chapter 3, any organizational change requires some mech-

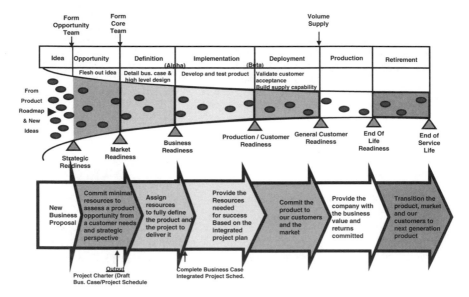

**Figure 7.1** Nortel: Time to Market

anism for leading and managing the process. In the context of new ventures, this process must be capable of defining the new venture opportunity, developing the new venture, and ultimately launching it and tracking its success. For new ventures, the process is generically known as the New Product Introduction Process. Corporations have many specific variations on this theme, such as Nortel Networks' Time to Market[3] (see figure 7.1). Xerox has experimented with many approaches over the years, one of which is known as the Corporate Innovation Committee (CIC).[4] Regardless of the variation, the most successful are those that are kept simple.

As a case in point, one of the most straightforward and effective product introduction processes was developed by Colin Patterson, a cofounder of Gandalf Technologies, one of the first high-tech darlings in the Silicon Valley North in Ottawa, Canada. In the early days of the firm, once significant success had been achieved with its first product and venture capital was plentiful. With the abundance of money available, each engineer was able to fund his own pet project. But a strange thing happened. The more money Gandalf had, the fewer new products there were coming out of all of these projects. What had occurred was that there were many projects, each with some resources, but no big projects, with a critical mass of resources. Patterson instituted a product development process, which he called the Carrot Approach to New Product Development. The concept was simple. If you plant a bunch of seeds and do not selectively weed and feed them, the result at the end of the season will be carrots, but typically long, thin ones that don't have much taste. If, however, during the growing

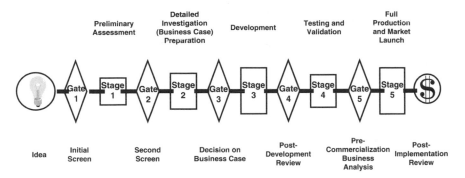

**Figure 7.2** The Generic Stage-Gate Process

season, the maturing plants are selectively fed and the stragglers are weeded out, then the result will be a crop of fat, tasty carrots. By the end of his first growing season at Gandalf, Patterson had his own crop of healthy new products.

Many variants of the product introduction process trace their roots back to Robert Cooper's pioneering work, which he named the Stage-Gate process.[5] His concept was simple: each developmental stage was followed by a gate, at which a decision was made to proceed with the project to the next developmental stage, disband the project, or further develop and come back again. Projects could not proceed to the next stage unless the requirements for the prior gate were met. Cooper's Stage-Gate model is depicted in figure 7.2.

All gating processes share a number of common elements:

- A series of developmental stages, each building upon the previous one.
- A series of checkpoints defined by specific criteria where go/no-go decisions are made.
- Appropriate resources are allocated to move the product forward to the next gate.

Many of the world's most innovative corporations adopted Cooper's model or a variant of it, during the late 1980s, but most have now abandoned it. The problem lay not so much with the process itself, but the ways in which companies used it. Corporations refined and elaborated the process so that the number of gates and subgates became a bureaucratic nightmare. Correspondingly, far from being enablers of product introduction, the gates became hurdles to be overcome and introduced delays in the process. Some corporations actually started to refer to the gates as "kill points," not at all what Cooper intended. In fact, gating can play an important role in the new product process, but only if the gates are associated with ensuring quality of execution in the development process and deadlines are met for certain stages of development. The question then becomes, What do we have to do, and what resources have to be committed to get the development to this stage, by this date?

## Managing New Ventures—The Corporate Venturing Group

The traditional new product process works well for most types of new ventures, particularly those that are clearly within the scope of the current core business. But what about those new ventures that either threaten the core business, manifesting Joseph Schumpeter's powerful concept of "creative destruction"[6] (e.g., eSchwab), or are clearly outside or peripheral to the current core business, (e.g., General Motor's OnStar)? Given the standard gates and go/no-go criteria at each gate, these latter two categories of new ventures most certainly would be rejected within the traditional model. As such, there needs to be a process that complements a type of Stage-Gate process, one that provides another avenue through which new ventures can be pursued. This complementary process often functions more as a new venture incubator than a simple decision-making process.[7] Many corporations have such groups, including:

- Procter and Gamble's Corporate Venturing Group, a group that was instrumental in creating reflect.com, an early e-business venture focused on providing custom cosmetics to consumers.
- Nortel's Business Ventures Group, a group responsible for nurturing and eventually spinning out numerous stand-alone new ventures.

The outcomes from the activities of corporate venturing groups are typically more varied than those for new product development processes. They include not only new products, but also licensing, creation of a new business unit, and subsidiary spin-off. Given this alternative range of outcomes, a different approach to the management of the resultant venture is also required.

## The First 100 Days

In defining, developing, and launching new ventures, whether they are line extensions, new products, or new lines of business, objectives and timelines should be consistent with those utilized and realized by new venture specialists—the venture capital community. In reviewing a typical venture capital decision process, table 7.2 outlines the typical timelines for decision making.[8]

**Table 7.2** Average Venture Capital Deal

|  | Total | Elapsed Days |
|---|---|---|
| Business plans | 500 | 1 |
| Meetings | 100 | 15 |
| Serious investigations | 50 | 15–45 |
| Extensive due diligence | 15 | 45–60 |
| Term sheets | 12 | 60 |
| Investments | 10 (2%) | 90 |

These are average timelines, however, and new ventures can proceed much more quickly. Andrew Waitman, managing partner of Celtic House International, one of North America's most successful technology-based venture capital firms, consistently shortens this timeline to weeks rather than months, even when the technology is complex.

As with other change initiatives, the first 100 days need to be focused on generating speed. This requirement for speed translates into the following objectives for the first 100 days:

- Initial business case completed.
- Product/service specifications determined.
- Embryonic team established.
- Lead customer(s) identified.
- Initial funding secured.

The initial business case provides an initial statement of answers to the four key questions posed earlier. A typical business case has the following key elements:

- Product description.
- Statement of customer need.
- Target markets and customers.
- Product specifications.
- Marketing requirements.
- Manufacturing requirements.
- Anticipated risks and mitigation strategies.
- Anticipated financial returns and benefits.
- Required resources.
- Core team members.

## The Second 100 Days

During the second 100 days, the challenge is to build a critical mass of resources and create momentum behind the new venture. Regardless of the venture type, objectives for the first 100 days largely remain the same. It is during the second 100 days that key objectives differ significantly across venture types. For a biotechnology venture, it may take several years to work through the science. Similarly, in high-tech ventures such as semiconductor design, it may take over a year to translate a design into an actual product. There are many organizations, such as Hewlett-Packard, that can and do create and launch new products within a 200-day period. For these companies, key objectives for the second 100 days include:

- Definition of an initial business plan.
  - Manufacturing/service delivery capability scoped.
  - Marketing and sales plan defined.

- Initial product in the market with lead customers.
- Business team established.
- Additional funding secured.

For those ventures for which the time horizon for product introduction is beyond a 200-day period, objectives for the first 200 days tend to be very tactical in nature and are typically focused on meeting the next development milestone. In addition to design/development-related activities, the team needs to be concerned with constantly validating their original assumptions regarding market window, customer requirements, etc. In short, objectives for the second 100 days should be:

- Definition of an initial business plan.
  ○ Design/development milestones cast.
- Continuing feedback from lead customers.
- Development team established.
- Additional funding secured.

## Establishing the Winning Conditions

Improving the odds of success for new product introductions and corporate venturing groups, requires the establishment the ten Winning Conditions. The following sections discuss in detail how each of these Winning Conditions applies to new ventures.

### 1. Correct Diagnosis of the Change Challenge

In diagnosing the change challenge for a new venture, the two dimensions to consider are depth and breadth. The diagnosis is all the more critical because the depth largely determines which process, new product introduction or corporate venturing, the initiative should proceed through.

New ventures can be considered in terms of their overall impact on the organization. Some have a relatively shallow impact and simply require operational adjustments. Others, however, are so radically different from the core business that they cannot be addressed within the existing organization and require a completely new paradigm to be commercialized successfully. Using the model that we developed in chapter 2, the four levels of change with respect to new ventures can be viewed as follows:

1. *Operational*: New ventures in this category most often take the form of line extensions. For example, when Procter and Gamble added Spring Fresh Tide to its portfolio of Tide products, the resulting change was primarily operational in nature—the same production line, same distribution channel, same basic packaging, changes to fragrance, but little else.
2. *Strategic*: New ventures in this category often take the form of a new

product category within a core business. For example, when Acklands-Grainger added electrical products to its catalog, the revenue growth opportunity was significant and required considerable strategic effort across the organization, including the redesign of warehouse facilities, training of branch personnel, and changes to the catalog itself. However, the basic values and behaviors required to sell this product line were the same as for the company's traditional product line.

3. *Cultural*: At this level of change, completely new lines of business are added that involve significant change in value and behavior if they are to be successful. They may be related to the core business. For example, when Nortel Networks added software development to its business portfolio, significant cultural shifts were required to move from a "hardware only" shop to one more broadly conceived. New lines of business can also be added that are unrelated to the core business or businesses. In this situation, such as when General Electric began growing GE Capital, cultural shift is essential, in this instance away from a manufacturing culture to that of a relatively cutthroat financial services orientation.

4. *Paradigm*: At this fundamental level of change with respect to new ventures, it is almost inevitable that an entirely new organization must be created. As a classic case in point, when Schwab decided it needed to become e-enabled and move to a discount brokerage value proposition, it spun out a firm called eSchwab and let it grow to a critical mass that enabled it to acquire its parent company. eSchwab could have never happened within the Schwab organization, and it only thrived because it was nurtured outside the parent.

In addition to the depth of change associated with the new venture, there are also breadth of impact issues to be considered when diagnosing the change challenge. Unlike some other types of change, new ventures frequently impact almost every part of an organization:

- Operations groups may have to add production capacity and/or reallocate existing capacity.
- Marketing groups may have to undertake market research, redesign promotional material, and launch new campaigns.
- Sales groups may have to retrain sales representatives on new product features, hire more and different salespeople, and set up new channels of distribution.
- Human resource groups may have to redesign sales compensation schemes, reallocate personnel, temporarily backfill positions for project team members, create new bonus structures, review pension requirements, and reconfigure more mundane activities from payroll processing to vacation entitlements.
- Finance and accounting groups may have to change financial reporting procedures, create new finance codes, reallocate capital budgets, review financial business cases, and possibly seek external forms of financing through investment banks or venture capitalists.

- Information systems groups may have to redesign web sites, provide additional technology support to the new venture team, or purchase new servers and PCs.

Clearly, new ventures create many headaches and typically have a broad impact across the organization. Without some recognition or organizational imperative associating with addressing these headaches, new ventures can die a slow and lingering death simply because the many and necessary details associated with taking them from concept through to commercial success just don't get done or done quickly enough. More than a few new ventures have failed in the marketplace because the customer facing part of the organization, the sales representatives, just didn't see anything in it for them to push the new product. Sad really, when the stakes are so high!

## 2. Early Development of Shared Understanding

There are two organizational processes that assist in the creation of shared understanding as it relates to new ventures. The first is typically strategic planning, which expresses the desire for growth and defines the vehicles through which it will be achieved. The strategic plan sets the target for growth and makes it an organizational imperative. In concert with this process are the new product introduction and corporate Venturing processes, where that target for growth gets translated into tangible and identifiable growth candidates. It is these processes that are most critical in creating shared understanding. As such, they must be concerned with two things:

- Systematically reducing the risk associated with new ventures by placing successive and increasingly large bets on a few likely winners
- Creating alignment among key stakeholders at every step of the decision-making and resource allocation process.

In the case of choosing and launching new ventures, the four generic components of shared understanding discussed earlier translate into a series of questions that must be answered. Because each venture is different, there is no standard set; however, the critical elements to be addressed are usually along the following lines. Vision can be an inspiring statement of what the venture might ultimately become, including statements about what the benefits are to customers and the value to the business. A typical mission statement for a new venture might cover a period of eighteen months and specifically focus on what has to be accomplished to ensure a successful start-up of the new venture.

Corresponding measures of success address the following question: How will we know if and when we've been successful? Dimensions can include market positioning (such as target segments), revenue growth, profitability, market share, being first to market, and acceptance among a group of reference customers.

Typical key programs and projects to be identified early include the market research that has to be undertaken, technology development, requirements for lead customer (beta project) testing, process development, and the makeup of the required business team. Corresponding enabling processes include those that we have identified already—new product introduction and corporate venturing.

In terms of who needs to be involved in shared understanding the answer is simple—just about everyone. In the case of new ventures, there is typically a great depth of understanding on the four areas outlined above among the new venture team and its sponsors and champions. Yet, in the other stakeholder areas—finance, operations, marketing, etc.—there is often a limited understanding of their roles in making the new venture a success. Without this understanding, as discussed earlier, valuable time is lost when critical new venture enablers are not ready quickly enough.

### 3. Enrichment of Shared Understanding

The new product introduction and corporate venturing processes themselves are the principal tools for maintaining and enriching shared understanding. At every decision point, new information is factored in, made sense of, and utilized to make the go/no-go decisions or refine the original concept. If the decision points are well defined, decision point criteria are well understood, and the right people are involved at the decision points, it is relatively straightforward to enrich shared understanding through these processes.

There is a danger of becoming too internally focused as new ventures proceed through the various development processes. These new product processes don't usually explicitly involve customers, although validated customer perspectives are supposed to be factored in throughout. In reality, customer perspectives can be lacking; if this occurs, it can negatively affect the entire venture.

Rarely does the original concept for a new venture proceed exactly as planned or the market turn out as predicted. For examples, Rogaine, a drug originally intended for heart treatment, became a blockbuster drug when it was discovered that a significant side effect was the growth of hair, for which there was a much larger market. A complete redesign of the marketing approach was required to capitalize on the market for these unintended effects. In short, critical shared understanding is most successfully maintained and enriched by ensuring appropriate involvement of stakeholders, including customers, throughout the development processes.

Equally important, yet somewhat more difficult, in new product development is to manage the shared understanding around *why* certain projects don't make it through a decision point. In this case, managing change is more associated with ensuring that the unsuccessful new venture team is reenergized and redeployed onto other promising ventures. 3M calls this "well-intentioned failure." There are no punishments associated with not making it through the entire process; rather, there is recognition of "nothing ventured, nothing gained."

### 4. Establishment of a Sense of Urgency

Unlike some of the other types of change we discuss, such as turnaround, culture change, and acquisitions, new ventures are generally perceived to be positive, energizing, and fun. Adding sales personnel is much more pleasant and satisfying than downsizing. As such, there is often no need to establish a sense of urgency, but there is a need to contain the unbridled enthusiasm of people for new products. This enthusiasm can be channeled into developing a sense of urgency with respect to bringing these ideas to commercial reality. Research and Development employees are known for their propensity to "play with" new product ideas for extended periods of time, seeking perfection rather than driving hard to get a first product into the market. This was the situation faced by Patterson at Gandalf. His people seemed to have much more fun generating new ideas than bringing them to fruition. Yet, he wanted them to have a sense of urgency about bringing new products to the market.

Why are people motivated to create and launch new ventures? Typical motivators include:

- Achieving corporate objectives (e.g., one of 3M's corporate objectives states that "30% of products will be new in the last 3 years").
- Beating a competitor to market to obtain coveted first-mover advantage.
- Passion of the inventor/originator for the idea.
- Financial rewards.

What we know from the world of new ventures is that successful entrepreneurs are intrinsically motivated to succeed and that extrinsic rewards such as money are not the primary drivers. Many successful entrepreneurs comment that "money is a way of keeping score" and that without an inner passion that drives them to see their venture succeed, they would have likely given up somewhere along the path from concept to commercial success. The key point is that you often don't need to establish a sense of urgency outside of traditional organizational levers with respect to bringing new ideas forward.

In contrast, employees not engaged in new venture work may view new ventures as irritants to the established order rather than as keys to the future. They may either starve these initiatives of resources and cooperation or place bureaucratic hurdles in their way. Corporations are likely to have to utilize whatever levers are at their disposal to generate a sense of urgency among key enabling parts of the organization. One is to put their employees on new venture teams. Another is to rate their performance in providing assistance to new ventures. Explicit recognition of the project team's contribution during celebrations of success can also be highly motivating.

## 5. Creation of a Limited and Focused Strategic Agenda

Gating and corporate venturing processes involve focusing limited resources on those product developments that have the best opportunity for success. Patterson's carrot theory of new product development clearly illustrates that an organization can't possibly nurture all of its seedlings. Without tough choices along the way as to which to fertilize and which to weed out, the crop will fail. Given this, an organization needs to decide how many and what types of new ventures can be reasonably undertaken at one time and at what stage of development. In a company like 3M, there may be hundreds of early-stage new ventures under way, but only a very limited number of major new product launches occurring at any one time. This reality is one of the reasons for speed. If a product can be taken from concept to launch in a period of, say, three months, and if the organization can handle five major launches simultaneously, then there can be twenty major launches per year. However, if this same process takes a year, then a corporation could have twenty new launches simultaneously eating up resources and competing for management attention. Most likely, the failure rate would be high in this situation.

Clearly, there is a limit to the capacity of an organization to undertake this range of new ventures at any one time. In the world of academe, we refer to this capability as "absorptive capacity."[9] In the business world, it is referred to colloquially as "bandwidth." At a certain point, the organization cannot absorb anything else new. Nowhere is the bandwidth issue felt more keenly than in the enabling functions of Information Technology, Human Resources, and Marketing and Sales. Hence, it is critically important to ensure a highly focused agenda of new venture projects at or near the commercialization stage, when resource requirements are highest.

A risk/return portfolio approach is one useful way to categorize projects. A desirable portfolio would be one that has a few projects with very high risk and very high returns, many with moderate or low risk and high returns, and relatively few with high risk and moderate or low returns. Another useful classification differentiates between incremental, "outside the box," and "new box" developments. As an example of how this can work in practice, consider the situation of car manufacturers. Incremental new ventures are typically associated with model redesigns and additional features and benefits such as sliding doors on both sides of a van. "Outside the box" new ventures include such things as washers, dryers, televisions, and VCRs in vans and SUVs. Included in the "new box" category are the launches of a model line such as the SUV, a complete redesign of an existing model, and entirely new but related ventures such as General Motor's OnStar system.

## 6. Rapid, Strategic Decision Making and Deployment

To execute new ventures rapidly through building speed and momentum, two fundamental conditions must be satisfied. First, a parallel-deployment methodology is required, rather than the traditional linear, sequential approach.[10] Many corporations implemented gating and corporate venturing as linear, sequential processes. The first decision point was focused almost entirely on technical feasibility: does the science make sense? The next decision point focused on manufacturability: could the product be produced economically? Not until the end of the process were questions about the size of the market and such things as channels of distribution really hashed out. What often happened was that technically superb whizbang products were fully developed before critical market

| Principal Role | R & D | | Demonstration    Piloting | | Operations |
|---|---|---|---|---|---|
| PROCESS | Exploratory Process R& D | Process Performance Targets | Engineering and Piloting of Critical Elements | Total Operation System Design and Specification | Process Technology Package |
| MARKET | Marketing Specifications | | Market Test Design | Demonstrate Product Performance | Technology Market Package |
| PRODUCT | Exploratory Product R&D | Alternative Product Forms | Market Testing | Product Application System Design | Product Commercial- ization |

**Figure 7.3** Concurrent Product Development

information was considered. If the market information was poor, then it was back to the drawing board for another go. Valuable time was lost, financial resources were wasted, and, most likely, the window of opportunity had passed.

In contemporary approaches, product, market, and process development proceed simultaneously. An embryonic business team is established early in the process. Information on all these aspects of the project are factored in at every decision point because the relative emphasis and certainty of information change as the process unfolds. For example, market information may be sketchy in the early stages, but some preliminary indicators of whether or not there even is a market should be crucial to the go/no-go decision at the first gate. A framework useful for understanding the concurrent nature of product development is depicted in figure 7.3.

Enabling this concurrent development approach requires a strategic decision-making process, which can produce decisions, resource reallocations, and action quickly, rather than a traditional resource allocation process such as annual budgeting. In practice, this means that:

- The process cannot become bureaucratic. In some firms there are only three decision points and three developmental stages. Time frames for development are explicit and the review sessions are regular—one per month in some cases.
- Decision makers at any stage should be those who control the resources required to fund the project at the next stage of development, not those who have to go through another level of approval before they can commit.
- The mix of decision makers needs to change as the process unfolds to correspond to decisions that are made at a given review. For example,

relatively more scientists and engineers would be involved in the early decision points and more marketing and sales personnel in the latter stages.

- The decision criteria must be made explicit for each review so that submissions address all possible questions. If this is not done, valuable time can be lost because no decision is made and project teams retrench to gather the information they require.
- Not all new product development funds should be allocated at the start of the budget year. A significant proportion may be held back to fund initiatives that emerge during the year.

We are frequently asked how long a new product development should take. Many people think in terms of months and years when, in fact, it may be a matter of days or weeks depending on the situation. As an example of how this process can work, and work quickly, consider Eureka Ranch, a company based in Cincinnati, Ohio, that specializes in fast-paced, three-day product development sessions in which clients:

- Brainstorm new product ideas.
- Choose the most promising from among these.
- Sketch out initial product concepts that include, in some cases, prototype packaging.

A profile done on Eureka Ranch by the Canadian Broadcasting Corporation's *Venture* show features the Long-Term Research and Development group of Tyson Food Company, the world's largest producer of beef, pork, and chicken. The group is showcased as it undergoes one of these three-day sessions.[11] The group selected other Tyson personnel (e.g., from sales and marketing) and external experts (e.g., on children's food) to participate. The team met for three days at Eureka Ranch to come up with new ideas for chicken and lunch products. On the first day, the group brainstormed hundreds of new product ideas. The second day saw a smaller group of decision makers meet to weed out the less-promising ideas and agree on a few promising ones. For the ideas that were deemed to be promising, new product pitches were created overnight, complete with pictures and packaging, so that on the third day, further progress could be made. The result at the end of the session was a considerable number of new product ideas that would then go into consumer testing. We use the video of this session in our MBA and executive program courses on New Venture Management to illustrate how quickly this process can work. It does not need to take months, only weeks or even a few days. Setting expectations appropriately is critical in this stage.

## 7. A Human Flywheel of Commitment

In a new venture, there are two human flywheels that need to be considered. The inner flywheel relates to the venture itself and the team leading the venture. The outer relates to the broader organization and the individuals who, although not directly engaged in new venture projects, can directly and indirectly influence the outcomes.

In the core team, you want to have people involved who are passionate about the venture and who will do whatever is required. There should be no 20-70-10 principle operating within new venture project teams; rather, the project team should represent a portion of the high-energy 20 percent group within the organization. These are the true believers who will spend sixteen hours a day, if necessary, to make the venture a success. Two serious mistakes that organizations make in creating the new venture team are to remove the originator of the idea from the project team and to "allocate" resources to the team rather than allow the team to "attract" resources.

In his article "Bringing Silicon Valley Inside," Gary Hamel comments that many new ventures within organizations need to mimic, as much as possible, the elements that form a center of entrepreneurial activities like Silicon Valley.[12] One of these elements is the ability of new ventures to attract resources rather than take what is allocated to them. In Silicon Valley–type corporations, the market for human capital is just that—a market. World-class engineers and marketers are free to choose the ventures that fit their interests and expertise and that unleash their passions. Promising ventures attract the best and the brightest. The team is almost always made up of the true believers. Yet, in corporations bound by their organization charts and hierarchies, project teams are created by allocating resources. In some cases, team members may not actually be that interested in the venture itself, except as a source of steady income. Without people who truly believe and who will go to exceptional lengths to see their ideas through to fruition, new ventures are less likely to succeed.

In spite of having the right people, new venture teams may still fail to convince others of the merits of their venture. Table 7.3 provides a summary of the most common reasons that this occurs. In summary, new venture teams need to speak in plain language, hit stakeholder "hot buttons," and demonstrate passion and commitment.

Complementing the team's ability to "pitch" the venture is the organization's ability to ensure that incentives are aligned, appropriate processes exist, and pertinent skills are available in the enabling functions such as Information Technology, Human Resources, and Marketing and Sales.

**Table 7.3** Reasons that the Business Plan "Pitch" Fails

- Poor rationale—just a bad idea
- Poor timing
- Wrong people
- Failure to hit "hot buttons"
- Inappropriate language (e.g., too technical)
- Poor presentation style
- Inability to answer key questions
- Lack of credibility or lack of passion

Individuals in these groups are key players in the outer flywheel of a new venture. Although they may have limited day-to-day contact with the initiative, they ultimately have a defining role in determining the outcome by virtue of the service and support they provide for the new venture. For example, is the Human Resource team willing and able to locate and recruit new personnel with appropriate skills in the time frame required by the venture? Can the Information Technology group develop any necessary applications software in the required time frame? The ability of these groups to fulfill new venture requirements is determined not only by their attitudes, but also by their structure and capabilities. For example, in some corporations, both of these groups will have employees who are dedicated to supporting new venture initiatives.

## 8. Identification and Management of Sources of Resistance

As with any other type of change, there will likely be a large group of employees, perhaps up to 70 percent, who appear to be indifferent to new venture activities. They may be viewed as resistant to the success of new ventures but, in reality, they may have different and perhaps conflicting priorities:

- Operations personnel may have the view that "This new venture is going to disrupt my operation and my bonus is based on efficiency and output. There is a disincentive for me to help."
- Sales personnel may think, "I have my quotas and they don't include spending time and effort getting up to speed on this new stuff. I'm going to stick with what I know."
- Human Resource personnel can take the position that "This new venture is going to create headaches for me. If the people involved are successful, they're going to want some sort of monetary rewards, to become members of a new company if one is going to be created. I'm going to have to backfill their regular jobs. This is going to be one monumental challenge for me."
- Financial personnel may be of the opinion that "This is too risky. I don't see the return. I'm going to have to add new product codes and tracking mechanisms. The venture needs money and our capital budgeting process is not in sync with their requests. This is just creating too many problems."
- Managers may well ask "Why should I fund this? I have limited resources. If it doesn't go well, am I going to have egg all over my face? It's not worth the career risk."

Who are the real resisters of new ventures? Why do these saboteurs wreak havoc? Most of these individuals can eventually be brought to support new venture activities through a combination of leadership, shared success, and changes to key organizational enablers. For example, if it's clear that the executive team strongly supports new ventures, part of this group will fall into line. In addition, if some of these employees can be provided with an opportunity to share in the success of new ventures, they are likely to align more strongly with them. One way to accomplish this is to ensure that each new venture team has at least part-time members from each of the key facilitating functional groups. Additionally, as we will discuss shortly, aligning key enablers, such as recognition and reward, policies, and education, with the requirements for new venture success can be extremely effective.

As a final commentary on why these people appear to resist, there is one cultural barrier that often needs to be addressed: the punishment for failure—real or perceived. In practice, this "punishment" for lack of success with a new venture can take many forms:

- Poor performance evaluations.
- Sidelining from the career fast track.
- Rumor-mill commentary ("so-and-so is a loser").

It is incumbent upon the leadership to ensure that these punishments are not used because they are a sure way to kill the entrepreneurial spirit forever. Firms like 3M understand this reality and take extraordinary measures to ensure that when the inevitable happens and a new venture is not successful, the new venture team is not punished but rather lauded for doing everything they could. The culture recognizes risk taking as part of its lifeblood and rewards it on an ongoing basis.

A small minority of employees, up to 10 percent, will be strongly opposed to new ventures as the wrong thing to do. Their deeply held beliefs take the form of comments and thinking such as these:

- "It's not fair that someone is going to win big [money or recognition] if the new venture is wildly successful. Better for everyone to be mediocre rather than have a few winners."
- "It's just too risky [every new venture gets the same comment]."
- "If I can't win in this new venture, then no one else will either, and I'll make sure of it."
- "It's too competitive. My new venture idea shouldn't have to compete with others in the new product process. I should just get the resources I need and to hell with everyone else."

With thinking like this, it is clear that short of a brain transplant, these individuals are unlikely to change their minds. Remember that the people in this category can rarely be brought onside. Any attempt to do this requires enormous effort and may be futile because of deeply held attitudes and beliefs that cannot be changed, or cannot be changed quickly enough in relation to how quickly the venture needs to be launched.

There are two organizational implications of having individuals with these attitudes. First, as it relates to success in launching new ventures, is to make tough decisions regarding them. As discussed in chapter 2, these decisions include removal of the individual from contact with the new venture or a career move to another organization.

The second implication relates to the recruitment and promotion criteria and policies of the organization. If the ability to create and launch new ventures is to become a repeatable process, then attitudes and beliefs about collaborative competition (not an oxymoron) and risk taking must be factored in to hiring decisions. There is nothing wrong with internal competition as long as it doesn't become dysfunctional. Similarly, if people aren't willing to take risk, then not much will happen. If an organization is to have an entrepreneurial culture, these two attitudes must be explicitly considered, particularly when hiring or promoting senior executives but also when hiring new employees generally.

## 9. Follow-through On Changing Organizational Enablers

For new ventures, key organizational enablers need to be considered on two fronts: as they relate to the new venture team itself and as they relate to the parts of the organization outside the team. These key organizational enablers include rewards and recognition, horizontal processes (e.g., hiring and capital budgeting), training, and organizational structure.

First, let's consider the new venture team. We know that successful entrepreneurs are those individuals who are intrinsically motivated to see their new ventures succeed. Given the nature of successful entrepreneurs and their intrinsic motivation, the implications for rewards and recognition are simple. Dee Hock, founder of Visa, had it right:

> Money motivates neither the best people, nor the best in people. It can move the body and influence the mind, but it cannot touch the heart or move the spirit; that is reserved for belief, principle and morality. As Napoleon observed, "No amount of money will induce someone to lay down their life, but they will gladly do so for a bit of yellow ribbon."[13]

Clearly, there has to be something in it for the entrepreneur and his or her team, and yellow ribbons will not work for everyone. Organizations often err, however, in assuming that the rewards need to be monetary and the recognition must be individual. Nothing could be further from the truth. The most successful entrepreneurs (there are, of course, exceptions to the rule) are team oriented and intrinsically motivated. The operative principle here is that organizations need to have a portfolio approach to rewards and recognition when it comes to new venture teams. Table 5.3, which showed a framework based on individual and group recognition and financial reward, provides a useful way to approach this subject.

On the issue of rewards and recognition, let us return for a moment to Colin Patterson and his carrot theory. To provide some fun and motivate the Gandalf engineers to see their ideas through to commercialization, Patterson created the Golden Carrot Award for successful ventures. Engineers who were successful in their quest received an eighteen-carat-gold lapel pin in the shape of a carrot and were inducted into the Gandalf Carrot Hall of Fame. It was as meaningful as Napoleon's yellow ribbon and became a highly coveted symbol of success within the organization.

At a more well known level, 3M has a variety of ways to recognize successful new venture achievement. For example, membership in the Carlton Society, a sort of internal Nobel Society, is accorded only to those involved in initiating a new venture and making it commercially successful. The inventor of the Post-it Notes adhesive is a Carlton Society member. In addition, there are Genesis Awards for promising new proposals and the Golden Step Award for new venture teams that reach a certain revenue volume.

Other critical organizational enablers for new venture teams include horizontal processes, training, and team structure and membership. Key horizontal processes are primarily associated with the new venture team's ability to tap into expertise and capabilities in other parts of the organization. In one organization we studied, a team working on a new product was consistently stymied by the vice-president of sales as they tried to ensure that new and different channels of distribution were being set up. There needs to be a clear and unequivocal message sent across that organization that priority new ventures get needed resources. This, of course, assumes that these resources exist; this will be discussed further in the following sections.

In terms of training, several types are typically required. First is training on high-performance teams. Successful new ventures depend on teams. The most successful new venture teams are diverse because specialized knowledge needs to be combined with marketing, production, and logistics expertise. We know that the best-performing teams are diverse but also that the worst-performing teams are diverse. The magic lies in integrating that diversity, and integration relies on team skills. So, the first priority for training is creating a high-performance team.

The second training issue relates to the team's ability to have the requisite skills. Many newly formed new venture teams are heavy on specialized knowledge and somewhat light on business acumen. The "build it and they will come" phenomenon prevails. Business-plan preparation, negotiation, communication, sales, and informal influencing skills commonly top the list of missing skills. It is crucial to ensure that technically sound ideas can be translated into viable business propositions.

The flip side of business training is technical or specialized training. For team members from the business side of the organization, comfort and competence with specialized knowledge is important. Thus, training may entail activities associated with technical issues as well.

One of the major enablers for successful new ventures is an organization structure and style that allows a business team to be developed around any new venture rapidly and effectively. Unfortunately, many organizations have such deep silos between Research and Development and functional groups such as Operations and Marketing that a cross-disciplinary business team simply cannot come together rapidly. Unless there is a Product Development group that is relatively self-contained with respect to these skills, as some indeed are, the organization must be able to facilitate the horizontal transactions that allow these teams to be assembled expediently and effectively. Perhaps the best situation is one in which employees throughout the organization are made aware of the need for new teams and can volunteer for them.

From a broader organizational perspective, and outside the new venture team, the same categories of enablers apply. Incentives must exist for those outside the new venture who assist in making the venture a success. What's in it for the operations manager to disrupt his production line? Why should a sales representative push the new product? How can a finance manager find the time to provide financial advice to the team? Without answers to these questions, critical time and resources will not be made available. The solutions are not simple, however, and they require explicit actions. For certain, there must be incentives for these groups to provide their time and expertise. But incentives are useless if there are no resources, such as time and money, to work with.

Organizations must operate and serve existing customers with quality products and services. Yet, there has to be time and money available to try new things. This dynamic has been well understood for many years, and a leading economist, Edith Penrose,[14] coined the phrase "organizational slack" to capture the resource issue. Slack can take the form of either people with time or available seed money for new ventures. Without slack, there can be limited assistance. With limited assistance, there can be fewer new ventures. Without successful new ventures, there can be no growth. The flattening of organizations and the push for efficiencies that re engineering has brought on have worked to strip out slack in the belief that it is a bad thing. In the world of new ventures, the reverse is true; slack is a great thing. Kodak's Office of Innovation understands this well, and they state as one of their innovation principles that "the most effective way to proceed is not necessarily the most efficient."

If an organization has slack, the issue of incentives can be discussed. For enabling organizations, there can be intrinsic motivations that can be tapped into—the excitement of working with a new venture team, personal satisfaction, skills development, and the like. Of more interest, though, are the extrinsic motivators. 3M has something called the "15 percent rule," which states that certain personnel, the enablers, are expected to spend up to 15 percent of their time working on a project for which they are not directly responsible. In principle, it is designed to have key individuals reach out beyond their day jobs to assist in new venture creation. In practice, this "rule" is reinforced through the performance management system, in which annual performance appraisals include an assessment of whether or not this 15 percent of time has been utilized.

Other organizational enablers include horizontal processes, which work with and complement the new product, and corporate venturing processes. For example, a capital budgeting process that occurs once per year is of little use to a new venture that requires additional, unanticipated resources six months into the year. Similarly, recruitment approaches that are lengthy and cumbersome do not fit well with the fast pace of most new ventures. Corporations need to examine these and other organizational processes to ensure that they are not barriers to new venture creation but, instead, reinforcers and enablers.

## 10. Demonstrated Leadership Commitment

Last, but not least, is the issue of demonstrated leadership for new ventures. Again, leadership in this arena must be considered at two levels: leadership of the venture itself and leadership within the broader organization, particularly at senior levels.

A great deal has been researched and written about the characteristics and attributes that successful entrepreneurs share. There is no definitive answer, but a synthesis of over fifty studies suggests that successful entrepreneurs share characteristics that can be broadly grouped into six themes or traits, summarized in table 7.4.[15]

An overriding characteristic, however, is that successful entrepreneurs are passionate about their ventures and use that passion to drive commitment from team members, the organization, and customers. As a matter of fact, the most important element for venture capitalists when considering investment opportunities is the new venture team and its leadership. [16]

We like to show our students a short video to illustrate the six themes outlined in table 7.4. It is a video that depicts the story of Second Chance Body Armor, a midsized North American company that designs and manufactures bulletproof vests.[17] The inventor and founder, Richard Davis, started with $70 and a passion for protecting the human body against bullets. His passion was born out of a near life-ending encounter with a bullet during a pizza shop holdup. Davis's insight into protective body armor was that most police officers who died from bullet wounds did so because they weren't wearing bulletproof vests. They didn't wear vests because they were plastic and uncomfortable.

Davis set out to create comfortable and flexible vests made from ballistic nylon, a fabric name more generally known under the brand name Kevlar. His biggest challenge was to convince police officers that the seemingly flimsy vests actually worked, but he had extremely limited financial resources to undertake any sort of sophisticated marketing. So Davis did the next best thing—he hit the road, donned his vest, and proceeded to shoot himself in the chest at short range. The vest worked (of course), the police officers were convinced, and the rest of the story is a fairy tale case of new venture success. Richard Davis took extraordinary measures to demonstrate his belief in and commitment to his product. He comments that the money is nice, but his true feelings of success stem from the number of lives he has saved—Second Chance keeps track of each and every one of them. Thus, the larger issue for new venture leaders is that they similarly *demonstrate* passion and commitment to their ventures, because that is how teams are built and customers are convinced.

Executive leadership for new ventures and the changes they create requires a demonstrated passion and commitment to promoting individual initiatives, as well as to keeping the pieces of the new venture success formula together, particularly the cultural aspects. Senior executives demonstrate their personal commitment to new ventures in a variety of ways. Most directly, some CEOs sponsor new products in their corporations. They meet frequently with the teams, ensure

**Table 7.4** At the Heart of It All, the Entrepreneur

| Theme | Attitude or Behavior |
|---|---|
| Commitment and Determination | • Tenacity and decisiveness, able to decommit/commit quickly<br>• Discipline<br>• Persistence in solving problems<br>• Willingness to undertake personal sacrifice<br>• Total immersion |
| Leadership | • Self-starter; high standards but not perfectionist<br>• Team builder and hero maker; inspires others<br>• Treat others as you want to be treated<br>• Share the wealth with all the people who helped to create it<br>• Integrity and reliability; builder of trust; practices fairness<br>• Not a lone wolf<br>• Superior learner and teacher<br>• Patience and urgency |
| Opportunity Obsession | • Having intimate knowledge of customers' needs<br>• Market driven<br>• Obsessed with value creation and enhancement |
| Tolerance of Risk, Ambiguity, and Uncertainty | • Calculated risk taker<br>• Risk minimizer<br>• Risk sharer<br>• Manages paradoxes and contradictions<br>• Tolerance of uncertainty and lack of structure<br>• Tolerance of stress and conflict<br>• Ability to resolve problems and integrate solutions |
| Creativity, Self-Reliance, and Ability to Adapt | • Unconventional, open minded, lateral thinker<br>• Restlessness with status quo<br>• Ability to adapt and change; creative problem solver<br>• Ability to learn quickly<br>• Lack of fear of failure<br>• Ability to conceptualize and "sweat details" (helicopter mind) |
| Motivation to Excel | • Goal-and-results orientation; high but realistic goals<br>• Drive to achieve and grow<br>• Low need for status and power<br>• Interpersonally supporting versus competitive<br>• Aware of weaknesses and strengths<br>• Having perspective and sense of humor |

*Source:* Jeffry A. Timmons, *New Venture Creation: Entrepreneurship for the 21st Century* (New York: IRWIN/McGraw-Hill, 1999), 221. Used with permission.

that resources are provided, and may offer specific assistance, such as arranging meetings with lead customers. Others will go out of their way to periodically visit teams that are working on new projects to encourage and recognize their activities. In addition, many executives establish rewards for achievements in the new ventures field.

Beyond personal leadership, there are leadership challenges related to creating and maintaining an appropriate environment and culture in which new ventures can flourish. Specifically, these challenges entail:

- Setting challenging targets for new venture creation.
- Encouragement of not just new ideas, but new ideas that can lead to commercial success.
- Policies that explicitly state a tolerance for failure and mistakes.
- Championing the existence of organizational "slack" as a good thing.
- Keeping shareholders happy by balancing the quest for quarterly returns against the requirements for funding new venture creation.

New venture leadership is not for the faint of heart, and it requires a constancy of commitment that once undone is extremely difficult to regain.

## In Summary

Generating a continuing stream of successful new ventures is one of the toughest challenges any corporation faces. New ventures introduce disruptive changes that must be welcomed and valued if sustained success is to be achieved. We have demonstrated how the Winning Conditions create an appropriate framework for driving the changes required of successful new ventures. Important themes to remember are:

- The importance of two complementary, new product introduction processes—a Stage-Gate–type process and a corporate venturing process.
- Developing speed to market via these processes.
- Establishing a business team early, one that includes the inventor/founder.
- Building a team through "resource attraction" rather than "resource allocation."
- Involving lead customers early and keeping them close.
- The role of enabling functional groups that support the new venture.
- Celebration of both success and "well-intentioned failure."
- Demonstrating leadership passion for new ventures.

Rapid new venture creation has been made to appear extremely difficult, almost a mystical art, by many management gurus. As we have shown, it's really not that difficult!

# 8

## Rapid Introduction of New Information Systems

Successful deployment of information technology is one of the most important sources of advantage available to corporations. These systems provide the foundations for superior customer service, more-effective utilization of resources, and new areas of growth. In addition, information systems are often key elements that facilitate organizational change. So pervasive have these technologies become that in 1991, for the first time ever, companies spent more money on computing and communications gear than the combined monies spent on industrial, mining, farm, and construction equipment.[1] In fact, investments in computers and telecommunications now amount to at least half of most large firms' annual capital expenditures.

Investments in information technology can benefit organizations in four fundamentally different ways:

- Providing infrastructure.
- Offering operating advantage.
- Offering a point of differentiation for existing businesses.
- Providing new lines of business.

At the most basic level, organizations invest in information systems simply because they must. Like the plumbing and electrical systems in your house, these are the classic infrastructure investments that don't provide any sort of visible or immediate advantage but that must be made. Upgrades to communication networks and the latest version of Microsoft Windows are examples of these types of investments.

At the operating, or functional strategy, level (the level at which most information systems investments are considered), information systems investments can streamline operations and reduce administrative and operating costs. Investments in Enterprise Resource Planning (ERP) systems, such as SAP and Oracle, or Human Resource Management Information System (HRMIS), such as PeopleSoft, are examples of this type.

At the business strategy level, information systems can be used to create competitive advantage for existing businesses. As we know, competitive advantage can be achieved in any number of ways. Wal-Mart's investment in inventory control systems, warehouse management systems, and other related store management systems, has enabled it to be a low-cost retailer. Lands' End, the catalog retailer, has used the Web to create an online shopping experience that far surpasses that of its competitors, offering such possibilities as shopping with a friend, virtually trying on clothes, etc. In these two examples, the nature of the business remains the same, but advantage is created and sustained through their uses of information systems.

At the corporate strategy level, information systems can provide opportunities to create new businesses. The Sabre Reservations Systems, created by parent corporation AMR, is a classic case in point. American Airlines was the first airline to create online reservations systems for use by the travel industry, the result of which was the establishment of a brand-new line of business, one that today is the primary contributor to AMR's bottom-line profitability.

Despite these success stories, many organizations struggle to properly envision and deploy information systems, in the end generating little value for either the people who must use them or the corporations that fund them. A 1994 landmark study of 8,000 information systems projects, conducted by the Standish Group, revealed some ugly truths:

- Nearly 33 percent failed outright.
- More than 50 percent were over budget.
- Only 16 percent completed on time and on budget.
- In large companies (with revenues greater than $500 million), only 9 percent of projects were successful.[2]

With statistics like these, it's no wonder that the acronym CIO—usually used to refer to the chief information officer—became synonymous with "career is over." As bad as these statistics are, the reality is even worse because this study doesn't cover the true cost of delays to critical organizational change initiatives that are dependent on information systems as key enablers.

Why is this still the case after so many years of experience with information systems? The reasons range from poor technological choices to an inability to properly incorporate new technologies into the fabric of the organization. In particular, the overwhelming focus on the part of many champions who drive implementation of new information systems is to strive for technical perfection and spend as little time and/or money as possible considering or acting upon the inevitable organizational changes that any new information system requires.

Typical failure modes tend to exhibit a number of common characteristics:

- *Poor systems design*—the operational system fails to meet users' specifications because it was designed in relative isolation by technical specialists who don't know the business or the users' requirements and who fail to understand the application.

- *Inadequate resources allocated to major initiatives*—people with the requisite technical skills are costly, and IT departments frequently commit the major part of their resources to maintaining and upgrading legacy systems, which doesn't leave much to allocate to major projects.
- *Technological obsolescence*—implementation schedules are so long that by the time the system is implemented, the technology is obsolete. Technology projects frequently exceed their projected implementation schedules by a factor of two or three.
- *Search for technological perfection*—there is a certain amount of functionality that everyone can agree on, but then individual desires and requirements take over and the additional functionality takes too long to implement to everyone's satisfaction. The classic 80:20 rule prevails in this instance.
- *Inadequate training*—numerous studies and a continuing flow of horror stories indicate that inadequate training continues to be a problem. Either the training is not budgeted for in the first place, or at the end of the project when other elements have exceeded their allocations, training gets cut. The result: suboptimal utilization.
- *Lack of end-user acceptance and use of new systems*—this is often a result of several of the above problems. Systems are launched inadequately, so they are immediately characterized as unreliable and unsuccessful, a stigma from which they usually never recover.

These are but symptoms of deeper problems. A stream of projects that are late, over budget, and nonconforming to specifications is an outcome associated with some less well understood root causes. In particular there is often a lack of shared understanding among key stakeholders of what it *really* takes to design and implement a system, lack of appropriate involvement of key personnel, failure to redesign core business processes and practices, and a "system" that is too big and unwieldy in the first place. Information systems personnel often take the heat for these failures, when in reality the blame needs to be shared equally with business leaders.

This reality is reinforced by the findings from a study of knowledge management (KM) undertaken by Ernst & Young Center for Innovation in 1997.[3] Their study of 427 firms found that among the greatest challenges in KM projects, "overcoming technological limitations" was eighth on a list of eleven items. The rest of the challenges were related to organizational issues, not technology issues. Table 8.1 summarizes the study's findings, and suggests that executives in these successful organizations recognize that anticipating and managing the concomitant changes that these information systems inevitably produce are critical steps to implementation success.

Successful organizations insist on speed in the implementation of new technology. Many demand that tangible deliverables must be achieved within six months. These firms also believe in intelligent momentum. At the outset of major

**Table 8.1** Greatest Knowledge Management Challenges

| Barrier | % of Respondents Having This Challenge |
|---|---|
| Changing people's behavior | 56 |
| Measuring the value and performance of knowledge assets | 43 |
| Determining what knowledge should be managed | 40 |
| Justifying the use of scarce resources for knowledge initiatives | 34 |
| Mapping the organization's existing knowledge | 28 |
| Setting the appropriate scope for knowledge initiatives | 24 |
| Defining standard process for knowledge network | 24 |
| Making knowledge available | 15 |
| Overcoming technological limitations | 13 |
| Identifying the right team/leader for knowledge initiatives | 12 |
| Attracting and retaining talented people | 9 |

initiatives, there is substantial time invested in managing expectations and developing shared understanding among key stakeholders, especially executives, managers in the information technology function, users, consultants, and vendors. This shared understanding is then translated into operational commitment that takes the form of timely and sufficient resource allocation such that momentum is built and sustained to deliver results in the expected time frame.

## Implementing Information Systems—The Management Process

Information systems, no matter how simple, introduce change into organizations. To understand the nature of their impact, though, we first need to clarify what we mean by "information systems." Some people talk about information technology, information management, and information systems interchangeably. In this chapter, information systems refer to both hardware and software—the boxes and equipment, as well as the applications or programs that run on them.

As with any specific type of change, processes must exist that are capable of identifying the need for new information systems, prioritizing this need, developing the system, and ultimately implementing it. For information systems, there are typically two interrelated processes that accomplish these tasks. The first is the strategic planning process—corporate, business unit, or functional—that generates the requirement for the new system. For example, a line of business might identify customer loyalty as a focus for driving market share. It might then identify a key action of creating a customer information system. The creation of the system, in turn, becomes an objective for the Information Systems group. Table 8.2 illustrates how the strategic plans for these groups would be linked in this scenario.

The benefits of such a linkage are:

**Table 8.2** Linked Strategic Plans

| Business Strategy | IT Strategy |
|---|---|
| *Vision/Mission Objective 1:* Increase market share 5% | ***Objective 1:* Create customer information system** |
| Strategic Thrust A: Develop customer loyalty program | *Strategic Thrust 1:* Build client/server infrastructure |
| ***Action 1:* Create customer information system** | *Strategic Thrust 2:* Create data warehouse |
| *Action 2:* Conduct market research | *Strategic Thrust 3:* Identify management applications |

- Creation of a clear context for the new system because it relates to achievement of a business objective—market share increase—and is not an "orphan" system standing on its own.
- Buy-in and commitment from the business.
- Clear prioritization of the importance of the system.

More often than not, however, such clear linkages do not exist, and this creates problems throughout the development and implementation of the system.

At the same time, however, there are instances in which information systems investments are not tied to business strategy. For example, the need to upgrade infrastructure (e.g., communications networks or operating systems) is often driven by the Information Systems group. In cases such as these, the change challenge is more difficult because the importance of such investments may not be obvious to everyone, no matter how critical they are. It's like not making changes to a building's electrical system until the lights actually go out.

The reality today is that strategic planning and operational planning in most organizations generate a plethora of information systems requirements that often overwhelm the capabilities of the Information Systems group. The Standish Group survey discussed earlier indicated that 93 percent of the organizations surveyed have a three-year development backlog, and at least 75 percent of information systems professionals' time is spent on maintaining and tweaking existing systems, leaving relatively little time to support new initiatives. Therefore, a sound prioritization system is required to determine which development to undertake in any given time period. In some extreme cases, it may be necessary to cut off support to legacy systems in order to provide a critical mass of resources for the implementation of major new systems.

Once a decision is made to undertake the development of a system, the concept becomes a project. Thus, complementing the strategic planning process is a project management process that takes the information system from concept through to implementation. The project management approach is usually made up of two groups, the project team and an oversight body (often called a steering committee), each with their own, but linked, decision-making processes. It is through the project management process, and the interaction between the team and the steering committee, that information systems move from paper to reality.

## The First 100 Days

Once a decision is made to proceed with a major information systems initiative, three parallel sets of activities must be undertaken. The first relates to the project itself and the activities related to planning for, developing, and ultimately implementing the system. The second set relates to the creation and management of the project steering committee. The third relates to the management of the end users, other employees, and even external stakeholders, such as customers and vendors, who will be affected by the new system. It is around these categories of activities that the objectives for the first 100 and 200 days are cast.

Very early on in the first 100 days, the members of the project team have to be selected and assembled. Some of these team members are likely to be full-time on the project, but others are likely to play only a part-time role. In addition to development staff, the team is likely to contain user representatives; individuals from groups that have a key supporting role to play, such as Purchasing and other functional areas and representatives from key vendors. The probability of a successful launch will be enhanced if an initial team-building session is conducted to focus and align all participants. Some part of this process can be devoted to getting acquainted, but the most powerful team building occurs if the team works together to define a shared mission, objectives, and plan for the project. It may be that vendors are not selected until later in the process, at which time their representatives need to be inducted into the project team.

The Steering Committee also has to be created and its mandate and mode of operation agreed upon. Some training may be necessary to ensure that members understand their role; one of the problems encountered with these groups is that they lack a true understanding of their role, and the committee attempts to manage rather than steer the project.

In one large, Australia-based mining company that experienced a "worst-case scenario" in implementing a new financial system, the steering committee was responsible for several of the problems encountered. It looked great on paper—all of the key executives controlling all of the necessary resources—but functioned very poorly.[4] Committee members didn't understand their roles and tried to micromanage the development process. Worse still, there was almost no shared understanding among the members as to what the new financial system was intended to achieve. Some thought it was for automating some financial reporting, and others viewed it as a significant driver of cultural change because the new system would allow for detailed comparisons of financial results across operating properties, something not easily done with the current system.

Thus, an early task for the steering committee is to clearly articulate its mandate, then ensure shared understanding of the task ahead. In addition, the committee needs to review the project plan, ensure that a thorough risk assessment has been conducted, and put strategies in place to mitigate the critical risks.

Early involvement of end users and other stakeholders is also required. They provide valuable insight into the development challenge and can be instrumental in ensuring that the project plan is realistic and achievable and that enabling resources outside the project team's direct control are identified.

With these activities under way, the project should have developed a considerable degree of speed, if not momentum, by the end of the first 100 days. Objectives for the first 100 days might include:

- Freezing specifications.
- Identifying and securing key external resources.
  ◦ Vendor resources.
  ◦ Consulting resources.
- Completing risk assessment.
  ◦ Identifing major risk factors.
  ◦ Developing and implementing mitigation strategies.
- Identifying and assigning project resources.

Once these objectives are met, the basic Winning Conditions for successful development and implementation have been established.


## The Second 100 Days

If the first 100 days is focused around building speed, planning, and creating a strong sense of shared understanding among the various stakeholders, then the second 100 days is focused around creating a critical mass of resources behind the project, obtaining tangible near-term demonstrable outputs, and gaining widespread acceptance of the new system within the affected parts of the organization.

During this period, continued communication among the various stakeholders is critical. This is a phase in which the project team is likely to be so heavily engaged that the team members do not feel there is time to communicate. Failure to communicate causes many projects to lose direction and support among the end user community. Almost inevitably, there will be design and programming changes that may affect the ultimate functionality of the system. Communication among the various groups is key to ensuring that these changes are understood and accepted. "Scope creep" is a major killer for many information systems projects because every end user wants to ensure that his or her individual needs are met. The best project managers contain scope by continually communicating the implications of changes and modifications to both the budget and the timeline of the project. In one organization, a seasoned project manager prepared a very brief financial analysis for every change request he received. His standard line was as follows: "Sure, we can make the change, but here's what it will cost in time and money. You make the call." Through focused communications activities and vehicles such as these, end users realize the impact that their "wish lists" have on the overall delivery of the project, and they typically come to recognize and buy in to the system's functionality.

A critical mass of end users can be achieved if tangible parts of a new system can be demonstrated. There are many different approaches to developing systems, and it is well beyond the scope of this chapter to delve into these approaches. It is important to understand, however, that some approaches can provide tangible outputs early on in the development process, whereas others can't. In the early days of systems development, the development process worked like this:

- A systems analyst worked with end users to identify their needs for the new system.
- The analyst drafted a document that outlined these needs.
- Users signed off on the system specifications.
- The information systems group designed and developed the system.
- The information systems group presented the system and turned on the switch.

As it turns out, organizations have experienced huge problems with this approach for the following reasons:

- Users aren't very good at defining their needs at the outset.
- Analysts aren't very good at translating needs into system specifications.
- There is no opportunity to factor in user input as the system is being developed; it is an "all-or-nothing" approach.

It is, in fact, very difficult to identify what you need until you see what's possible. That's when a more contemporary approach to developing information systems, known generically as a prototyping methodology, comes in handy. In prototyping, systems development is a much more iterative and tangible process, one that provides for user input very early on. It works like this:

- A systems analyst works with end users to identify their needs for the new system.
- The information systems group creates a prototype based on the needs analysis (e.g., what the screens look like).
- Users review the prototype and provide their feedback. The systems analyst refines the prototype for another review. This continues until users are satisfied with the proposed functionality.
- Users sign off on the final system specifications.
- The information systems group designs and develops the entire system.
- The information systems group presents the system and turns on the switch.

As you can see, the prototyping approach is much more inclusive, works to create buy-in through the development process, and results in systems that actually fit the needs of end users. What a novel concept!

In addition to ensuring that the development approach is appropriate, the project team needs to interface with the steering committee to ensure that the project remains on schedule and focused on deliverables. To do this, regular meetings between the steering committee and the project manager are required. Depending on the rate of progress and the scale of the project, these meetings may be as frequent as every week, and should be at least every month, perhaps with a weekly progress report circulated to the members. In addition, the steering committee should periodically review and update the risk assessment. At an engineering consulting firm that we studied and worked with, these regular meetings didn't occur. Steering committee members constantly cancelled review sessions because they were "too busy" to attend. Serious issues needed to be resolved early on in the project, and these cancelled meetings ended up delaying the implementation of the system by several months.

To summarize these activities, by the end of the second 100 days, the following should be achieved:

- Prototype complete and reviewed by users.
- Training plan created.
- Implementation plan created.
- All development program milestones met.
- Secondary team building undertaken.

Accomplishment of these objectives should ensure that sufficient intelligent momentum has been generated to propel the project through to a successful conclusion, even if it is ultimately a year or more before the entire system is complete.

## Establishing the Winning Conditions

In reviewing information systems fiascos, it is relatively easy to track these failures back to the absence of one or more of the ten Winning Conditions. From the preceding discussion, it is clear that a solid project management team and a great steering committee are the two overarching vehicles through which the Winning Conditions are established. The following sections describe how these vehicles work to create the context for successful implementation.

### 1. Correct Diagnosis of the Change Challenge

Although the introduction to this chapter provided insight into what an information system might do for an organization, it is not particularly enlightening regarding how the systems will affect the company. For example, even an apparently minor infrastructure change, such as moving from WordPerfect to Word, can introduce significant cultural change if there are strongly held employee values and beliefs to be addressed. Some employees love WordPerfect and hate Word, and vice versa.

Because of the complexity of information systems, it is instructive to look at specific examples of information systems–related projects in order to fully understand how the dimensions of change—depth and breadth—interact with respect to diagnosing the true change challenge. By way of example, a key priority for many organizations these days is KM. Anyone involved in this field knows that an integral part of executing on this priority is investment in enabling information systems. There are many activities involved in KM, and a simple way of thinking about these is to reflect on the life cycle of knowledge in an organization:

- Acquisition or creation.
- Organization.
- Retrieval.
- Distribution and use.
- Maintenance.

There is clearly overlap among these different activities, and information systems that serve one can also serve others. The 1997 KM study by the Ernst & Young Center for Innovation found that the majority of activities were focused around four types of projects: creating an intranet, creating knowledge repositories, implementing decision support tools, and implementing groupware to support collaboration.[5] Given these four types of KM projects, how do you effectively diagnose the true change challenge of each one?

We differentiate among the levels of change by considering the information system's impact on business processes and end-user behavior using the framework that we developed in chapter 2. Specifically, does the information system require changes to underlying business processes? Does the information system require end users to alter their behaviors (i.e., routine of accomplishing a task)? Using these questions and others like them, it is relatively easy to diagnose the depth of change involved.

At an operational level of change, information systems automate existing processes and typically require only minor or tactical behavioral changes. An example of this level of change is the posting of meeting minutes on an intranet, a simple case of making them available electronically.

Strategic change is involved when information systems require relatively high levels of expenditure and make significant differences to existing business processes, yet still only require minor, tactical behavioral changes. For example, the creation of a knowledge repository and the provision of sophisticated search capabilities allow employees to file and retrieve reports electronically (automating a manual process) and therefore enable faster and richer access to the information contained in those reports (via the search tool). Shoshana Zuboff, a noted information systems authority, coined the term "infomate" to describe information systems that accomplish this task. They make information available in a more timely and useful fashion to more people, thus enabling better and faster decision making.[6]

At the level of culture change, information systems typically "infomate" an existing process but require significant behavioral changes involving shifts in attitudes and beliefs. For instance, the successful implementation of expert systems in a variety of applications demands significant shifts in employee behavior. In the banking sector, Credit Scoring systems (an example of an expert system) automatically approve or reject a loan application, thereby removing the decision-making capability from the loan officers. Essentially, they are being asked to believe that the system provides better guidance than they are capable of themselves. In many situations, employees will either ignore the expert system or attempt to second-guess its output. These systems only function effectively when this kind of behavior is eliminated.

At the deepest level of change, paradigm shift, organizations are required to either create a new process or redo an existing process that completely changes the nature of the activity and requires both behavioral and attitudinal changes. Staying with the same knowledge repository example as above, if a collaborative groupware system is tacked on top of the basic system with the expectation that it will enable research and development twenty-four hours a day, seven days a week, clearly a new research and development process has been created, as well as a new way of working with other people.

Information systems affect underlying business processes and require significant changes to individual behavior, but they also vary in their impact on different parts of an organization. The broader the impact of an information system, the more complex its implementation becomes and the more difficult the management of the resultant change becomes. Four basic categories of breadth of impact are easily identified:

- Impact within a work group, unit, or function.
- Impact across work groups, units, or functions but within a business unit.
- Impact across business units but within an organizational entity (e.g., a corporation).
- Impact across organizations (e.g., across corporations or with alliance partners, vendors, and customers).

Thus, diagnosis of the change challenge involves assessing the breadth and depth of the impact of the information system while considering issues peculiar to information systems, as discussed above. As with all change initiatives, diagnosis is a critical activity in managing change because it provides initial guidance. But more important, it provides insight into the approaches and levers that will be most appropriate and effective in driving the change. A useful method for summarizing the change challenge is provided in table 8.3.

In addition to identifying the difficulty inherent in the change, the above diagnosis provides insight into the relative importance of the management processes involved in implementing information systems, namely, end-user management, project management, and steering committee management. For

**Table 8.3** Diagnosis of the Change Challenge

| | | Breadth of Change | | | |
|---|---|---|---|---|---|
| | | Intraunit | Cross-unit | Cross–business unit | Interorganizational |
| Depth Of Change | Operational | Simplest | | | |
| | Strategic | | Challenging | | |
| | Cultural | | | Very challenging | |
| | Paradigm | | | | Positively scary |

example, for information systems that introduce operational change contained within a unit, good, solid project management will be most important because end users likely won't be very concerned with the system and all end users are contained within one group. Contrast this example with an information system that introduces cultural change across business units. In this instance, the best project management in the world won't matter unless end users are managed well and the steering committee works to resolve any political issues or cross-business-unit conflicts. Yet, in many organizations, project teams proceed blindly in the hope that as long as the project plan is executed well, the rest will come. This is frequently a fatal assumption.

## 2. Early Development of Shared Understanding

Once the diagnosis and a thorough review of the change challenge are complete, the next imperative is to ensure that there is a true understanding of all of the components that lead to success. The importance of this aspect of the process is illustrated by the following comments by senior executives who participated in our research program.

A senior vice-president of logistics for one of the largest grocery retailers in the United States noted, "Lots happens between a good systems idea and execution . . . the vision part is well understood and there is no loss of purpose or commitment, these [information systems] are just huge things to realize . . . they die under the bureaucracy of the business, the complexity, the politics." The CFO of another large U.S.-based corporation commented on what understanding needs to be shared: "Right in the execution expectation stage, that is where things can fall apart, but it takes somebody's willingness on the business side to dig down in the low-level details."

Without an initial agreement on the key elements of shared understanding, we know that success in implementing information systems is low. Interestingly enough, understanding in certain categories matters more than in others. An in-depth study on the relative importance of the four dimensions of shared understanding (cf. figure 2.2) found that the key dimensions in predicting information systems success were key programs/projects and enabling processes. The study also found that organizations in which corporate executives and information technology managers possessed a greater shared understanding of issues related to these two dimensions were consistently successful in their implementation of information systems.[7] To quote a common saying, "the devil is in the details."

Creating shared understanding with respect to information systems means that the key players have a shared sense of the answers to the following questions:

- What is the vision for the information system? For example, is it to enable better, faster decision making? Or is to provide anytime, anywhere access to corporate information?
- How will success be measured? Is it on time and on budget? Is it related

to achievement of a strategic objective? Is it related to end-user acceptance and use?

- What are the projects and subprojects that must be undertaken to take the information system from concept through to implementation? What resources will be required?
- What business processes must be redesigned to support the information systems?

The next question relating to shared understanding is, with whom should the above understanding be shared? An information systems vice-president of another large grocery retailer summarized the situation quite nicely:

> Here is what you've got. You've got the business side and you have the technology side. You have the general manager and you have the Chief information officer. Under the general manager you have some kind of business manager, and under the CIO you have an analyst. All of the communication is typically going on between the business manager and the analyst on this tactical execution stuff. But if the decisions have to be made between the general manager and chief information officer, you're going to have a guaranteed disconnect between these two and between the business manager-analyst as well. In fact you're also probably going to end up with one between the general manager and the business manager and between the chief information officer and the analyst. What is the hope for this? Zero!

What this convoluted quote serves to illustrate is that there are many stakeholders to consider in implementing information systems, and a breakdown between any two of the parties can be problematic. On the information systems side, stakeholders include vendors' sales representatives and technical specialists, consultants such as the lead partner and implementation specialists, senior information systems executives and personnel including software developers and hardware technicians, and project participants such as systems analysts. On the noninformation systems side, there are corporate executives, business-unit executives, end users, and project participants. The final stakeholder is the CEO or head of the organization, a person ostensibly in neither category but actually at the top of both.

If you look at the number of parties likely to be involved, the minimum number of relationships is $2^{13}$, or 8,192. Clearly, a corporate executive and a vendor's technical specialist will have limited interaction, so the issue of shared understanding among parties is not quite as daunting as it appears on the surface. However, it may be important for the vendor's technical specialist to clearly understand the strategic importance of the project to the customer's executive team. In fact, it is often in the details that projects fall apart because key technical issues and their potential organizational impacts get lost in the maze of relationships and filters between the technologists and the senior executives. In the Australian mining company described earlier, when the new financial system was finally ready for widespread rollout, it became clear that there was not enough storage capacity available on the existing hardware, a technical "detail" that could have and should have surfaced much earlier.

What is critical with so many parties potentially involved in the development process is to ensure that all stakeholders understand the project plan, the critical milestones, and the issues related to achievement of those milestones. As the next section discusses, stakeholders need to maintain an understanding of these issues as the project progresses.

## 3. Enrichment of Shared Understanding

What does enrichment of shared understanding really mean with respect to information systems development? Naturally, there are monthly steering committee meetings and periodic reports, but all too often, these are merely reporting out sessions. Fundamental problems are not discussed broadly, and change of scope and design are not communicated. In these projects, enrichment of shared understanding means that what is being learned as the development progresses—about the system itself, the development process, and the future application—is shared among the stakeholders. Appropriate decisions can then be made based on this understanding.

There are three parallel processes useful for fulfilling the requirement of enriched shared understanding. Project processes must include frequent meetings to ensure continued alignment among the team members. End-user and external stakeholders, like vendors and consultants, must also provide for frequent two-way communications with the project team and the end users. These processes might be relatively formal and include the review of prototypes, or they can be informal and take the form of brown-bag lunches. The key is to keep the lines of communication open among all the various stakeholder groups.

In addition, the periodic meetings of the steering committee can be used as an opportunity for a more strategic review of the initiative, following which adjustments can be made in scope, resources, and schedule. In one high-performing steering committee in our study the chairman of the committee established a routine whereby the project manager provided the committee with a list of items he needed to be resolved. The list served to focus the steering committee's efforts and greatly sped up the meetings.

## 4. Establishment of a Sense of Urgency

In implementing an information system, there are two issues to be addressed with respect to urgency. The first is ensuring that the initiative receives an appropriate priority ranking on the organization's strategic agenda. It is highly unlikely that an organization will cease to exist because an information system, such as an HRMIS, is not implemented quickly enough. Thus, in the face of a multitude of competing initiatives, how do information systems become a priority?

The ultimate priority endorsement comes from senior executives. Yet, these people are often nowhere to be seen in major information systems initiatives because they delegate away the responsibility. A senior vice-president of information systems at a major U.S. retail organization that has built a considerable competitive advantage around its information systems commented on the value of unequivocal statements from the chief executive officer: "Our CEO is the big cannon in the corner office—a strong and vocal advocate for common systems, common data and common business processes. He has been very consistent and never once wavered."

Such statements are reinforced if the initiative is one of the three or four critical initiatives, or a key element in one of these, within a strategic plan— whether it's at the corporate, business, or functional level. A HRMIS that is not tagged as a priority within the human resource strategy is doomed to failure. Yet, how frequently are HRMIS implementations driven by the Information Systems group? The Human Resources group is only marginally engaged; instead, they have a different set of more-traditional strategic priorities such as an overhaul of the performance measurement system and succession planning. Without this clear and logical link, the needed resources in the Human Resources group have a much lower probability of being available.

What about a situation in which the information system is clearly linked to the strategic plan for the organization, but the organization still doesn't seem motivated? One public-sector organization we've worked with has struggled for six years to implement a new financial information system. Progress has proceeded at a glacial pace. Project managers have come and gone, and the project has been renamed several times in an effort to relaunch and to create enthusiasm. Not much was happening with the latest relaunch, however, until the new project manager did some homework and discovered that this particular government ministry was the only one of its type in North America that did not currently possess the capabilities that the new system would provide. This one simple fact unlocked a sense of professional pride, and the latest relaunch shows signs of success.

Other approaches commonly utilized to inject a sense of urgency and set the bar appropriately include:

- *Publication of studies.* Studies conducted by information systems specialty research organizations such as Gartner Group, Forrester Research, and International Data Corporation (IDC) can serve to establish benchmarks around time frames for systems development and provide competitive information.
- *End user as project manager.* An end user who drives the project team, especially one whose bonus is tied to the achievement of a strategic objective enabled by the new system, has a terrific effect on the level of urgency.
- *Specific performance incentives.* When Jack Welch wanted to "digitize" General Electric, he stated that any executive who wanted to advance his career needed to be engaged in driving one of the digitization projects he'd identified. Needless to say, there was no confusion about the urgency of these various projects.

### 5. Creation of a Limited and Focused Strategic Agenda

Large information systems projects can take some time, in some cases up to two years, before the final value is truly realized—a long time in today's business environment. Shorter technology cycles promise that by the time the entire system is in place and is delivering the intended outcomes, the technology is obsolete. So how does one manage the apparent disconnect between these two realities?

The most successful organizations recognize that although the end goal is a complete system, there are usually well-defined parts that contribute to the complete system. As such, system implementation can be reduced to a series of well-defined implementation campaigns, with each campaign contributing to the overall system. Benefits of such an approach include easily identifiable milestones and value-adding pieces, as well as the opportunity to celebrate success along the way.

More specifically, for large information systems projects, breaking the project into a set of discrete deliverables with defined outcomes and tangible benefits to the organization is appropriate. In several organizations we've worked with, chief information officers stipulate that no deliverable can take longer than six months to realize. Successful CIOs often use analogies to great advantage in communication of the need for such discrete deliverables. The story goes something like this: the ultimate goal may be to build a two-story house with attached garage. It might take a year to complete the whole project, but the garage will only take a few weeks, and the first level only a few months. As long as these pieces are built, the family will have a roof over their heads and a place for the car. The house certainly looks like a house, it is just missing a second level. Large information systems can work the same way: build the foundation pieces for the entire system, but break the project into discrete deliverables that add value as they are completed.

### 6. Rapid, Strategic Decision Making and Deployment

To rapidly execute a large information technology initiative and its attendant changes through building speed and momentum requires that two fundamental conditions be satisfied. First, a parallel-deployment methodology is required, rather than the traditional linear, sequential approach. Enabling this are decision-making processes that can produce decisions, resource reallocations, and action much faster than many companies appear capable of, even today.

A parallel-deployment methodology generates speed in the planning and execution of information system developments. As we demonstrated in figure 2.3, four parallel streams of action are required: executive actions, substantive initiatives, organizational enablers, and communication. The following example of how these four streams can work and work well in practice describes the experience of a large Canadian insurance company that made the decision to replace the mission-critical information system that managed all of their policies.

## Executive-Level Actions

The CEO sent out an all-employee memo regarding the importance of having a new information system. At this point, the actual software vendor hadn't been chosen, and the project team had just been formed. Nevertheless, the CEO felt that it was critical to prepare the organization and provide a rationale for why the new system was required at that time. All-employee memos were a rarity in the company, so the significance of the memo sent a clear message to the entire organization: be part of this initiative. In addition, he indicated that he was personally going to chair the steering committee, which further demonstrated his personal commitment to the initiative. Each executive was tasked with holding day-long sessions with their subordinates to ascertain "what it was going to take" to make the project a success. There was little confusion throughout the management ranks as to the career implications of not being 100 percent committed to the project.

## Communications

The CEO wanted the new system to become top priority across the organization. More important, he wanted the project to invigorate the organization and even be perceived as fun and rewarding. Like high-performing athletes who prepare for months or years for the Olympics, the CEO wanted all employees to be part of the preparations and know that they were shooting for gold. He borrowed a long-standing United Way campaign tactic and instituted the "thermometer" reading for tracking progress on the project. The various project deliverables, rather than dollars, formed the bars on the thermometer. In this way, every single person in the organization knew the various project parts, such as selecting a vendor and completing a prototype, their target completion dates, and their actual completion dates. The thermometer appeared in strategic locations, such as in the lunchroom and above the photocopier, and was unavoidable. In a remarkable achievement, not one deadline was missed. More important, people throughout the organization who were involved at different times and in different deliverables were instantly recognized for their contributions. They were recognized informally, because everyone knew who was involved in what, and more formally through small celebrations and personal communiqués from the CEO that were provided at the end of each deliverable. In the end, the project took a lot of hard work, but a postaudit revealed that those involved felt it was extremely worthwhile and, yes, even fun.

## Substantive Changes

Although there were no substantive changes to the business—it would still be writing policies—the process of assessing risk and writing policies was substantially changed by the new system. Various studies had been undertaken over the years that looked at different ways of doing things; rather than start from square one, a decision was made to move forward with the most obvious of the various changes that had already been proposed and agreed to in principle. Any new system was going to have implications for their network of independent insurance brokers, and immediate steps were taken to redesign the organizational interface with the broker network. There would be no going back.

### Changes in Organizational Enablers

Perhaps the most significant and symbolic change that occurred at the beginning of the initiative was the redeployment of human capital and financial resources within the company. The organization made the decision to halt all efforts associated with maintaining the current system and tweaking other systems and to redeploy the resources to planning for and implementing the new policy management system. Although this seems like an obvious decision, many organizations have dozens of miniprojects under way at any one time all of which take on a life of their own and require resources.

Along with rapid and parallel deployment of activities such as those outlined above, it is necessary to ensure that decisions that affect the implementation of new information systems are made in a timely fashion. In large information systems initiatives, there are typically four interrelated decision-making processes at play: strategic planning, project team processes, steering committee processes, and end-user processes. Decision-making failures, as well as disconnects, in any of these processes are problematic.

A typical example is the case of a major industrial distributor that identified an e-commerce capability as a major future source of competitive advantage. It was cast as one of four strategic objectives for the organization, and the vice-president of marketing was made accountable for the deliverables. Speed was of the essence if the company was to be first to market with the concept. A team was put in place to execute the project as planned. Progress was tracked and reviewed at the quarterly strategic planning meetings.

During the project initiation and scoping phases, critical issues were identified that had not been considered during the strategic planning discussion when timelines were set and resources were allocated. These were significant technology-related issues, as well as issues related to inventory information, such as ensuring consistent product numbers and pricing for both the traditional line of business and the Web site.

The responsibility for initiating action and allocating resources to resolve these issues was outside of the marketing vice-president's control and required a reallocation of resources, as well as some refinement of timelines. Although the project team identified these issues within the first month of the project, they were not resolved until the next scheduled strategy review almost three months later. The outcome was three months of lost time, a delay that in the end proved to be very costly. The issues could have and should have been resolved as soon as they were identified. Yet, the decision-making body, in this case the executive team, was not suitable for the task. A better approach would have been to create a steering committee to guide the project, rather than rely on the executive team.

A great steering committee can vastly improve the speed of decision making; however, it is also common to see instances in which superb steering committees are effectively neutered in their ability to make timely decisions by the inability of the project team to surface issues when they need to be surfaced. The following scenario illustrates the point:

> In a large, geographically diverse engineering and design consultancy, a strategic initiative to implement a standard project costing system across the organization was identified in a strategic planning retreat. Recognizing the importance of the project, a subset of the executive team formed a three-person steering committee to oversee the project. The steering committee was empowered by the CEO to make key decisions around scope and resources for the initiative. A project team was formed and they quickly engaged a consultant to assist in the vendor selection process. The vendor selection process became the priority for the project team. Critical issues around team membership and different costing practices in the geographically separate business units were not raised and discussed at the project level until several months into the project. By the time they were brought to the steering committee, several potential team members had been assigned to other important projects for clients and were no longer available. In addition, the business units were up in arms about rumored changes to their project costing practices. The project never recovered and the steering committee shut it down.

In this scenario, the communication failure at the project level was the root cause of the problems. Comprehensive project planning methodologies, as well as steering committee probing and vigilance, are the solutions in cases like these.

End-user decision processes are primarily concerned with having proper representation on the project team and/or links to the project team. This often doesn't happen, as the following experience recounts:

> On paper, we had great end-user support for the project. In reality, we'd been assigned a very junior person to interface with, and every time we asked him a question or needed a decision, he had to go off and check with someone. It was ridiculous. We needed a half-day turnaround on something and instead we'd have to wait for a week. It just about killed the project.

To summarize, these scenarios illustrate the importance of having not only rapid decision-making capabilities within the processes, but also alignment among the processes. Excellent steering committees, superb project management capabilities, and strong links to end users are the three "tickets" to rapid decision-making nirvana.

## 7. A Human Flywheel of Commitment

Information technology often evokes extreme emotional responses from people. Many people just completely hate it, and not necessarily for any rational reasons. At the other extreme, some people are so in love with the technology that they lose sight of the real business purpose of a new system. In sifting through the

**Table 8.4** Attitudinal and Motivational Characteristics of Participants

|  | Low-Ability | High-Ability |
|---|---|---|
| High-Willingness | **Easily salvageable:** Want to participate/contribute, but lack the skills, tools, and know-how. | **Nirvana:** Understand the technology and the business. Have time and interest to contribute. |
| Low-Willingness | **Lost Causes:** Want nothing to do with project and can't contribute anyway. | **Special Attention:** Want nothing to do with it but possess valuable capabilities if they can be engaged. |

reasons—rational and otherwise—they generally fall into one of four categories, as shown in table 8.4.

In the "nirvana" category, one finds the relatively limited set of people who are constantly called on to represent their organizations on various project teams. These are the technologists who understand the business inside and out, as well as the business people who are competent in the technology arena. They don't fear technology, they embrace it. They perceive competence in managing information technology as a good thing rather than a necessary evil, and they are both intellectually and operationally committed. These are the people who typically form the core of the organization's approximate 20 percent of employees who champion change and who are certainly the most visible.

Most employees who are unwilling to make an early firm commitment to an initiative can be categorized into one of two groups: the "easily salvageable" group or the "special attention" group. Here, it is critical to differentiate between those who are willing but not able to contribute and those who are able but not willing; the conversion strategies need to be very different.

For the "easily salvageable" category, the prescription is clear: provide the right type and appropriate amount of training. In this group, attitudes and beliefs are in alignment with the value of the new technology, but there is a lack of knowledge or skills. It is from this group that some of the most powerful advocates can be drawn. Their position is clear: "We agree in principle but we lack crucial know-how to move forward."

In the "special attention" category, training is typically not very effective because this group already has technical competence. The problem is their demotivating career-related concerns, such as returning to the mainstream business once the project is complete. The very real question for some is, "If the project fails, will I be blacklisted?" Another frequent concern relates to available time. Employees may be asked to continue doing their regular jobs while participating in this project. In this situation, the employees feel that they can't do both and do both well.

### 8. Identification and Management of Sources of Resistance

In the "lost causes" category depicted in table 8.4, one generally finds people with the following excuses, excerpted from various interviews held over the years:

- "I've been successful thus far in my career without embracing technology, and I'm not about to do it now."
- "I really have no time for this stuff. I don't understand it, I don't want to understand it, and more importantly I hate dealing with those technology geeks. They talk in acronyms and generally work to make me look stupid."
- "It will be a cold day in hell before I'm part of any activities associated with the Department of Profit Prevention [i.e., the technology group]."

With strongly held beliefs like these, no form of reasoning will be effective. At work here are deeply held values that are not easily, if ever, reversed. These are the people who are typically in the small minority but who will actively resist involvement in a new information system. If the CEO falls into this group, then the organization is likely to be in some trouble. There are tough decisions to be made concerning these individuals. The ideal solution is clear: removal of the individuals in question. However, it is highly unlikely that individuals who are great marketers, for example, are going to be discharged because they have a technology aversion.

A simple strategy is to ensure that these individuals are isolated from development and implementation efforts. If they have to be involved with the operation of the new technology, alternative methods of accomplishing work (I.e., methods not related to the use of the new technology) should be eliminated. Of course, it is also possible to mandate that these individuals use the new system. However, it is not unusual for people with these characteristics to be incredibly creative at finding ways to demonstrate that the system really doesn't work. A last resort is to explicitly tie use of the system or outcomes of system use to individual performance measurements and rewards.

### 9. Follow-through on Changing Organizational Enablers

As we've discussed already, information systems often require changes to many organizational processes to facilitate the creation of a culture of acceptance. Process changes range from the simple, such as submitting expense forms online, to the complex, such as integrating the supply chain. Consequently, there may be many significant changes to the way an organization operates in order to extract value from the new system. Drawing again from the 1997 Ernst & Young KM study, table 8.5 summarizes the perceived causes of the unwillingness or inability of employees to change behaviors.[8]

A review of table 8.5 clearly indicates that the barriers to knowledge sharing, a necessary antecedent condition for any KM approach, are culturally and not technologically based. What is also clear is that near-term organizational deci-

**Table 8.5** Common Impediments in Knowledge Management Projects

| Impediment to Knowledge Sharing | % of Respondents with This Impediment |
| --- | --- |
| Culture | 54 |
| Top management's failure to signal importance | 32 |
| Lack of shared understanding of strategy or business model | 30 |
| Organizational structure | 28 |
| Lack of ownership of the problem | 28 |
| Nonstandardized process | 27 |
| Information/communication technology restraints | 22 |
| Incentive system | 19 |
| Staff turnover | 8 |
| Configuration/physical features of workspace | 5 |

sions need to consider two issues: disabling the old approach and enabling the new approach. Specific tactics within each category address the issues typically raised by the "perceived" resisters.

Disabling activities are focused around the removal of supports for the old way of doing things. These typically include limiting access to an old system and reducing support resources—dollars or human resources. As an example of how this works in practice, one organization, in implementing an organization-wide change to the way expense forms were approved and paid, reduced the expense claims administrative personnel from three to one, stopped the issuance of checks and moved exclusively to direct deposit, and collected and destroyed paper expense forms from every department in the organization. Those who had stockpiled forms and/or refused to change saw an increase in the turnaround time for payment from an average of one week to three weeks. Needless to say, the holdouts adopted the new system fairly quickly thereafter.

Removal of supports for the old approach can, of course, backfire and do so dramatically unless accompanied by enablers of the new approach. For information systems, these key enablers include training, mentoring, and technical support. Training is always a subject of hot debate as it relates to enabling information systems. It is critical to success, yet it is often not allocated the budget it requires to be truly effective. The simple reality is that extensive and ongoing training is required to extract value from the new system. Limited or no training results in failure.

One-on-one mentoring can also be very effective because it can reduce the fear factor in a low-key, nonthreatening manner. For example, in an effort to get General Electric's senior executives knowledgeable about the Internet and engaged in Internet-related projects, Jack Welch requested that each one select a young company employee to be a personal mentor on this important technology. Technical support is also a critical enabler in the launch of new information systems. Help desk support is, in fact, a life line for employees who are using a new system for the first time.

**Table 8.6** Roles for Senior Executives

| Role of the CEO | Role of the CIO |
|---|---|
| Position IT and CIO as change agents | Focus obsessively on the business |
| Focus on effectiveness, not efficiency | Educate the management team |
| Instill value and understanding of IT | Manage executive relationships |
| Include CIO on executive team | Deliver as promised and communicate |
| Manage IT as integral, not as adjunct | Concentrate IS development effort |
| Create a shared vision for the role of IT | Create a shared vision for the role of IT |

## 10. Demonstrated Leadership Commitment

For a successful stream of information systems to be introduced in an organization, leadership is required at the organizational, steering committee, and project levels to create an appropriate climate and culture for acceptance of these often disruptive changes. Rarely is visible business leadership as important, and paradoxically so lacking, as in information systems projects. There is frequently a high quality of technical leadership in these kinds of initiatives, but all too often the organizational leadership is entirely missing:

> Most companies run information technology projects the way we used to manage Research and Development when it didn't work. They leave the leadership up to a bright technical person who unfortunately doesn't have a clue about the business. In Research and Development we've learned that we need technical leadership, but the overall leader has to be a business person.

In one of the most powerful demonstrations of organizational leadership for a major information systems initiative, the CEO and CIO of a large U.S.-based retailer held a joint all-employee update session to kick off the new system. The fact that the session was jointly chaired was symbolic. But more important, was the fact that the CEO fielded all the technology questions and the CIO answered all the business questions. The message was clear: they were a team, and they were committed. Table 8.6 summarizes the leadership roles for CEOs and CIOs.

Even if the CEO is, and is seen to be, 100 percent committed to the information system initiative, there still needs to be strong leadership from the project's steering committee. What this means in practical terms is that the committee needs to have the following attributes:

- A clearly defined mandate. The steering committee is not there to run the project, it is there to resolve issues brought forth by the project manager. The most successful steering committees we have worked with went so far as to indicate to the project manager that at every review, they wanted a short status report followed by a focused set of issues that required resolution.

- Empowered to make decisions and resource allocation shifts related to the project. If the steering committee has to convene a meeting of the entire executive team every time there is a major decision to be made, they're not much use.
- Small in size, operating as a team, with an organization-level perspective. In one particularly dysfunctional steering committee, the project review sessions usually devolved into a finger-pointing exercise and a grandstanding opportunity for the various committee members. The project manager came to dread the reviews and felt that they were a significant drag on the project rather than a key enabler.
- Regularly scheduled review meetings with the project manager and periodically with the entire team. High-quality steering committee members are usually busy people. We have encountered numerous instances in which steering committees are formed with the best of intentions, but the logistical challenges of finding mutually agreeable meeting times derail these good intentions and the reviews don't happen often even when they are most critical.

And finally, information systems leadership must occur at the project level. There has been a great deal of research focused on identifying the attributes of exceptional project leaders.[9] Most executives would agree that the following qualities make a highly effective information systems project manager:

- A business background, as well as technology know-how.
- Planning skills—realistic plans versus optimistic plans.
- Capability to utilize leading-edge systems development approaches.
- Leadership skills—to gain consensus among groups of people with differing aims and priorities.
- Effective communication skills—in plain language, not "technobabble."
- A working knowledge of the proven formal techniques of project management, such as scope management and change control.

Leadership in information systems must occur at all of these three levels, and each and every one is critical.

## In Summary

Expertise in developing and implementing information systems is a key management and organizational competency for the twenty-frist century. Indeed, it will be increasingly difficult for organizations to be successful without capabilities in this area. Critical characteristics of a successful approach are the following:

- Employ a leading-edge systems development approach, such as prototyping.
- Have solid project management discipline.
- Disperse information systems leadership throughout the organization (i.e., ensure that it's not focused solely in the Information Systems group).

- Create focused project steering committees with clearly defined mandates.
- Involve end users and other key stakeholders throughout the development process.
- Adequately resource training activities.

Information systems initiatives represent significant investments for organizations, yet they often suffer from what we call the "iceberg" phenomenon. Like the part of an iceberg, that is visible above the waterline, there are obvious activities associated with an information systems initiative, such as the purchasing of hardware and the selection of software vendors. But it's what's not evident above the water that sunk the Titanic. There is often limited effort expended on less visible or intangible activities, such as team building and training, yet it is these "below the waterline" activities, many of them elements of the ten Winning Conditions, that can ultimately make these investments an outstanding success.

# 9

## Turnaround—Getting Back on Track Fast

In this chapter, we explore the challenge of another critical change initiative: business turnaround. Turnarounds are high risk, and they often fail. We tend to hear about the spectacular successes, such as those engineered by Lee Iacocca at Chrysler and by Larry Weinbach at Unisys, but not the hundreds that don't turn out so well. In fact, the statistics are pretty grim. A major study found no instances of successful turnaround among the weakest companies in eight industries.[1] This type of change is frequently the toughest and most gut-wrenching any executive has to undertake: "You have between thirty and sixty days to make an impression as the new leader, to convince everyone that you're the right person, and to show people that you are doing something. To make a difference, you have one year."[2]

Faced with this situation, how do you make an impression within thirty or sixty days, particularly one that will have lasting positive outcomes? Whereas at the outset, there is usually an overwhelming sense of urgency associated with turnaround, it is often not sustained because of the relatively short-term, operational nature of the corrective process. Too often, once the crisis has passed, behaviors return to their former mode, and although the organization may survive, it does not continue moving forward. In fact, performance may decline again, leading to another turnaround within a relatively short period of time.

Executives in the private sector are not the only ones who face the challenge of turnaround. Many organizations in the public sector, as well, require a turnaround, although they are unlikely to go bankrupt. However, public-sector executives frequently move into situations in which the organization is so broken that if it were in the private sector, it would be out of business. Many of the concepts and frameworks we discuss in this chapter are also applicable to these situations, although the up-front emphasis on cash-flow management may not be so great, and public-sector executives usually face more constraints than their private-sector counterparts concerning downsizing and the removal of nonper-

**Table 9.1** Sample Indicators of Impending Trouble

*Strategic*
- Loss of market share or key customers
- Profit margin erosion
- Defection of distributors or agents to competitors
- Functional obsolescence of plant, equipment, and systems
- Negative trend in debt : equity ratios
- Financial instability at a major customer or supplier

*Operational*
- Negative cash flow
- Quarterly or monthly financial losses
- Increasing levels of sales, general, and administration expense (overhead) as a percentage of revenues
- Unacceptable levels of customer dissatisfaction
- Loss of key employees to competition

forming employees. We have worked with several public-sector executives who have made a difference within the first 100 days, and their experiences are reflected in the chapter.

*How did we get in this position?* This is the most commonly asked question by executives who discover that their company is either in receivership or in need of a turnaround. In many companies, the specter of insolvency or business failure comes as a complete surprise to most employees and, not infrequently, the executive team as well. In many smaller enterprises, all of the fundamentals may look sound—satisfied customers, revenue growth, accounting profits—but suddenly, the business is out of cash and cannot pay its creditors. In many larger firms, satisfactory operating results may mask a deteriorating strategic position, which suddenly and dramatically becomes evident in a massive collapse of some key performance variable, such as revenues. Then, of course, there is the situation in which a fundamentally sound business is placed in jeopardy by the failure of a large customer or key supplier.

The first lesson of bankruptcy or turnaround is quite simple: *don't go there.* In our experience, many firms in need of turnaround could have avoided being in this unpleasant situation if their executives had heeded the early warning signs of impending trouble. These indicators can be either strategic or operational; the former usually provides a leading indicator of potential problems ahead, and the latter is much more immediate.[3] Table 9.1 provides a list of some sample indicators that executives might use. Each business should know which three or four are critical in its own industry and track them regularly. When they start to show signs of deterioration, action should be taken immediately rather than waiting until a turnaround is necessary.

Executives with experience in this field know that the first 100 days of such a turnaround largely determines the ultimate outcome. In this chapter, we examine the traditional model of turnaround—stabilization, gaining control, operational improvement, and strategic repositioning—and find it too slow for today's environment. Executives, and companies, cannot work through these stages in a linear fashion if turnaround is to be achieved expeditiously. Progress must be achieved on a number of fronts simultaneously to produce a successful outcome.

Supporting our case with specific examples, we demonstrate that our parallel-deployment methodology is capable of achieving significant results much more rapidly than the traditional approach. Given the relatively low proportion of payroll costs to total costs for many companies, we show that head-count reduction can often be an inappropriate focus for early-stage turnaround. We also demonstrate that a turnaround strategy can produce lasting change more rapidly if the approach builds, rather than destroys, employee commitment, as the traditional "lean and mean" approach tends to do.

The traditional model of turnaround proceeds in a relatively linear fashion: operational stabilization and improvement, strategic repositioning, then cultural change.[4] A variant on this model is efficiency-oriented turnaround followed by entrepreneurial turnaround.[5] Many executives we have spoken with view this approach as simplistic and unworkable in today's business environment. There are a number of reasons for this outlook. First, simply working at the margins and making operational improvements may be insufficient to produce the required degree of improvement fast enough. Second, there are often some initial strategic and cultural changes, such as narrowing the focus of the business, that can be made rapidly, that do not need intensive study or planning, and that can have dramatic impacts on organization performance.[6] Third, once operational results have been achieved and the organization is out of intensive care, without some implementation of culture change, there is a high probability that the behaviors that produced the problems in the first place will not change, and the next steps of organizational realignment will not take place.

There has been a tendency to characterize the requirements for a successful turnaround as stabilizing the situation by raising cash, improving controls and operating performance, then repositioning the business strategically. This view assumes that in all turnaround situations, there is some kind of operational crisis of confidence in the firm. In reality, turnarounds are often required in firms that have no short-term cash crisis, but may, for example, have a desperate need to rapidly reverse a declining strategic position before the inevitable operating crisis arrives. The toughest turnaround to lead is a company in which most employees do not perceive a problem, but very tough decisions, such as closing plants and eliminating products, must be made quickly before the situation translates into disastrous operating performance.

As outlined in figure 9.1, turnaround can be considered as a sequence of parallel strategic and operational moves to reposition the business. Unlike traditional models, this approach suggests that strategic action to make fundamental changes can start early in the process. The initial challenge for executives is to determine where they are starting from in the chain. Is this a turnaround with a real cash crisis, pending insolvency? Or is it a turnaround in which tough decisions must be made, but short-term insolvency is not a threat?

Ford's successful turnaround in the early 1980s is an example of this second type. Although the company was unprofitable and its strategic position was

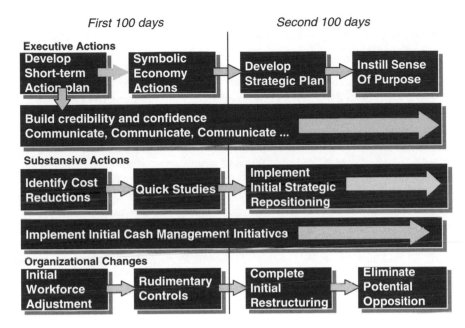

**Figure 9.1** Parallel Deployment of Turnaround Initiatives

weak, it was not in immediate danger of insolvency. Consequently, while its executives acted rapidly to close plants and downsize the workforce, which significantly lowered the corporation's break-even production level, they also moved quickly to increase investment in employee training and development, product development and plant modernization as key elements of their turnaround strategy.

Inexperienced executives frequently make a number of serious errors when they attempt to lead a turnaround. The most common include:

- The wrong diagnosis—adopting a panic, slash-and-burn approach that destroys fundamental value in the business.
- Failure to raise cash (don't fire the credit manager).
- Increasing revenues rapidly—often worsens the cash crisis as accounts receivable grow.
- Eliminating investment spending (e.g., market development) when not absolutely necessary.
- Slashing service to customers—may only increase their defection rate.
- Moving too rapidly to downsizing—may not be important, and severance payments may increase short-term cash drain.

Some companies will seek to grow revenues as a way to raise cash. In most cases, increasing sales creates a short-term demand for cash to meet accounts payable, and unless sales are for cash or a cash equivalent, rapidly increasing accounts receivable will actually worsen the cash crisis.

An inappropriate focus on reducing payroll can be fatal if the cash-flow benefits are minimal but customer service suffers a major decline. There are many companies in which total payroll is less than 20 percent of total costs, so a 10 percent reduction in head count only improves the bottom line by 2 percent, even if there are no costs associated with these severances, which there usually are. Did the repeated 5 percent head count reductions of innovative corporations such as Nortel and Lucent during the telecommunications downturn of the early 2000s solve the companies' financial woes? They certainly sapped morale and destroyed organization vitality and value. In fact, there is little evidence that layoffs unaccompanied by other forms of organizational change result in improved financial performance. Studies appear to show that layoffs produce little direct impact on financial performance.[7]

Even adopting a draconian downsizing approach in this situation—say a 40 percent staff reduction—will likely reduce labor costs very little in the short term. The reduction in overall costs will be an insignificant amount—8 percent at best. In addition, as morale sags and employees struggle to adjust, customer service levels are likely to decline. In this situation, it may well be better to use voluntary approaches to staff reduction, such as early retirement, and focus the remaining employees on finding ways to significantly reduce the 80 percent of costs that are not payroll related. That being said, however, sometimes executives have no choice but to resort to a dramatic downsizing activity if they are to save the business.

## Downsizing

What if you must downsize? If payroll costs are a high proportion of total, costs maybe in excess of 50 percent, there is little option but to quickly reduce the workforce. In this situation, mental toughness is essential. If a union is involved, it is a time for complete openness and candid conversations if any jobs are to be salvaged. This is also a time to employ a few proven rules of thumb because there is no exact science in this process. The following are some guidelines that experienced turnaround executives have found useful:

- *Do it quickly*—don't hold the sword of Damocles over the organization for a long period of time.
- *Do it hard*—cut deeper than you think you need to. It's demoralizing to go back a second and third time, and you can always add new people if you need to later.
- Reduce overhead staffing more than the field—this is both symbolic and realistic from a cost perspective to ensure that overheads do not rise as a proportion of total costs.
- Don't let friendship get in the way.
- Pick up survivors and move forward—don't allow employees to remain in limbo after this exercise. Communicate, engage them, and exploit the survivor mentality.

There are certainly benefits if the process is carried out rapidly and thoroughly. The most tragic types of corporate culture are those in which the annual 5 or 10 percent head-count reduction has become ritual. As one manager noted, "It's like being nibbled to death by ducks."

This tough approach was judged to be necessary by the new CEO of a major Canadian mining company with over ten thousand employees and payroll costs that amounted to 54 percent of total costs. Within three months, the CEO reduced employment in the head office by 55 percent, in the process losing the services of seven out of twelve vice-presidents, most of whom the corporation had to pay for another eighteen months. He also reduced employment at the company's major operation by 40 percent, approximately fourteen hundred employees, without incurring any short-term loss of production. While prices remained low for the next few years, the company was able to survive and reposition itself to take full advantage of the next period of high prices. By that time, it was capable of sustained, low-cost production.

Not all downsizing has to be accomplished with great rapidity. In many situations, a gradual reduction in employment levels is preferable for all stakeholders. For this purpose, a variety of alternatives to layoffs are available, including outsourcing, early retirement, reduced workweeks, retraining, and temporary labor pools.

Corporations have taken to outsourcing functions when third party providers can provide cheaper and possibly higher-quality service. In these situations, it is not unusual for employees to move from the client to the provider, albeit at reduced levels of salary and benefits in many cases. Some companies will create temporary labor pools to which surplus employees can be transferred until they either find alternative employment within the firm, which usually involves retraining, or become eligible for early retirement packages.

## How to Improve Profit Margins

As we have seen, the initial challenge in many turnaround situations is to raise cash but not worry primarily about profitability. However, opportunities to improve profitability during the first 200 days should not be missed. Profit improvement can be derived in two ways: raising prices and reducing costs.

Although most firms believe that they have little opportunity to raise prices to improve profit margins in the short term, there are a couple of instances in which these opportunities may exist. One situation, which is remarkably prevalent, involves an incentive structure for sales employees that rewards revenue generation but has no factor for profit margin. This type of plan encourages them to make sales that don't produce a profit, and that may actually increase cash losses for the firm. Consequently, some companies have found that a refocusing of sales incentives to encourage only *profitable* sales can improve earnings dramatically in the short term, even though revenues may decline for a period. A side benefit is that selling costs may also decline as the variable portion of sales compensation declines.

Another situation with occasional opportunities to raise prices is in relatively young companies that have a tendency to underprice their products to gain customer acceptance and market share. One small Canadian software producer that experienced losses and contemplated layoffs instead took the bold step of raising the prices to its customers, large telecommunications suppliers. The company discovered that its customers were relatively insensitive to its prices, so it instituted two 5 percent increases, six months apart, which made a significant contribution to improving its profitability within the first 200 days of its turn-around initiative. The company avoided the unpleasant task of laying off highly committed employees.

In reality, though, most companies in trouble have little opportunity to improve prices, so improving profit margins involves insight into the cost structure of the business, which many executives fail to grasp. For example, if 70 percent of the firm's costs are incurred in the form of purchases from suppliers, then internal budget slashing, even if successful, will have a relatively marginal impact on the firm's cost structure. Sustaining successful turnaround requires that executives begin to understand the true controllable cost drivers in their business and focus their cost-reduction activities around them. Initiating an approach in which cost management is focused around innovation and involvement, resulting in a culture that is *lean and keen* rather than *lean and mean* is also appropriate for the long term, because it can generate a positive attitude toward cost reduction among employees.[8]

## The First 100 Days

As suggested by the word, turnaround implies not only moving in a new direction, but also reversing inherent momentum in the wrong one. The objectives for the first 100 days relate to stopping the momentum toward the edge of the precipice and developing speed in moving away from it. Of course, if the company's operating health is sound, and it is a strategic turnaround that is required, then the executive team has time to develop a more proactive game plan. For the moment, though, let's consider the worst case, one in which both strategic and operational health are bad. Larry Weinbach, CEO of Unisys, talking about his turnaround experience:

> So the first 100 days is important, but . . . the first day is important just to give people confidence you have a plan . . . The first day . . . when I joined the company I went on Business Television and told our employees . . . there are only three things that were important: customers, employees and reputation. . . . The second thing I did on day one is I went on actual television . . . the syndicated business shows, and I said that this company was committed to repaying a billion dollars in debt in less than two years, and that we were motivated to do it and that we were going to get the employees behind that. . . . I then got on a plane and visited about twenty thousand employees in the first 100 days and I basically told them that the challenge here was, without selling off assets, we had to pay off a billion dollars of debt.

If the organization stands at the end of the precipice, then much of the effort of the first 100 days has to be directed at retaining the confidence of key stakeholders whose support is required to keep the organization viable. For example, banks and creditors have to be convinced to continue the flow of funds. Suppliers have to feel that they will be paid for their shipments. Customers have to be convinced to continue buying and not switch to competing brands. This state of affairs will not come about unless the leadership team rapidly develops a plan of action to stabilize the situation and generate cash. It is not unusual in this situation for the CEO to personally sign every check, as a form of rudimentary cash control.

Alongside the cash management task, this period should see a thorough analysis of the organization's cost structure and the identification of initial opportunities to reduce cost and break-even volume. This may lead to some rapid, strategic decisions such as a major restructuring of the workforce, the closure of plants and other facilities, and the elimination of product lines. There are usually at least a few opportunities to implement these kinds of decisions rapidly.

Typical objectives for the first 100 days include:

- Retaining the confidence of banks, creditors, and customers.
- Implementing basic cash controls.
- Moving toward a positive cash flow from operations and through current asset liquidation.
- Reducing break-even volume.

If these objectives can be met within this period, then the speed that is generated can be rather easily turned into a process with significant momentum during the second 100 days.

How does the leadership team bring about these initial results so quickly? The key enablers for this period include:

- Developing the key elements of a short-term strategic plan that creates shared understanding and a sense of mission and purpose.
- Restructuring and streamlining the executive team.
- Developing a sense of urgency and focus among the workforce.

During the first thirty days, a short-term survival plan with a time frame as short as six months, should be developed through a process that lasts as little as a few of days. The mission is survival. The objectives are specific and quantitative. The strategies are short term and capable of rapid deployment. Frequently, self-styled turnaround leaders come in and impose their own action plan on the organization, but we have found that even in this case, the process is far more effective if the leadership team has the opportunity to buy in to the approach through a focused session, even if the CEO is highly directive during the process.

This process also provides an opportunity for the leader to size up the executive team. One of the challenges of the first 100 days is to ensure that the leadership team is made up of executives who are competent and have the will to win. Allowing those who are not contributing to remain on the team adds drag to the process and an unnecessary drain on cash flow. One of the challenges of the executives who are committed to the process is to impart a corresponding sense of urgency and priority among the workforce. Not infrequently, rank-and-file employees are woefully ignorant of the parlous state of the organization, and even if they are aware of the situation, they lack a clear understanding of how they can contribute to survival. A face-to-face communications initiative, rapidly implemented, can make a considerable difference in this period.

## The Second 100 Days

During the second 100 days, the purpose must be to build momentum away from the precipice and consolidate the progress made already. During the first 100 days, the focus has been on survival, but after this period, most organizations will know if they are going to survive. Therefore, it is time to extend the strategic horizon to eighteen months or two years. In addition, this is a period in which commitment to tough decisions can be demonstrated by following through on commitments made during the first 100 days. This is not a time to allow executives and employees to create delay by questioning key decisions that have already been made; rather, it is a time to demonstrate resolve by pushing ahead with implementation. Typical objectives for this period include:

- Resolving the short-term cash-flow problem.
- Initial closures and divestments of noncore assets and businesses.
- Improved operating profit margin through price and cost.

In this period, if sufficient progress has been made in the first 100 days, it may well be possible to initiate a restructuring of the organization's cash position. At the very least, the cash-flow crisis, if there is one, should be resolved so that the focus can return to the business fundamentals. During this period, strategic restructuring decisions made in the first 100 days can be completed, which will demonstrate the leadership team's commitment to follow-through on tough decisions. Finally, in this period, it should be possible to produce tangible improvement in operating margins, although the overall bottom line may still be negative due to one-time costs and write-downs.

Key enablers for this period include:

- Developing a longer-term strategic plan (eighteen months to two years).
- Completing any initial organization restructuring.
- Instilling a sense of purpose and financial accountability within the organization through implementation of basic control processes.

A longer-term strategic plan, with a horizon of up to two years, is important during this period to break the organization out of its crisis-oriented mentality. The message has to be, *"We have survived."* The content of this performance improvement plan should be a strategic agenda focused around key metrics such as return on assets, profitability, service levels, and employee performance. The communication of this plan demonstrates the intent of the executive team not

**Table 9.2** Strategic and Operational Health

|  | Strong | Weak |
|---|---|---|
| Strong | Monitor performance<br>Execute well<br>Avoid complacency | Operating performance may<br>mask deteriorating strategic<br>health<br>Reformulate strategy |
| Weak | Avoid long-term pain for short-term<br>gain<br>Operational program: Improve mar-<br>gins, costs, productivity | Turnaround required: Improve<br>operating performance<br>Reposition the business |

to allow the performance improvements secured during the first 100 days to either stagnate or slip back. Along with the completion of any organizational restructuring, this can significantly reduce the level of uncertainty for most employees.

Also in this period, it is important to ensure that work on instilling a sense of control and accountability throughout the organization is maintained. Usually, organizations get into trouble, in part, because of poor control and accountability, and during the first 100 days, only the most rudimentary processes can be put in place. During the second 100 days work should be initiated on reviewing control processes, performance measurement, and reporting, as well as recognition, reward, and compensation practices, to ensure that these are all aligned with future strategy.

## Establishing the Winning Conditions

### 1. Correct Diagnosis of the Change Challenge

Our model of the depth of change (see figure 2.1) applies extremely well to turnaround. This is another situation in which the correct diagnosis of the level of change required is critically important at the outset. Turnaround can involve different levels of organization change. In its simplest form, the strategic position of the organization is sound, but its operating performance is weak (see table 9.2). In this case, an operating turnaround is appropriate—improving efficiency and margins while maintaining strategy and culture. In this situation, the danger is in "throwing the baby out with the bathwater," or losing the strategic and cultural strengths of the organization by making inappropriate cuts and changes. At the other extreme, the situation is so bad that drastic changes are required, even to the fundamental paradigm of the business itself. This is the most challenging, riskiest, and least successful turnaround scenario, and the one that incumbent executives are most averse to adopting.

A useful way of thinking about the nature and scope of the turnaround required is to objectively evaluate the strategic and operational health of the business, which in practical terms may require the use of consultants or outside board members, and determine in which areas performance is unacceptable. As shown in table 9.2, broadly speaking, there are three possible diagnoses.

*Strategic Health Is Sound—Operational Health Is Poor.*

This diagnosis suggests that, even though the business may be bankrupt, the long-term prospects for the business are good if short-term problems can be addressed. In this situation, turnaround requires rapid improvement in operating performance and, usually, cash flow. The risks are either that the operating problems do not get resolved rapidly enough, or that the measures taken to resolve the operating difficulties erode the company's strategic position.

This was the situation of a growing, dynamic software services provider with sales of around $10 million when they discovered that they were within weeks of exceeding their bank line of credit following several quarters of unprofitable operations. Overall, their strategic health was sound, with little direct competition in their market niche, a base of satisfied customers, a good service offering, and loyal employees who worked long hours for modest salaries. However, they had been unable to generate a positive cash flow, overhead expenses were relatively high, and gross margins were much too low.

*Strategic Health Is Poor—Operational Health Is Good.*

A large number of corporate failures occur suddenly and dramatically when a deteriorating strategic position that has been masked by apparently sound operating results translates into rapid deterioration in operating results as well. In this situation, the turnaround challenge is to identify and address the strategic issues while there is still time. The risks are failure to identify the emerging issues in a timely fashion and the tendency for operating results to deteriorate as executives and managers focus on the strategic priorities.

This challenge faced the executive team at the Canadian equipment manufacturing subsidiary of a major European conglomerate. A strategic planning activity, long overdue, revealed that operating margins were satisfactory, but the company's recent focus on large systems orders had led to the erosion of the company's bread-and-butter line of business in individual unit sales and the repair and maintenance business. In addition, failure to address operating problems at a number of installations was leading to a dramatic decline in the reputation of the company. The analysis carried out for the strategic plan suggested that unless the company could turn around this weak strategic position, it would be in serious crisis within eighteen months.

*Strategic Health Is Poor—Operational Health Is Poor.*

This situation is the most challenging because of the scope and rapidity of the action that will be required to save the business, unless it is already in receivership. One of the first questions to ask is whether the business is worth saving or whether options, such as sale or liquidation, should be considered. This is also the classic situation in which many companies seek bankruptcy protection to provide them with the time to reorganize and reposition the business. The risks in this situation are either that good money will be thrown after bad or, in the case of a business unit within a larger corporation, that there will be a huge drain on executive time and energy for the failing business that could create far more value if applied to successful units.

Late in 2001, a quick assessment of the situation that faced the new CEO of one of North America's leading electronics manufacturing companies indicated that not only was the company within three months of running out of cash, but also its relative cost position was disastrous—the company was losing 33 cents on every dollar of revenue on a cash basis, and there was no likelihood that prices would rise in the near term to alleviate the situation. Dramatic action on both strategic and operational dimensions was clearly required if the company was to survive.

Making the correct diagnosis in situations like these is critical because it determines the degree of urgency in the situation, the scope of action required, and the appropriate tools to use. Unfortunately, faced with the specter of a turnaround, many executives switch into panic mode in which, to quote one knowledgeable observer, "they have a hammer, and everything looks like a nail." The most commonly made mistake in this state of affairs is an immediate to downsizing of the workforce as a way of cutting costs. If payroll is a relatively minor business cost, then all that results are a quick cash drain due to severance costs, and short-term reductions in customer service, and loss of productivity, which simply makes the situation worse.

## 2. Early Development of Shared Understanding

Quickly building shared understanding plays an important part in turnaround. Depending on the situation, however, rather than develop a shared vision, the executive team simply needs to develop an initial sense of purpose. This may be embodied in a set of shared objectives for the immediate future to ensure the survival of the organization, manifested in some specific measures of success. A shared understanding of the key initiatives required to achieve these results is also important, as is agreement on the process to be followed.

Part of building this shared understanding is carrying out an assessment of the team and the situation at the same time as creating a plan of action. The assessment of the team includes determining their degree of commitment to the task and the capability of individuals to contribute to the turnaround. This activity has to be carried out within the first sixty days. Individuals who are incapable of contributing to the future strategy have to be released quickly, and on equitable terms. In addition, initial decisions have to be made to bring in new people to contribute needed executive capabilities.

Shared understanding itself is created in a series of short, focused planning sessions undertaken within the first thirty days. Although the information required for a comprehensive assessment and analysis of the situation is unlikely to be available at the outset, the shared knowledge of the team and quick studies are usually adequate to provide the basis for taking initial actions. Elements of this assessment include cash position, cost structure, market position, core capabilities, and identification of major problem areas. The tough decisions that have to be made to ensure survival need to be addressed during this process. The outcome is a focused, short-term strategy, maybe with a time horizon as short as six months, targeted on survival through cash management, cost improvement, and initial repositioning.

## 3. Enrichment of Shared Understanding

Turnaround is one change initiative that is likely to have only weak shared understanding of the challenge at the outset. The initial diagnosis has to be undertaken rapidly, and it is probably based on significantly incomplete information. The possibility of a wrong diagnosis and failure to take appropriate action is therefore quite high. In this situation, shared understanding has to be enriched quickly and continually over a compressed period of time. For example, in an initial period of downsizing, it is quite possible that the corporation's strategic capabilities may be destroyed if key units such as research and development and marketing are decimated in the process.

Faced with this challenge, experienced turnaround leaders establish what is akin to a war room. The tactical information, such as basic financial statistics and operational data, is likely to be readily available. What has to be created is a shared understanding of the strategic position and potential of the business. As we noted earlier, in today's fast-paced environment, this cannot wait until the operational turnaround is complete. In one major technology-based corporation that faced a turnaround, an executive commented:

> Initially, our gut feel was to downsize across the board by about 40 percent, and we started off in that direction. However, over the first couple of months, we came to realize that the real problem was that there were two of our five business units that simply were not going to make it. One of these was our original core business. As well, there were areas of R&D where we needed more people, not less. Meeting frequently, within ninety days we had taken the decision to divest these two units and protect the staffing levels in the key areas of R&D, which meant actually hiring back a couple of key people who had already decided to leave. By the end of the second 100 days, we had firm deals for the business units we wanted to sell.

This approach contrasts sharply to that adopted by a global mining company that faced a similar situation. In this case, the CEO was forced to cut deeply into employment levels and virtually destroyed the corporation's marketing, R&D, exploration, training, and corporate capabilities, but made much smaller cuts in the operational workforce. The company had a strong ore reserve position, sufficient for over ten years of production, and the leadership team viewed the crisis as an opportunity to subsequently restaff and rebuild these corporate functions around the few key individuals they retained.

In both cases, the leadership team met every sixty days for two full days to discuss and enrich their understanding of the business, its current position, and future prospects. These meetings were in addition to weekly and sometimes daily meetings early in the process. The first three or four meetings focused on what the corporation had to do to survive. After this, the focus was on what the company had to do to be successful and to ensure no repeat of the financial crisis.

Part of the continuing sense of enriching shared understanding is to spread this throughout the organization. Almost inevitably, successful turnaround embodies a degree of cultural change, and part of the task is imparting to all employees an understanding of new behaviors that are required if the organization is to prosper in the future.

## 4. Establishment of a Sense of Urgency

Surprisingly, there may well be a need to communicate a sense of urgency in a turnaround situation because most employees may be totally unaware of how bad the situation is. However, it's not that difficult to create a sense of urgency through a basic communications initiative, preferably face-to-face. Some executives refer to this activity as "sharing the pain." Many employees will be galvanized by the simple facts that the company may cease to exist and that their continued employment is in jeopardy. In fact it is likely that a sense of crisis may take hold that could cause employees to make ill-considered decisions. In this situation, communication is likely to be about defining what's wrong with the organization, building awareness and understanding of what's required for survival, and creating a common sense of focus and purpose.

In the first thirty days of turnaround, it's important for the senior executive team to be visible to employees. This is not a time for hiding in the office or the conference room. Formal, periodic presentations and communications are important. A monthly update for all employees is helpful. There is also much to be gained during this period from informal interaction with supervisors and wage-roll employees, particularly those who are likely to be among the 20 percent who will dedicate themselves to the turnaround task. These are the employees who really know what the problems are and very often what's required to fix them. A weekly executive walkabout that lasts a couple of hours is a good way to accomplish this task.

Without exception, executives who lead successful turnarounds, such as Larry Weinbach, Lee Iacocca, and Ray Lane, state that it is critical to develop effective communications with customers and creditors to retain their confidence. Customers who sense that the business is in crisis may switch to alternative suppliers. Creditors have to be convinced to continue to fund the company, which will ensure a continued flow of input materials and services to sustain the business. A communications strategy, at all levels, that imparts a "business as usual" message is important at this stage.

During the second 100 days, communications with employees need to focus on ensuring a sense of continuity, demonstrating success, and recognizing outstanding achievement, particularly if downsizing has been an integral part of the first 100 days. The clear message has to be, "We've survived, but let's not go back there again." Employees need to be reassured that their efforts are yielding results, even if the process is painful. Effective communications through this period are open and frank—both the good news and the bad news have to be relayed.

## 5. Creation of a Limited and Focused Strategic Agenda

One mistake made by executives who are inexperienced at turnaround is to try and change everything at once. This is a recipe for disaster. When the organization is already in serious trouble additional changes can seriously impair customer service, the sales effort, and operational performance. This is a time for a highly selective, well-prioritized change agenda that targets only the areas that will yield maximum returns for the turnaround effort.

In some situations, a strategic turnaround is required, either complementary to an operating turnaround or by itself, if, as in the case of the Canadian equipment manufacturing company referred to earlier, the corporation's current operating performance is satisfactory. This company's chief operating officer realized that the company's strategic health was weak, and he organized a series of strategy review sessions, at which the magnitude and scale of the problem was revealed:

- Revenue growth of 50 percent in the last twelve months with no corresponding increase in profitability.
- Rapidly declining backlog of medium-sized orders—the bread and butter of the business.
- Inadequate and inexperienced marketing and sales activities—little contact with existing or potential customers.
- Substantial customer dissatisfaction with the performance of some of the company's recent equipment installations.
- No clear sense of direction among the executive team.
- Inadequate management development.
- Research and development activities that lagged those of the competition and were poorly targeted.

In his estimation, these problems would start to seriously affect the company's performance within twelve to eighteen months. In other words, what was required was a strategic turnaround carried out in an anticipatory manner.

Within the next 100 days, applying the principles shown in table 9.3, the executive team moved rapidly to reposition the business. They developed a limited set of three focused corporate and business-unit initiatives aimed at reestablishing the company's market position, enhancing product technology efforts, and starting to develop the company's potential middle-management strength. A recovery plan was established to rectify the deficiencies of recent customer installations. Spending on market and technology development was increased, funded through savings from a cost-reduction initiative focused around employee

**Table 9.3** Principles for Repositioning

---

- Establish a focused strategic plan for the business
- Identify desired competitive positioning with respect to customers and competitors
- Evaluate investment spending in terms of sufficiency and focus
- Identify target margins required to sustain investment programs and satisfactory returns for investors
- Establish a continuous improvement culture in which quality improvement and cost reduction are complementary
- Build partnerships with selected key strategic suppliers
- Define and establish cooperative relationship with employees and unions
- Ensure an appropriate capital structure for the business

---

involvement. A key enabler for these strategies was an initiative to strengthen the company's middle-management cadre through selective recruitment and an accelerated training and development activity.

## 6. Rapid, Strategic Decision Making and Deployment

Leading a successful corporate turnaround is one of the most challenging and exhilarating tasks any executive can experience. Success in this endeavor requires decisiveness and mental toughness. This is a time when demonstrated leadership, not just corporate rhetoric, is appreciated by all stakeholders in the organization. In our experience, successful turnaround executives substantially follow ten guiding principles, especially when cash is tight and creditors are at the door:

- Maintain credibility with customers, creditors, and the banks.
- Manage cash flow personally, even signing checks if appropriate.
- Make a rapid and concise diagnosis of the fundamental problems.
- Have a well-focused game plan with an appropriate time horizon.
- Don't wait to make strategic moves that are self-evident—cut unprofitable products and operations as soon as practical.
- Take along no passengers on the executive and management teams even if they are personal friends.
- Downsize quickly and communicate, communicate, communicate to the survivors—involve them in the solution.
- Once cash flow is positive, be prepared to sacrifice short-term dividends and use cash to reinvest in building the strength of the business.
- Ensure that the situation never repeats by establishing appropriate leading indicators that are routinely monitored and by building a culture that is cost conscious.
- Ensure that employees who exceed what is required of them are appropriately recognized and rewarded once the turnaround is consolidated.

**Table 9.4** Emergency Action Checklist

---

*Symbolic Actions*
- Cut out corporate jets, limousines, and club memberships
- Reduce expense accounts
- Reduce shrinkage—eliminate waste and theft
- CEO signs all checks

*Communications*
- Convince creditors to extend lines of credit
- Personal requests to major customers for prompt payment
- Ensure that all employees know to minimize cash expenditures

*Substantive Actions*
- Raise cash—stretch accounts payable, age accounts receivable, pressure delinquents, liquidate excess inventories, and, where appropriate, reduce head count
- Eliminate unprofitable assets—close losing businesses and discontinue unprofitable product lines

*Organizational Changes*
- Change spending authorities
- Delay, and tighten up, incentive payments
- Downsize

---

Surviving a financial crisis when insolvency is probable has been likened to a corporate heart attack. If the patient survives, he or she is likely to be weak, but also prepared to make a change in lifestyle. The challenge that faces many executives is to make sure that corporate lessons are learned from this life-threatening event, which helps to ensure that there will be no recurrence.

In the height of the financial storm, the CEO's main function is to maintain the financial credibility of the corporation with its bankers, customers, and suppliers. Monday-morning checklists for CEOs who are new to this situation include meetings with bank executives to ensure that lines of credit are maintained and meetings with the executives of key suppliers to maintain their confidence. Rhetoric isn't enough in these meetings; creditors want to see a practical recovery plan and they want to hear about tangible actions taken to move the company forward and improve its cash position.

In this respect, the checklist presented in table 9.4 suggests a number of ways in which companies can deploy parallel initiatives to rapidly reverse a negative cash flow, which should always be the first goal of management in this situation. As this table demonstrates, most companies have the potential to raise cash quickly if they are willing to make some tough, and possibly humbling, decisions. It is simply a matter of knowing where to look. If management does not, then the insolvency specialists will, when they arrive.

Some of these actions, such as liquidating inventories and collecting accounts receivable, can occur rapidly, but others, such as selling or closing unprofitable businesses or operations, may take several months and require the board and management to accept that they will not receive full value for some of them.

## 7. A Human Flywheel of Commitment

The worst thing a leadership team can do is disengage the human flywheel, which is almost certain to exist within the organization, through taking an inappropriate course of action. This can happen in a number of ways. The first is simply to deny that there is a major problem. With a view to retaining investor, customer, and supplier confidence, executives may repeatedly deny that there is a major crisis within the organization, thus breeding a sense of complacency and planting the seeds for a subsequent breakdown in trust between employees and management. This happened to a major Canadian charter airline, Canada 3000, late in 2001. Management issued denial after denial of a financial crisis until the morning that the airline ceased to operate, leaving thousands of stranded passengers around the world. Afterward, employees commented that if they had known the real situation, they may have behaved very differently.

The other approach that often disengages the flywheel is a top-down, autocratic style that appears to punish employees for the situation that the company is in. In this case, the entire turnaround approach appears to focus on middle management and rank-and-file employees for cost reduction, even if the cost structure does not warrant this. If, at the same time, senior executives appear to be unwilling to restrain their own lavish ways, it is almost certain that a flywheel of commitment will not develop. In fact, the best people start to look for other employment, and the organization goes into a virtually unstoppable death spiral.

When this happens, once employees—and, to a large degree, stakeholders outside the organization—are informed of the situation, many of them are likely to be willing to engage in the change activity, even if tough measures are required. Once they have a sense that the leadership team has a plan, they may be willing to implement whatever course of action is decided upon, particularly if it is a matter of survival.

## 8. Identification and Management of Sources of Resistance

Surprisingly, there may be considerable resistance during the early stages of a turnaround. For most people, this is likely to arise from ignorance of the reality of the situation and can be quickly addressed through a communications blitz. However, even then there may be employees who, for one reason or another, may feel that they would benefit from the failure of the organization. For example, some employees may feel that they may be better off if a new ownership or leadership team takes control. Others may feel that there will be a lucrative payout if employees are offered severance packages. However, these individuals are likely to be in the minority. Most apparent resistance in this situation arises from a lack of awareness and understanding.

Of course, in many organizations, resistance to the actions required during turnaround may be offered by unions that attempt to prevent a membership decline or genuinely believe that the proposed actions do not serve the best interests of their members. If not effectively addressed, this brake on the pace of change can slow the whole process significantly or even lead to the collapse of entire rescue packages.

Most of the resistance encountered during the early stage of turnaround can be addressed through the simple process of opening the books to employees and the union. There are no doubt risks in doing this, but usually the benefits outweigh them. The perceived risks include suppliers and creditors learning the true financial situation of the company and sensitive information leaking out to competitors. However, the benefits of providing a credible and compelling financial picture to employees and the union often outweigh these risks. Apart from building awareness and understanding, this act can go a long way in overcoming cynicism and negativity, particularly if the commitment is sustained in the long term.

### 9. Follow-through on Changing Organizational Enablers

Turnaround is unlikely to be successful unless there are corresponding changes in key organizational enablers such as policies, recognition and rewards, and information systems. Formal systems may need to be changed, or even abandoned rapidly, particularly if they are promoting behaviors that are leading to the need for turnaround.

Not infrequently, reward and recognition systems contribute to decline by creating the wrong type of behavior throughout the corporation; for example, sales compensation that rewards revenue generation and maintenance behavior rather than profit contribution and sales growth. Once again, it is the folly of rewarding A while hoping for B.[9] Similarly, a lack of appropriate incentives can lead to indifference and apathy in the face of declining performance. It's unlikely that a sophisticated new system can be created within the first 100 or 200 days of a turnaround, but it is imperative to eliminate the dysfunctional ones and replace them with something that may be relatively crude and informal, but that starts to generate appropriate performance. Given that this is a time when money is likely in short supply, low-cost recognition approaches, such as pizza lunches, token employee and team awards, and personal recognition, are appropriate and useful in maintaining morale in a tough period.

There are also policies that have to be changed in this situation, especially those relating to financial control and expenditure. Most likely, one of the contributing factors in this situation is that information systems have not been providing the right kind of information to executives. Although it's not possible to implement sophisticated new systems within the first 100 days, rudimentary controls have to be established, particularly for cash management. In addition, it is necessary to generate information that indicates the primary source of trouble. Which operations, products, and customers are unprofitable? Which elements of the cost structure are out of line with industry norms? This information is required to enable repositioning decisions to be made quickly and with a reasonable probability that they are correct.

In the early stages of turnaround, all expenditure policies have to be reviewed, as do spending authorities. Turnaround executives commonly find out that there is no accountability for cash management in the organization. Standing orders, credit cards, spending limits, and entertainment and travel policies all have to be reviewed. Some CEOs go so far as to demand that for a period of time they personally sign every check, even for pencils! Alongside these reviews, executives have work assiduously on a restructuring of the company's debt portfolio.

If downsizing is an appropriate strategy, experienced executives insist on reducing corporate and administrative staff, including executives, by a greater percentage than that imposed on operating units. In part, this is symbolic, but it also reflects these executives' keen interest in reducing overhead costs in proportion to direct costs. A few executives even have three categories of employees to which they are willing to apply increasing levels of reductions:

- Employees who either produce or directly interact with the customer.
- Employees who directly support these producers.
- All other employees.

However, this taxonomy should be applied with discretion. For example, in companies with a high technological component, serious reductions in product development and engineering may do irreparable harm to the long-term prospects of the business.

## 10. Demonstrated Leadership Commitment

Pending insolvency should act to focus the mind and sharpen the pencil. In this situation, there is not a lot of time for detailed analysis and reflection; rather, it is a time for tough decisions, objectivity, and action, recognizing that mistakes are likely to be made, which hopefully will not prove fatal. The board is often faced with deciding whether the CEO and the executive team, which led the company into the mess, are the right people to rectify the situation. If a relatively inexperienced team is left in place to lead the process, then consulting assistance from people with relevant experience should be sought.

Choosing the right leader, quickly, is key in this situation. History shows that incumbent CEOs experience great difficulty in leading a crisis-driven turnaround, because they have difficulty being objective and making firm, sometimes unpleasant decisions that reverse earlier ones that they made.[10] In this situation, companies often resort to executives with considerable turnaround experience to resolve the crisis, again with mixed results.

Some of these turnaround executives appear to be capable of rapidly assessing the situation and demonstrate great insight and flexibility in tailoring their rescue strategies to individual firms, often with considerable success. There are others, though, who have a standardized lean-and-mean approach to turnaround, which in some circumstances can be exactly right but in others can simply accelerate the decline. Another quality to look for is the ability to calm nervous investors and customers and quell internal bickering in order to make tough decisions and move forward. Finally, many turnaround leaders are authoritative but can also be fun to work with. We have heard these leaders described by their subordinates as individuals with a capacity to be tough when required, but who, in the darkest moments, have a great ability to sustain the spirits of the team.

When dealing with the executive and management teams, it is often necessary to carry out a rapid assessment of the capability of each individual to contribute to the turnaround task. In this situation, expensive passengers, or worse still, passive resisters, cannot be tolerated. New CEOs faced with this situation discover that either they cannot find up-to-date performance evaluations or all evaluations read "fully satisfactory." The rough assessment framework that one CEO uses in this situation, and demands that his subordinates also adopt, is as follows:

- Incompetent to the point of being dangerous to near-term survival.
- Incompetent with little hope of improvement.
- Incompetent at present, but with hope for improvement.
- Competent, but lost the will to win.
- Competent and ready to act.

Crude it may be, but in his opinion there is no place on his turnaround team for the incompetents who are "dangerous" or have "little hope." Those who have hope for improvement are given six or nine months to raise their performance to required levels.

The first 100 days of turnaround is a time when executives must lead by example in terms of no-frills management by eliminating visible excess and possibly even accepting reduced salaries for a period of time. This was the approach of the executives of the Canadian software service company that required an operational turnaround. Faced with possible insolvency, the executives spent two days over a weekend examining the firm's cash flow and cost structure. They immediately identified the potential to generate $200,000 in cash within 30 days. They also collectively took salary and fringe benefit cutbacks, saving a further $8,000 per month. They eliminated executive-class air travel, expensive lunches and dinners except when entertaining clients, and health club memberships.

With this type of leadership, it was not too difficult to encourage other employees in the firm to join in the task of raising cash and reducing costs. As a result, the company improved its cash flow and reduced costs by between 10 and 15 percent over the following three to six months, which made the difference between a modest profit and corporate failure. They accomplished this task without firing any employees and without cuts to the level of customer service.

## In Summary

The most important element in turnaround is to ensure that crisis does not turn into panic and chaos. If the organization is already in bad shape, a change program that worsens an already poor operating performance will almost certainly kill the business. Effective turnaround requires:

- Correct diagnosis of the nature of the need for turnaround.
- Rapid development of a survival plan.
- Faced with insolvency, rapid cash generation through a parallel approach.
- Making key strategic repositioning decisions as rapidly as possible.
- Understanding the true cost drivers in the business and targeting these initially, rather than making cuts across the board.
- Quick decisions on which members of the executive team are competent to play a role in improving the situation.
- Once survival is assured, development of a strategic plan that strengthens the business and improves profit margins by raising prices and reducing costs.

Finally, although turnaround is generally viewed as a negative endeavor, many people tell us that, with the right leadership, it can be an exhilarating and rewarding experience—a career highlight.

# 10

## Mobilizing for Culture Change

Culture change is wrapped up in many strategic initiatives, but it can also be an end in itself for an organization. Culture is all about people, what they value, what they believe, and most important, how they behave collectively. Culture change is deeper than strategic change because rather than just changing direction and the deployment of resources across the organization, executives are now dealing with humanity. In this situation, the behavior of the leadership team is critical to the outcome. To restate a simple truth, when change is occurring at this depth, *either the leadership has to change or the leadership has to be changed.* Concerning culture change, Paul Tellier of CN commented, "The first lever is changing the team—people are key in shaping culture. . . . I reluctantly terminated eight senior executives out of a group of approximately twenty-four in the first three months."

Many executives continue to adhere to the conventional wisdom that deep cultural change takes multiple years to implement. It is not unusual to hear five to ten years mentioned as the typical time required for a large corporation to implement this type of transformation. In our view, however, this time frame is no longer an option, and we present an innovative approach based on the best of practical experience that can bring about cultural transformation in a relatively short time frame—in months, rather than years.

Research has identified a number of factors that inhibit the ability to change culture rapidly. These include complacency or arrogance that results from an extended period of success,[1] habitual routines that are difficult to alter,[2] and stale top management executives who are unwilling to act.[3] However, even allowing for these factors, there is substantial anecdotal and written evidence that even long-established organizations, when properly led, can change their culture rapidly.

How long does it take for an organization to develop an innovative culture? In the case of one public-sector organization, it took as little as six weeks. Faced with a looming budget crisis, the executives of the City of Ajax in Canada decided that instead of adopting the traditional approach of cutting service and raising taxes, they would first see if any of their 250 employees, most of whom were unionized, had any thoughts on how to deal with the situation. At the time, the majority of the employees were totally disengaged from any improvement activities, and morale in the organization was low.

Working together over a period of a few weeks, a team of managers and employees put together a framework for a cost-improvement initiative that promised speedy implementation of proposals and various forms of recognition and rewards for employees who involved themselves in the activity. Cornerstone principles of the activity were no cuts in service and no layoffs as a result of implemented proposals. Within six weeks, this organization produced 2,200 proposals for process and service improvement. Seventy percent were implemented within twelve months, which resulted in the elimination of the potential budget crisis. The process provided a vehicle through which the entire culture of the organization changed within ninety days. Much more important, short-term improvements in morale were dramatic and positive changes in employee behavior were sustained in the longer term—to the point that the city came to be regarded as a role model for other municipalities in Canada.

What are the messages in this example? First, no one went around preaching a new set of values to the employees. Although the most senior executives had in mind a broad set of behaviors and benefits that would emerge from the process, they did not impose these up front. Second, the culture change was developed around a specific, tangible initiative that required behaviors to change if it was to succeed. Third, time was taken at the outset to convince employees of why this activity was important. Fourth, things got better visibly, tangibly, and fast. Fifth, involvement was recognized and rewarded.

Culture change can happen fast in large corporations as well. We were struck by the comments of two executives from a leading international bank that had just replaced its autocratic, directive CEO with one who had a human resources background. We asked these executives how long it would take for the new CEO to repair the damage to the bank's culture that had been wreaked by his predecessor. We expected the answer to be two or three years, at least, but instead, both executives said "forty-eight hours." When we inquired further, it became apparent that the appointment of the new CEO was in itself so significant that employee behavior had changed almost instantaneously. As one executive said so succinctly, "The fear has gone—overnight." In this example, the desired values may have been present all along, but the former CEO's leadership style submerged these values and caused behavior that established a low-performance and dysfunctional culture.

One of the most frequently cited examples of an effective cultural revolution is that of Ford in the early 1980s, which was accomplished in less than thirty-six months. Ford changed from a conflict-based culture with low employee engagement to one of union-management cooperation and a highly engaged workforce convinced that "Quality is Job 1." Unlike Ford, Unisys, CN, and scores of other organizations that made cultural change happen quickly, too many cor-

**Table 10.1** Major Elements that Determine Culture

| Soft Elements | Hard Elements |
| --- | --- |
| • Beliefs | • Structure |
| • Values | • Communications |
| • Symbols | • Education and training |
| • Heroes and heroines | • Policies |
| • Ritual and ceremony | • Recognition and rewards |
| • Myths and legends | • Objectives |

porations subscribe to the conventional wisdom that deep change must take several years. In this chapter, we set out explicit procedures for successfully driving rapid culture change that will have a lasting impact. Again, we demonstrate the need for a parallel-deployment process with a heavy emphasis on coaching, communications, and appropriate recognition and rewards.

## Creating a Culture

What do we mean by organization culture in the first place? If we are to talk meaningfully about changing it, then we need to be clear about the notion of culture. For the purposes of our book, we define the concept as a set of common behaviors determined by the interaction of history, values, and principles, as well as structure and enabling processes (see table 10.1). In some organizations, the influence of culture can be so strong and positive that it can make up for weak strategy and provide a distinct competitive edge. In others, though, negative aspects of culture can neutralize even the most brilliant strategies. In large organizations, there are likely to be many cultures. The engineering group's culture is probably different from the accounting group's culture, which is almost certain to be different from the sales group's culture. In multidivisional firms, cultures will vary from division to division. However, from a corporate perspective, the most important features are the few key behaviors and corresponding values that span the entire organization and influence its overall performance.

Culture is wrapped up in what people believe and, more important, how they behave. Executives can espouse values, beliefs, and principles for their organization, but unless these become embedded in behaviors, they do not define a culture. In fact, it is not unusual to read one set of values on the walls of an organization and see a totally different set acted out in the corridors. Many people view culture as largely being determined by the soft elements shown in table 10.1, but these are often the outcomes of behaviors determined by the hard elements. For example, many of the heroes and heroines in a corporate culture only emerge because policies, as well as recognition and rewards, make it possible in the first place. Of course, there are always those who emerge in spite of these elements, just as there are always some people who are willing to ask for forgiveness rather than permission!

The elements of culture need not be captured in a formal statement. For example, at Queen's University in Canada, there is a strong culture that values teaching, lifelong friendship, and community, as well as research. It is not written down anywhere, but corresponding behaviors can be seen all over the campus. On the other hand, some organizations, such as the auto-components giant Magna, have a formal, documented cultural philosophy that prescribes executive, management and employee behavior. Attempting to change either type of culture would be an extremely challenging exercise.

What defines a culture? Ignore what it says on the wall or the little card. What do you see and hear? Traditionally, culture has been thought to be shaped principally by behavioral factors. Clearly, the history of the organization influences culture. The values of the founders of the business often have a lasting impact. Traditional values and beliefs play a role as well. But most important, it is how people behave that defines culture. How we work together. How we resolve conflicts. How we deal with customers. How we make decisions. How we respond to new ideas and innovations. How we reward and recognize performance. The words can be on the wall, but unless people actually demonstrate the desired behaviors, the declarative statements mean nothing.

In reality culture is formed by both the hard and the soft elements that we identified in table 10.1, although some academics view culture and formal organization elements as quite distinct. For example, in *Breaking the Code of Change*, Michael Beer and Nitin Nohria state, "Organizational change efforts vary in the extent to which they focus on formal organizational arrangements such as structure and systems and the extent to which they acknowledge and deal with culture."[4]

Culture is shaped by organizational structure and processes, as well as behavioral elements. Jay Galbraith, in *Designing Organizations*, argues that changes to formal structure and systems are central to strategic change.[5] Recognition and rewards also influence culture. Who wins, who loses, or do we all win together? The structure of these processes will dramatically affect behavior and, in turn, culture. Organization structure is a major determinant of culture because it can influence the formation of silos, the sharing of information, and how people work together. Communication systems are also important. Is information shared openly, and is there an infrastructure to sustain this? Or is information closely held and only shared on a need-to-know basis? Policies, decision-making structures, conflict resolution mechanisms, and employee training and development all influence culture through the way that they shape employee behavior.

Change itself is often a cultural issue. We deal with it according to our values and beliefs. For some, change is good, and for others, change is bad. These notions are unlikely to be altered simply by argument and analysis. The benefits of change need to be clearly demonstrated. Correspondingly, some organization cultures in which flexibility, openness, innovation, and risk taking are accepted behaviors are likely to be those in which change is more easily accepted. On the other hand, cultures that value stability, process, well-defined roles and responsibilities, and error-free work are likely to be much more resistant to change.

## The Challenge of Cultural Change

Culture is one of the deepest and most difficult forms of change for any organization to undertake. The executive challenge at this deep level is to alter the way that people think and behave, as well as what they value. This is the level at which executives, managers, and supervisors start to become very defensive because *they* have to change if the process is to be successful. Many executives believe that the best time to change culture is when there is some kind of organizational crisis that will stimulate employees to reconsider their values and behaviors. In part, they are correct. Culture change is *most* difficult under the following conditions:

- When there is already a strongly entrenched culture.
- When the organization views itself as relatively successful.[6]
- When there is no crisis.

Culture change demands a leadership team that is willing to spend considerable time creating awareness and understanding of the need for and the nature of change throughout the organization. Karl Weick calls this process *sensemaking*, which we view to be part of the enabling processes for shared understanding. He suggests that three of the key elements of sensemaking are a sense of direction, frequent updating, and candid conversation.[7]

The drawbacks of using crisis as a principal driver for cultural change are twofold. First, during a crisis, many executives demonstrate a coercive style of leadership that is top-down, directive, and insensitive as they drive for rapid performance improvement. This style may be diametrically opposed to the desired new culture. Second, any behavior change secured under these conditions may not be lasting. As soon as employees perceive the crisis to be over, their behaviors may revert to what they were prior to the crisis. This need not be the case, as demonstrated by Ford, but the way in which the crisis is handled must be appropriate. There must be rapid changes in leadership behaviors and the key organizational enablers to ensure that the new values and behaviors are reinforced once the crisis is over.

So what are the major mistakes that executives make when implementing culture change?

- Preaching the new values and behaviors rather than leading by example.
- Sending out mixed messages—taking actions and making decisions that are inconsistent with the proposed culture.
- Failing to address opposition and resistance that undermine the process.
- Failing to embody the desired culture in tangible behaviors and actions.
- Failing to align performance measurement and recognition and rewards with the desired culture.

Organizations have tried to define culture through statements of values and principles, but these statements are often made without much understanding of what the words really mean. Not surprisingly, perhaps, these statements often look remarkably similar from one corporation to the next. The following "values" appear repeatedly in these statements: innovation, learning continuous improvement, honesty, mutual respect, teamwork, accountability, customer service, and diversity. Often, the list will be long, with maybe eight or ten core values, which would require every employee to be a model of virtue, understanding, and tolerance. In addition, the list frequently bears little relationship to the strategy of the organization.

Posting a long list of values on the wall is not the way to bring about a cultural transformation. For employees increasingly jaded by the empty and broken promises of senior executives, these declarations are one more source of cynicism. Instead, what's required to bring about rapid culture shift is a change of behavior throughout the organization that is led by central personnel and supported by key enabling mechanisms such as appropriate recognition and rewards. Inform and educate. Do not allow opposition time to solidify. Change employees' behavior. Provide positive feedback. Sustain the behavior by recognizing and rewarding success. These steps can lead to rapid change in organization culture.

In the literature, there are different schools of thought about changing employees' values, beliefs, and behaviors. One school of thought maintains that values and beliefs must change first for the shift to last. However, how long does it take to convince an employee with twenty years of experience, and apparent success, that his beliefs and behaviors have to change, especially if there is no crisis? One executive that we interviewed likened this approach to trying to convince a Republican congressman to cross the House and become a Democrat. Impossible? No, but unlikely and time consuming.

This executive and others we have worked with use a more pragmatic approach. They realize that it can take quite a while to change an individual's value set by argument and persuasion. However, changing their behavior, then reinforcing that new behavior through performance evaluations, accountability and rewards and recognition, is a more rapid way to drive culture change. One executive described this approach as follows: "Some employees will always have wanted to do it the new way, and these are where I get the quick wins. Others try it, and many find that they like it, especially if they get rewarded for it. There's usually a few who won't, or don't want to change, but they usually don't stick around for too long." Electrons don't change their state by being talked to. They change their state by being acted upon by other forces. So it is with human behavior.

## Culture Change—The First 100 Days

If the first 100 days is all about speed, then the first challenges of rapid cultural change are about establishing the need for change and building awareness and

**Table 10.2** Behavioral Changes Required to Align with Values

- Management practices consistent with a respectful workplace
- More coordination of our work across product lines and between functional and service groups—breaking down silos
- More collaboration among executives and managers
- Increased delegation at all levels
- Adoption and use of advanced service practices by all employees
- Officewide allocation and reallocation of resources aligned with strategic priorities by executives

understanding through a multichannel communications blitz that reaches every part of the organization and every employee. This communication is necessary even if the culture change is being triggered by some form of crisis. The core messages have to be continuously and conspicuously visible. New behaviors have to be demonstrated by leadership and recognized when they occur elsewhere in the organization. In addition, those employees who are likely to be early adopters of the new culture have to be identified and mobilized. Accordingly, key objectives for this period might be:

- Broadening awareness of, and a powerful logic for, the change.
- Realigning recognition and rewards with desired behaviors.
- Establishing performance parameters for new behaviors.
- Identifying role models of desired behaviors.
- Aligning of senior leadership behaviors with the desired culture.

Culture change will only take hold quickly if employees have tangible signals that values and behaviors have changed at the top. As part of a change planning workshop following the appointment of a new chief executive, one government agency with a list of eight guiding principles, many of which were being ignored, such as respectfulness in the workplace, shortened the list to five values. The agency also prepared a short list of corresponding behaviors to be demonstrated by senior management immediately following the workshop (see table 10.2). Everyone on the team individually agreed, although with varying degrees of passion, that these were desirable changes. Three specific changes were targeted initially—increased delegation, reallocation of resources, and coordination of work—and measures were developed to track them.

The new chief executive made it clear to members of her senior team that she would not tolerate failure to act in accordance with this agreement. One of her closing lines in the workshop was, "I'm not going to give you a month to get your behavior in line with what we've agreed. I expect our employees to see the difference when we walk out of this meeting." Within the next forty days, as part of a strategic communications process, these cultural changes were communicated and discussed throughout the entire organization. Visits were arranged to a couple of organizations where executives and employees could experience this type of culture firsthand. The chief executive followed up with monthly individual discussions with each member of her executive team and a series of informal meetings with employees to discuss how the changes were going. By the end of the first 100 days, informal tracking measures were already picking up significant changes in behavior, and employees were commenting openly on the improvement in the culture of the organization. Asked about the changes, one long-time executive made these comments:

> We always used to talk about acting this way. But our chief executive made it clear to us that as long as she was around it would not be an option. What used to be an old boys club has changed rapidly into a much more diverse and respectful workplace, and you know what, all of us find it a much better place to work.

## Culture Change—The Second 100 Days

In the second 100 days, the intent has to be to create momentum around the culture change, which means that the human flywheel must be starting to take effect. In addition, sources of resistance have to be identified and initial steps have to be taken to address them. During the second 100 days, objectives are likely to include:

- Clearly communicating executive resolve and intent to all employees.
- Mobilizing the early adopters into activities that embody the new behaviors.
- Taking initial steps to deal with resistance.
- Broadly communicating and recognizing of initial successes.

Few culture changes will happen as rapidly as in the example just cited. In fact, it is more than likely that by the end of the first 100 days, desired values and new behaviors may be acted out by only a very small proportion of employees. The second 100 days has to see a continuing restatement of the desired change, as well as strong signals of an intent to persevere. This is the time to start talking about how acting out new values and behaviors has provided tangible benefits and successes.

It is also a time to deal firmly with flagrant violations of new cultural norms in order to demonstrate that senior management is resolved in its intent. This may, in some cases, mean the dismissal of a few employees who are not only acting inappropriately, but also encouraging others to do so. These actions may be tough to take, but they send out clear, unambiguous signals to the entire workforce.

## Establishing the Winning Conditions

### 1. Correct Diagnosis of the Change Challenge

The first step in successful cultural change in any organization is for the executive team to correctly diagnose the depth of the level at which they will be working. Executives should realize that when the proposed change initiative will significantly affect how employees behave, they are dealing with cultural change. The diagnosis can be made by asking a series of simple questions:

- Does the change require different values to be embedded in the organization?
- In what ways will employee behavior have to change significantly?
- What values and behaviors do we wish to maintain?

Of course, it is also important to define which key elements of culture need to be changed and which ones can remain the same. Usually, all organizations have some strengths in their culture that should not be lost, and it is important to recognize what these are.

Once it's clear that culture change is required, a second part of the diagnosis concerns how this can be brought about. In this respect, both stakeholder and force-field analyses are relevant. The difficulty and complexity of the change can be determined by assessing the probable effect on stakeholders and their degree of commitment to old values, beliefs, and behaviors. The force-field analysis identifies the drivers for change, as well as the barriers, obstacles, and resistance points. In every situation, the task is to use the diagnosis to determine which employees will be early adopters and advocates of the new culture and which ones will put up the greatest resistance.

From this analysis, an appropriate game plan can be developed. In the extreme, this can involve "blowing up" the organization or parts of it and rebuilding one in which there are a significant number of new employees with a new value set. Even if this does not prove necessary for the organization as a whole, it may prove necessary for the executive team if a number of key players cannot buy in to the new culture.

## 2. Early Development of Shared Understanding

It is particularly important in cultural change for the leadership team to have a true shared understanding of the nature of the anticipated change. In part, this is because of the difficulty of successful implementation of this level of change. An early part of this process is to identify, however imperfectly, how behavior has to change if the desired outcomes are to be secured. This is quite different from what happens in many contemporary planning processes.

Recently, a major global resources corporation was about to embark on a radical culture shift. Following the historic signing of a first-ever, collaborative union—management agreement to work together on improvement projects of mutual benefit, a hundred years of entrenched conflict had to be put in the past if real progress was to be made. An early step in this process was a facilitated two-day workshop attended only by the three union presidents, who were occasionally in conflict among themselves, and the senior members of the management team. During the first day, management provided the union with a candid presentation of the company's current position and future strategy. The union representatives apprised management of the personal challenges that the new agreement posed for them with their membership, who clearly viewed it as the latest "flavor of the month." Along the way, there was considerable rhetoric and taking of positions by both sides, but with that out of the way, by the end of the day, each side had a clear understanding of how collaboration would be possible and how it would not.

On the second day, the group worked together to identify charters for three major collaborative projects aligned with the company's strategy and the interests of the union and its members. This task was completed much faster than anyone in the room had thought possible, and without any real disagreement, which boosted the morale of the group considerably. There was agreement to launch these projects within thirty days of the first workshop, and an appropriate joint action plan was created to accomplish this. The remainder of the day was spent in defining the process for collaboration and, specifically, how the behavior of the individuals in the room had to change, as well as the behavior of others, particularly front line supervisors and union representatives, if the initiative was to prosper. Most important of all, the union presidents and management committed to improving communication and working together on issues that in the past would have created substantial conflict.

In planning for culture change, merely describing the desired values and principles is not sufficient. In fact, history suggests that this approach is only likely to result in cynicism and frustration throughout the organization. In this situation, planning has to include an identification of the behaviors that will physically manifest the desired culture change and consideration of the changes in organizational enablers that will facilitate these changes. What's the vision? What's the enabling process? We have found that executive teams that embark on this path not only discuss values, but also possess a clear, shared vision of future behavior patterns that will result from the process.

For example, if the executive team determines that the organization needs to become more innovative as part of its culture change, it is in no way sufficient to merely state, "Innovation is now one of our core values." As part of the planning process, executives have to identify what types of behaviors will correspond to this increased innovativeness. Is it asking more employees to propose new process improvement ideas? Is it creating multidisciplinary teams to generate a stream of new products into the marketplace? Is it requiring more customer focus to lead to creative business solutions to solve their problems? Is it all three? A vision of what the future will look like, one that is linked to clear measures of success, is required. Examples include an average of one implemented proposal per employee per quarter, 5 percent sales growth each year from new products, and perhaps a 20 percent increase in customer loyalty by better meeting their needs.

With some sense of vision and of how success will be measured, the executive team can then determine how behavior will have to change to bring about these outcomes. For example, if a higher rate of innovation is desired, then executives and managers are likely to have to become more tolerant of failure. A stream of new products will probably require employees to work more effectively across the organization. Facilitating these behaviors will almost certainly require changes in the key organizational enablers—structure, processes, and recognition and rewards. There is also likely to be a significant employee education task. For example, it is unlikely that rank-and file employees will start to generate worthwhile process-improvement ideas without some education in why they are important, where to look for ideas, how to propose them, and how to implement them.

It is equally important, when working at this level, that leadership behavior change, in line with the new values and beliefs that are demanded of the organization. Planning for cultural change has to go further and deeper than that required for operational or strategic change. In cultural change, the leadership team has to plan how its own behaviors will mirror the desired change in culture. If executives continue to behave more in line with the past than the future, the culture will not change for the better, and it is likely to change for the worse as cynicism takes hold among the rank and file. Thus, if executives demand innovation but react negatively to proposals, punish failure, and starve the process of resources for experimentation and implementation, then all they are likely to achieve is cynicism. There is good reason that at 3M, one of the world's most innovative companies, two of the most strongly held values are to never kill a good idea and to be tolerant of failure.

### 3. Enrichment of Shared Understanding

How does shared understanding become enriched during cultural transformation? For example, the union presidents and the management team of the natural resources company we just described recognized that one meeting would not bring about culture change. As a result, one of the outcomes of the initial workshop was an agreement to meet for a full day every sixty days for at least the first year to discuss mutual issues, opportunities, and concerns in order to ensure that shared understanding of their challenge continued to be enriched. As a symbol that things were changing in the company, the groups issued a joint communiqué to all employees that announced their intention to do this.

At Acklands-Grainger, the executive team thought the shift to a sales development culture required branch managers and sales employees to spend much more time with existing customers, get more of their business, as well as prospect for new accounts. The desired outcome was accelerated growth for the company. Initially, broad target measures were developed that corresponded to these expectations. For example, within a year, branch managers would be expected to spend at least 25 percent of their time outside the branch with customers. Sales representatives were expected to spend a majority of their time on the road making sales calls.

An initial surge in sales revenues following the launch of the strategy suggested to the management team that the new strategy was working and that the culture change was taking hold. However, within a relatively short period, it became evident to the whole of the executive team that sales was one area in which behavior change was not occurring as fast as desired. Discussions at one of the team's strategy review workshops identified the problems as a lack of clearly defined performance expectations and weak sales territory management skills. Consequently, steps were taken to define acceptable minimum sales call targets for every sales representative, branch manager, general manager, and executive, up to and including the president, Doug Harrison. In addition, the decision was made to implement a sales training initiative that had been delayed due to budget constraints. Within a very short time, sales performance improved significantly, and behaviors, reinforced by a new sales compensation plan, changed in the desired ways.

This example illustrates one of the real dangers in culture change—that initial changes in behavior will not be sustained. For example, one large telecommunications company that was noted for its ponderous bureaucracy instituted from the top down, and with much fanfare, a cultural shift that it referred to as its new "GO" culture. Behaviors in the new culture were to emphasize speed and responsiveness throughout all aspects of the corporation's business—decision making, problem solving, and dealings with customers, for example. Performance requirements were written into the accountabilities of executives and managers, the new logo was visible everywhere, and the new values and behaviors were front and center in everything that was undertaken. However, given the constant turnover in the executive ranks, many employees wondered just how long the approach would last. Would it be yet another corporate fad, forgotten within six months?

The only way to guarantee that it would last was to ensure that processes were in place through continual questioning, training, and communication that enabled every employee to gain a greater shared understanding of how to behave in the new culture. Allowing questioning up, down, and sideways enriches shared understanding of culture change by making people think about their behaviour, particularly if it is inappropriate. Training ensures that people acquire a richer understanding of what "GO" really means for they way in which the make decisions and carry out their work. Communication reaffirmed the value of new behaviors through the sharing of success stories, which created new myths and legends and also made heroes and heroines of people who went to extraordinary lengths to demonstrate the values embedded in the new culture.

## 4. Establishment of a Sense of Urgency

Cultural change will never happen unless there is a sense of urgency established at the outset. When some form of crisis precipitates this change, there is usually no doubt that behaviors must change for the crisis to be resolved. In this situation, the leadership team's task is to ensure that the changed behaviors that resolve the crisis are retained once the crisis is over.

It is much more challenging to secure cultural change when the adopted stance is proactive. In this situation, employees often perceive little reason to change their behavior and often adopt a "wait and see" attitude. In fact, there may be a strong belief that the current culture is the right one. Slow and steady will not win this race. Instead, a sense of urgency for behavior change must be established quickly. However, the temptation to create an artificial crisis should be avoided.

So how do you create a sense of urgency for cultural change when there is no crisis and not even a "burning platform" around which to focus? We have found that a powerful motivator can be the appropriate use of leading strategic indicators.[8] A powerful logic, to use Jack Welch's words, is, "Let's change before we have to." In this respect, employees can be powerfully motivated if they are made aware of, and helped to understand, the implications of changes in certain performance indicators. These might include measures such as customer complaints, satisfaction, and loyalty indicators that would suggest a need for change in customer-oriented behaviors. Declining margins might also be an indicator of the need to change cost-related behaviors.

Competitive intelligence can also be a powerful driver of cultural change, particularly if employees are directly exposed to it through benchmarking activities and visits. In the late 1970s, Ford sent not only executives and managers but also union representatives and rank-and-file employees to Japan to see firsthand how the competition operated. This created a climate in which ordinary employees were much more open to the cultural changes that were necessary. Major retail companies send their employees to Nordstrom to experience what a true customer-oriented culture is like. Manufacturing companies send their employees to Lincoln Electric to experience the reality of a high-performance production environment.

## 5. Creation of a Limited and Focused Strategic Agenda

Cultural change is one of those situations in which the temptation to change everything at once should be firmly resisted. Many organizations make the mistake of adopting a new set of values and then attempting to change them all at once. Widespread and simultaneous changes in values and behavior can result in chaos if the internal consistency and integrity of the organization are lost in the process. Because culture change is almost certainly accompanied by strategic change, it is also important to ensure a correspondence between major substantive changes and culture changes. It is important to determine a few, probably no more than two or three, core values and associated behaviors to address first. As much as possible, these should be mutually reinforcing. For example, delegation, employee development, and accountability tend to go together with a strategy focused on increased employee effectiveness through a flatter, more responsive structure. Similarly, innovation, risk taking, and tolerance of mistakes align with a strategy aimed at increasing the rate of new product introduction.

A number of the rules that apply to organizational change generally apply in this situation. For example, it's almost certain that some values and behaviors will be easier to change than others, so adopting these as the initial focus will provide some quick results and build credibility for the process.

In addition, using our parallel-deployment methodology will ensure that the key enablers are addressed simultaneously. For example, if the desired value and behavior change is toward a more sales-oriented culture, then priorities for training, adjustment in rewards and recognition, and policies can all be realigned with the new direction.

## 6. Rapid, Strategic Decision Making and Deployment

Effecting deep cultural change rapidly requires that key decisions be made expediently if the required parallel-deployment methodology is to be implemented. Paradoxically, however, the ability to act rapidly is, in itself, cultural. In some organizations, there is a strong belief that decisions have to be thoroughly analyzed and justified, be subject to due process, and have consensus. In this case, even small changes can take an age. One executive we know summed up the opposite tack: "If you've done your homework and it feels right, just do it."

An example of what this means in practice can be illustrated by considering the approach to human resource development activities in support of change initiatives in two corporations. In the first, Acklands-Grainger, the executive team decided that all branch managers required enhancement of their leadership skills if they were to become more effective at growing the branches profitably. Laurie Wright, the vice-president of human resources, immediately developed a four-day pilot program that was delivered to the company's newest branch managers within sixty days of the decision. Within 200 days, all branch managers had gone through the program, which was an outstanding success if judged by the subsequent performance of the branches.

The executive team of the other corporation made a decision on some supervisory development activities that were required to support an initiative to secure greater employee involvement in process and product improvement. However, in this case, the Human Resources group, following accepted practice, insisted on a thorough needs analysis first. As a result, the development program had not even been launched within 200 days, and the involvement initiative, which had been launched, was floundering, in part due to a lack of appropriate supervisory behavior.

In the early stages of the process, many employees are uncertain as to the real degree of commitment to change. Often, they've heard similar messages before, many times, but in the end things remained much the same. So how are they to know that this time it is going to be different? The answer is action, rather than talk. It may take some months to implement broad developmental and organizational initiatives that will make a major difference. However, much can be accomplished in the short term through a series of well-planned and well-communicated symbolic decisions and actions that signal commitment and intent to change behaviors.

Nowhere are symbolic actions, taken rapidly, as important as in cultural change. These actions, either small and intangible or, better still, large and substantive, create "buzz" throughout the organization. They get people talking. They energize people. They create the myths and legends that ultimately define a culture. A list of some of these actions was provided in table 5.1.

Executives in a number of organizations we studied reported that selective employee changes can have a powerful influence in the early stages of cultural change. Getting rid of one or two nonperforming employees quickly sends out a message, particularly if they are managers or supervisors who cannot exhibit an appropriate leadership style. Conversely, hiring one or two new employees who exemplify the kinds of behavior the new culture requires can be very symbolic. Changing the slogan also works. Think of the impact on Ford employees of the simple phrase "Quality is Job 1." Changed executive leadership styles, especially if they are highly visible, can also be powerful symbols. For example, in one government organization that was attempting to break down silos between divisions, two senior executives, previously antagonistic toward each other, met for two hours each week, over a period of two years, to demonstrate their commitment to working together. This move eventually paid off because other employees in the divisions realized that meetings of this kind were probably a good idea. Physical changes can also be symbolic. The new director of a corporate technology center, alarmed at the low state of morale in the dingy building, quickly put a new coat of paint on the walls, brought in plants, and freshened up the furniture. Within two months, morale and culture were noticeably improved.

## 7. A Human Flywheel of Commitment

Building the human flywheel is the single most important element in cultural transformation. More than in any other type of change, involving employees early is critical to rapid progress. However, it is likely that at the outset, a minority of employees will actually be directly engaged. Certainly, culture change cannot wait for everyone to be convinced before getting started. Jack Welch, discussing his early days as CEO of General Electric, noted that he took too long to get his change under way. In part, he attributed this delay to his desire to get everyone on board. The reality? As Jack Welch discovered, you never will. What's important is that a group of committed key players starts to act out the new behaviors, and those who cannot develop these behaviors have to go.

In the City of Ajax initiative described earlier, the rate and extent of involvement was unusual, but it perhaps reflects a latent demand for change that was preexisting with many employees. More typical is the situation in which perhaps 15 or 20 percent of employees are willing to move quickly in the new direction, but the majority remain unconvinced and therefore continue in their old behavior patterns.

Who are the key members of this human flywheel? Certainly the entire executive leadership of the organization has to be committed from the outset. Culture change cannot happen if one or more members of the leadership team are in disagreement and do not support the initiative with appropriate communications and behaviors. It is incumbent upon the CEO at the outset of deep cultural change to ensure that all members of the executive team are aligned with the new values and behaviors. During the first 100 days, a wise CEO will meet with his or her direct subordinates at least monthly, or more frequently if there are perceived problems, and offer coaching and advice. At the end of the first

100 days, if one or two members of the team appear to be incapable of adapting to the new style demanded of them, it is likely that a serious career discussion is required.

Beyond this group, the challenge is to identify the initial coalition that will support the transformation by becoming early adopters of the desired new behavior patterns. Sometimes, these individuals are to be found in relatively unexpected places and positions. For example, in one large accounting firm, the receptionist was the hub of the flywheel. She knew everything and everyone, and rank-and-file employees looked to her as a bellwether for developments in the company. Once she was on the team, the flywheel gathered momentum with incredible speed. In the first 100 days, the early adopters have to be encouraged to become participants in the process. They can join task forces or committees and simply exhibit the new values and behaviors in their day-to-day responsibilities. In the second 100 days, these champions have to be used to convert a majority of the remaining employees to the new approach.

## 8. Identification and Management of Sources of Resistance

Deep cultural change will not occur in any organization without experiencing resistance at all levels. Even when cultural change is being driven by a crisis that threatens the very survival of the corporation, there will always be those who oppose the new behaviors for one reason or another. For example, in certain circumstances, there may be a small minority of employees who feel that they will personally benefit if the corporation fails, through severance payments, for example. There are numerous reasons for this resistance, but the most common and the easiest to deal with is ignorance—lack of awareness and understanding of the need to change.

Falconbridge, one of Canada's leading mining companies, was within weeks of bankruptcy during the 1980s. The new CEO, Bill James, soon found out that 99 percent of employees were totally ignorant of the company's true financial situation and the need for deep change. That changed very quickly as James opened up the lines of communication, even talking directly to employees in the mines. Resistance to the company's survival plans soon evaporated. In this case, James's own ebullient, down-to-earth leadership style was a major factor in a cultural transformation that swept the company in the twelve months following his appointment. However, it is worthy to note that following sweeping cuts in the first 100 days of his tenure, during which his leadership style was highly authoritative and sometimes bordered on coercive, James moved to change the company culture to one in which engaged employees viewed productivity improvement and cost reduction as ultimately saving, not eliminating, jobs.

First- and second-line supervisors have been identified as major sources of resistance to cultural change. In fact, this level in the organization can be so resistant to communication and change that some executives refer to it as "the clay layer"—things go up and down to it, but nothing passes through. Absolutely, cultural change will not happen if a substantial number of supervisors have not bought in themselves. They will sabotage the message from management and filter the feedback on what is actually happening among the rank and file. In fact, it is not unusual for senior executives to have a totally false impression of the realities of the workplace unless they are clever enough to go and see for themselves.

How do you ensure that a majority of supervisors buy in to culture change? First of all, it's important during the diagnosis stage to understand how they will be affected and how much they will be able to influence the outcomes. Very likely, some supervisors will be unable to change as required, and they should be identified and offered appropriate exit packages or alternative employment opportunities (paradoxically, some older, senior supervisors make great coaches and mentors once they are taken out of a line responsibility). Some supervisors will be early adopters, and they should be engaged as champions of change initiatives. The remainder, those in the middle, have to be helped to change.

Relatively small things can make a difference in how supervisors respond—again, a number of them are cultural. For example, supervisors in many organizations feel caught in the middle—neither managers nor rank and file. A clear signal can often make a big difference. For example, one CEO told us of an important lesson he learned early in his tenure:

> I very quickly realized that immediately after I had met with employees, the first thing they would go and do would be to validate my messages with their supervisors. If this was the first the supervisors had heard of it, then the likelihood was that they would not be supportive, in fact, they'd be quite cynical. So what I started to do, and also encouraged my vice-presidents to do, was have a session just for supervisors a week or so before meeting with the rank and file. The outcome was completely different. Supervisors could appear to be "in the know", and became very supportive of my messages. Such a simple change.

This CEO told us that whenever he visited an operation, he always met the supervisors for breakfast so he could give them any news first. He also used the opportunity to find out what was going on in the operation and who he should talk to and provide recognition to as he made his tour.

## 9. Follow-through on Changing Organizational Enablers

Behavior changes are brought about by a reshaping of key organizational enablers, as well as by personal leadership. On this topic, Paul Tellier of CN commented

> Levers are important in changing culture. The first lever is changing the team—people are key in shaping culture—the right person in the right place at the right time is key. . . . The second lever is compensation: we spend a lot of time incenting employees—we now have stock options for six thousand out of our twenty-four thousand employees. There are $65 million on the table in bonuses this year. The third lever is training. For example we have put the entire senior management cadre through leadership training. The fourth lever is new blood. For example, even as we were downsizing, I insisted that we recruit university

graduates. . . . We now have a group of between 125 and 150 bright young people I refer to as "shit disturbers." The fifth lever is to build on success by amplifying success stories and best practices. At the moment there's not an employee in this company who is not proud of working for the top railroad in North America for the past fourteen quarters.

These outcomes cannot be achieved without the enabling programs and projects that permit the required behaviors to be manifested. In the case of Acklands-Grainger, it was necessary to take work out of the branches to free up the managers' time. In addition, it soon became evident not only that sales training was necessary for branch staff, but also that senior executives had to lead the way by spending more time with customers themselves. Once these elements were put in place, the desired behaviors started to emerge relatively quickly.

From our research and experience, we have seen that the inability to rapidly bring recognition and rewards into alignment with a new culture is a major cause of failure. For example, throughout the 1990s, the Canadian federal government asked its executives to lead their organizations in a more businesslike manner. They were asked to develop business plans, be more cost conscious, and seek out opportunities to recover costs for added-value services that they provided to citizens and corporations.

Many executives genuinely attempted to move their departments and branches in this direction. However, recognition and rewards, formal and informal, were never brought into line with these directions. The reward for beating your annual budget? You don't get the money next year. The reward for employees who proposed innovative ways to reduce costs? A long and tortuous evaluation and recognition process and possible put-downs from their managers. As a consequence, in most departments, the approach lasted as long as the budget deficit. As soon as a financial surplus was achieved by the government, revenue generation became a thing of the past and budget demands exploded. Culture change had not taken hold because the key enablers, such as rewards and recognition, had not been aligned with the desired new culture. Oh, the folly of rewarding *A* while hoping for *B*.[9]

How fast can recognition and rewards be changed? How long does it take to become growth oriented from a revenue maintenance culture? Acklands-Grainger wanted to shift from a sales maintenance culture to a sales development culture. To accomplish this task, they needed to get the company's 230 branch managers to believe that they owned their businesses and that it was their job to grow the business profitably. The challenge: get salespeople focused on generating new business, not on maintaining relationships with existing clients. Branch managers had to focus on growing branch gross profit margins.

Several key moves accomplished this task in months, rather than years. First, the message was clearly communicated as part of the company's strategy. Second, Doug Harrison quickly established a President's Club award program that rewarded high sales performers with a four-day all-expenses-paid trip with their spouse to a company retreat at a famous Canadian mountain resort. Overall reward and recognition programs were changed to reward salespeople on new business and branch managers on growth in their branches. In addition, part of their incentive was made dependent on how well Acklands-Grainger did as a whole.

The results? Although slow to start, continued executive team support for this initiative resulted in a rapid momentum build over the second 100 days. For the year, the overall President's Club target was exceeded by 300 percent, and forty branch managers received President's Club awards for being more than 25 percent over budgeted gross margin. Did everyone change? No, but by the end of 200 days, more people than not were saying that this was the right thing to do for the company, and the culture change was well under way. Was it a financial success? The cost of the trip was more than paid for before it even took place because of the resulting profit improvement.

## 10. Demonstrated Leadership Commitment

Responsibility for culture change cannot be delegated to a change committee. This form of change has to be led from the top, and it requires appropriate leadership styles and behaviors. This is one form of organizational change that cannot be preached—executives must model the way. Michael Beer et al. suggest that deep cultural change will inevitably fail if executives are perceived to be unable to change their behavior in line with the new culture.[10] Moreover, this leadership must have continuity.

Andrew Pettigrew and Richard Whipp identify the withdrawal of a key leader from a change team as a negative influence.[11] The reality in today's corporate world is that senior leaders change jobs on average once every eighteen months. As the senior team changes composition, it is essential that new members be quickly imbued with the values and style that have to be demonstrated.

Top-down leadership is only one element in this process. In fact, change efforts that are formula driven, focused around a single issue, and driven by top-down management fiat tend to be unsuccessful,[12] especially given the rate of turnover in executive roles. Successful cultural change requires continuity of leadership at all levels of the organization. Karl Weick argues strongly that the success of deep change initiatives is determined as much by choices made on the front line as by top management.[13]

These observations fit with our research findings and practical experiences. Deep cultural change works only if engagement can be secured throughout the organization. Rapid cultural change requires that leadership for the new values and behaviors quickly takes hold at all levels—executive, management supervisory, rank and file, and, if possible, union. Unfortunately, most organizations take far too long to engage the rank and file and the union in cultural change, with the result that speed and momentum build very slowly.

One of the critical tasks of leadership throughout the first 200 days of cultural change is communication. In this respect, most organizations woefully underestimate the amount and nature of what is required to build awareness and understanding. Frantically busy executives feel that they have little time to spend on communication during the early days of a deep cultural change initiative. In fact, the senior leadership of the organization may be even less visible during this period because they spend time in planning sessions, workshops, and seminars, as well as attend to their usual duties.

The reality is that deep cultural change will not happen fast unless executives are prepared, up-front, to put an extraordinary effort into communication. For example, in Ajax, where the employees overwhelmed management with good ideas, executives recognized that their own behavior had to change. An incredibly busy person, Barry Malmsten, the chief administrative officer for Ajax, asked employees to leave their proposals on his office chair if he was not there to take them personally. Within a week, each employee had a personal thank-you from him. A decision on each proposal was communicated within a month if it could not be done immediately. Frequently, though, department managers simply told the employees, "Just do it!" For over 80 percent of the approved proposals, employees were empowered to implement their ideas themselves.

One of the most glaring failures in a change initiative is the failure of second-tier executives and middle managers to follow up on initial communications by the CEO. After the CEO has taken the time to blitz the company with a series of presentations that outline the change initiative, it is critically important for other executives and managers to follow up with presentations and discussions with their own teams about the proposed changes and their implications for practices and behaviors in their own organization units. Unless this process is rigorously managed and led, implementation will be sporadic, at best.

The communication of deep cultural change is also not just a matter of what is said, but how it is said, and when. Cultural change requires a talent for speaking differently about what's important rather than merely arguing well. It is almost certain that presentations on cultural change by a CEO have to be reframed and restated to make them relevant for most rank-and-file employees. In addition, passion and the determination to persevere must be evident. The people in the best position to do this are committed leaders among the frontline supervisory group and the rank and file themselves. However, to be able to do this, they must clearly understand the nature and intent of the proposed change. Frontline culture change starts to take effect when it becomes the subject of everyday conversation.[14]

## In Summary

Cultural change can happen quickly. By the end of the first 100 days, role models who act out the new behaviors should be visible across the organization. By the end of 200 days, there should be a groundswell of stories about the positive impacts of the new culture and tangible signs of progress. Critical Winning Conditions to bring about this state of affairs include:

- An early definition of behaviors that embody the desired culture shift.
- Tangible initiatives that enable the desired behaviors to be acted out.
- Rapid creation of a human flywheel.

- Symbolic indicators of the new culture and promulgation of success stories.
- Early realignment of performance evaluation and recognition and rewards.
- Continuing, tangible evidence that the senior executives are relentless in their determination to make the changes.
- Tangible disincentives for individuals who continue to cling to old values and behaviors.
- Active support from first line supervision.

Finally, and most important, a nonnegotiable requirement for rapid culture change is a leadership team that is prepared to adopt a pacesetter style and lead through consistently demonstrating the desired behaviors.

# 11

## What Next?

So what happens after 200 days? How do you keep the process moving and continue to build momentum? Although it's important to secure results within the first 200 days of any change initiative, it's unlikely that everything will be nailed down by that time. A few major initiatives may last three or four years, even with a rapid start, and momentum has to be sustained throughout the period. It would be easy to suggest, "Just keep repeating what you've done so far," but it's not that simple. Even when you have built momentum, there are many ways in which change initiatives can still falter. One of the executives we interviewed explained:

> We had a great launch for the new strategy, and were going full speed ahead. About nine months into the process, though, our corporate parent suffered a major earnings blip, and their support for us all but evaporated. In fact, we were told to focus on generating cash, which put a real dent in our investment plans. The next five months were tough, but we managed to keep the process moving and finally came out the other side.

So what are the challenges? Some relate to holding the course, and others have to do with continuing to build momentum. No matter how well defined the strategy and how rich the degree of shared understanding, there is always the risk that, left to their own devices, task forces and committees will create their own agendas, especially when there is a lack of supervision. We have observed a number of situations in which a task force was provided with very specific terms of reference by the strategy team, but it returned several months later with something very different than what was asked for. In one case, a government organization was expecting a task force to return with a business case developed for a specific initiative. Along the way, however, members of the group decided unilaterally that a different initiative would be much more interesting to them. When the strategy team reconvened four months later, most members were astonished and quite a few were angry that the task force had gone off in a new direction with no consultation.

As the above example illustrates, there can also be a loss of focus due to unexpected crises or disruptions. Several government organizations in our sample had major problems staying the course on change initiatives because of the repeated crises they endured. This is especially true with portfolios such as immigration, health, and defense. Life for the senior executive teams in these organizations appears to be just one public relations crisis after another. As one executive commented, "My department is outstanding at crisis management. When there's a major disaster, we pull together extremely well. However, when it comes to organization change, we just never seem to get ahead."

We have also encountered similar situations in the private sector. In a number of project-oriented engineering and consulting firms, strategic change becomes a victim of the organization's task orientation. Similarly, in corporations in which new business comes in major chunks, the resources that are allocated to major change initiatives are often perceived to be the "slack" that is generally allocated to these new deals. No sooner is an initiative launched and resources allocated than the next major project or deal comes along and the key resources always seem to be pulled away from the strategic initiative to give to the client's agenda. This is particularly true if the leader of the initiative is a highly skilled project manager.

Unfulfilled expectations beyond the first 200 days can also be a major source of dissatisfaction. During this initial period, employees are often asked to engage in the change through taking part in surveys, focus groups, and task forces. All too frequently, the task force reports quickly but implementation happens slowly, or not at all. It only takes a few incidents of this kind for word to get around that management is not serious about their stated intention to change.

Another problem faced by all organizations after a period of time is that the strategy becomes "tired." At the outset, change is often fun, exciting, and challenging. However, after nine months or a year, a certain degree of fatigue can set in, even among the most enthusiastic teams. In part, this is often because project leaders or champions, and teams, are left unchanged in their role for too long. There is a definite life span in playing the role of a champion for a major organizational change initiative. As we discuss later in this final chapter, change champions need to be periodically refreshed in order to maintain the required momentum and enthusiasm for change.

This is also true for senior executives. Activities that initially seemed to be personally rewarding, even though they were hard work, can become much more of a chore over time. This is particularly the case with periodic presentations to employees. The first few rounds of these can be highly interesting and rewarding, especially if the employees are responsive and engaged. However, it's a hard slog to make perhaps a dozen or more presentations in rapid-fire succession every three or six months. After a while, many CEOs either delegate these activities or cease them completely. This action does not go unnoticed by supervisors and the rank and file, for whom this communication may have become important.

**Table 11.1** Maintaining
Momentum for Change

- Periodic updates (accountability)
- Frequent progress meetings
- Conference calls
- Highlight specific successes
- Symbolic acts
- Change champions periodically
- Celebrate successes
- Newsletter
- Change Web site on the Intranet

## Keeping the Process Going

To avoid some of the scenarios depicted above, successful change leaders use a variety of tools and techniques to ensure that the process takes precedence for the entire organization, as shown in table 11.1.

Continuing reviews of progress are critical to maintaining focus and enthusiasm for the change effort. In many organizations, these meetings last at least a day, often with a dinner the evening before so that participants can informally brief each other and socialize. The agenda elements for a typical meeting are shown in table 11.2.

These reviews, typically held at a minimum every three months, serve a number of important purposes:

- First, they act as an accountability framework and checkpoint. Participants report on progress against specific commitments made for the period just ended, and goals and key action plans with accountabilities are set for the upcoming period.
- Second, the discussion held during the reviews enriches shared understanding of the change challenge and provides an opportunity for double-loop learning to occur.[1]
- Third, they can play an important role in team building. In each quarterly

**Table 11.2** Three-Month Update Agenda

1. How do we *feel* about the process?
2. What are our achievements?
3. What has been accomplished?
4. What are the substantive issues?
5. What are the process issues?
6. How are we doing against our timeline?
7. What are our next three months' priorities?
8. What are our next three months' goals?
9. What are our next three months' action plans?
10. What could get in our way?

meeting, the strategy team should emerge with deeper insights into the nature of the process, the challenges (e.g., who is "tired"), and how to bring about success.

- Fourth and finally, these reviews facilitate the adoption of emergent strategies that fine-tune the process. These may be adopted due to change in the organization's external environment or new and richer insights into the issues that are underpinning the change initiative.

At Acklands-Grainger, Doug Harrison held such meetings for his strategy team every sixty days for the first eighteen months, the period of the company's first change mission, and thereafter every three months. Strategy team members included seven direct subordinates, six operating general managers, and nine director-level staff members from key enabling functions such as logistics, marketing, and finance. Asked about the value of the process, they commented that given the pace of the business, this was about the only occasion when they came together under one roof for any period of time and gained a complete picture of the current and proposed change agenda that they could then take back and communicate to their own staff.

In a number of other organizations that have a similar process, we have observed that attendance at these updates is not confined to executives or members of the change team. Union representatives, senior professional staff, supervisors, and even rank-and-file employees will be invited to sit in, participate, and familiarize themselves with what's happening.

Supplementing these quarterly sessions, shorter meetings can be held at more frequent intervals. We have observed organizations that have a monthly teleconference information session, lasting an hour or less, in which progress on major change initiatives is reported. Some executive teams review at least one specific initiative in depth each month for several hours with the deployment team. Some CEOs even meet weekly, for maybe an hour or so, with each of their direct subordinates, in part to discuss the progress of the change initiatives that they are sponsoring.

Aside from these ongoing reviews, other factors are important in ensuring continued momentum. Employees at all levels are energized when they see tangible evidence of the fruits of their labors. For example, visible signs of progress are a very powerful way to keep enthusiasm for a change initiative. In this respect, companies have been very inventive. For example, one corporation had signs and police tape wrapped around an area in an office building where a significant change-related initiative had been implemented. Another company sent home to each employee and also to its vendors and customers a calendar made up of photographs of teams with some representation of their successful change initiatives. Scorecards and other progress indicators in lunchrooms are also good for morale.

Symbols can act to maintain the momentum for change, but only if they are changed as time progresses. Otherwise they become stale. One executive, in the early stages of a major change, handed out lollipops to factory employees who were substantially contributing to a cultural change in the plant. After three months, he stopped handing out lollipops and moved on to something else. On subsequent visits to the plant, one of the first questions employees asked was, "Where are the lollipops?" He used this as a segue to talk about the next set of activities related to the change campaign.

Changing the leaders of the various change project teams can be a major contributor to maintaining momentum. In our experience, change champions can get burned out after about a year or eighteen months in a particular role. If this occurs, the effect on the rest of the team can be very negative. However, one can only change leaders if a suitable successor can be found. Thus, it is incumbent upon the executive team to assist these leaders in identifying and training their successors, thereby ensuring a smooth transition.

Recognition and rewards embodied in celebrations of success are also important elements of maintaining enthusiasm and, hence, momentum. Bonus checks are one thing, but organizations need to think about how to keep the reward impact going. For example, in one public-sector organization, a senior manager who had exhausted her discretionary financial resources got creative. She identified where employees had family members located across the country and aligned their travel schedules to these locations. Her thoughtfulness and creativity remains one of most talked-about items related to that particular change program.

As we have discussed before, newsletters can be an important source of information on a continuing basis. For example, a CEO column on change can become a regular feature. The CEO can use this method of communication to discuss particular aspects of change or to identify and recognize successful initiatives. Nowadays, these can be electronic, of course, and many corporations have a specific Web site for progress updates and recognition of specific achievements.

## The Longer Term

Although there should be continuing periodic reviews of the strategy every 60, 90, or 120 days, a major renewal point occurs when it is clear that the initial mission is close to attainment. This point is usually reached about twelve to eighteen months into the change process. At this time, the three or four initial key change initiatives should be substantially complete and operational. It's now time to identify the next mission that will create the next major strategic platform toward attainment of the vision.

This second mission may continue or build on initiatives from the first mission. For example, it is not unusual that cost reduction remains a continuing theme through more than one mission. However, the focus may change quite significantly. At Acklands-Grainger, the cost-reduction focus during the first mission was primarily internal; during the second mission, the focus switched more to external sources, such as suppliers and service providers. At this stage, the vision itself should be reviewed, possibly refined, and possibly even radically revised based on the experience of the past strategic time period, although a radical revision rarely happens in practice.

But while all this is happening, how is the organization's capacity for change developing? Organizations that are serious about the process leverage the know-how and experience that is continually being gained to build and maintain an organizational culture that is increasingly accepting and supportive of change.

## Building and Maintaining a Change-Oriented Culture

Throughout this book, we have applied the ten Winning Conditions to various types of organizational change. These conditions also serve as a framework for understanding how an organization can continue to build and maintain an increasing capacity for change, so that whenever a major initiative is undertaken, the organization can respond quickly and appropriately. The remainder of this chapter is focused on discussing the Winning Conditions as they apply to creating the organizational capacity for change.

### 1. Correct Diagnosis of the Change Challenge

Organizations need to be constantly polling their environments to obtain early warning signals of the need for change. Like the North American Aerospace Defense Command (NORAD) system located in northern Canada and Alaska that provides early warning signals for impending air attacks, organizations must have a similar "radar screen."[2] This radar screen needs to track both strategic and operational leading indicators for potential opportunities and threats. It must always be on. It should have a good range, as well, since it's often the blips at the edge of the screen that may have the greatest significance for future change.[3] Furthermore, the interpretation of the various blips must be solid and shared not only among the executive team, but also as broadly as possible throughout the organization. The Pearl Harbor attack in the Second World War might have been less successful had the radar capability of the American military in Hawaii been better prepared. The blips were there, but they were not well understood until it was too late.

### 2/3. Development and Enrichment of Shared Understanding

When we talk about shared understanding as one of the Winning Conditions, we usually refer to it around a specific change initiative. In the context of building a capacity for change, shared understanding still applies, although it is not focused around specific programs or projects. Rather, it can be focused around the leading indicators as noted above, but also what these indicators might mean for the organization. As a case in point, Arie De Geus, former strategic planner for Royal Dutch Shell, is credited with saving the company during the oil crisis of the mid-1970s.[4] What De Geus did that made a difference was force executives and senior managers to do scenario planning around some of the key variables in Shell's business model, such as extreme fluctuations in price. When one of the scenarios materialized, the organization had already considered its response and simply executed the game plan already created.

There is a lesson in this for building a capacity for change: anticipate a number of plausible future states and craft a plan for dealing with them. Not only can it help the organization respond quickly, but it's also a great way to develop executive and managerial shared understanding of the key success factors for the organization.

## 4. Maintaining a Sense of Urgency

We have said that change won't happen without a sense of urgency. However, every organization can't always be on a heightened state of alert. Like the small boy who "cried wolf" once too often, people stop responding if there's always a "wolf at the door." Have you ever visited an organization at which every customer order has a "rush" tag attached to it, or maybe "super rush," or even "super, super rush"? In this kind of environment, the value of the word "rush" has been degraded. Likewise, a sense of urgency can't always totally pervade an organization. What can exist, instead, is a sense that change is never over, that equilibrium is never reached, and that complacency is never a state of mind. In other words, just as in most businesses there will always be one or two rush orders that receive special attention, there should always be some sort of change activity under way with its associated sense of urgency.

In the spirit of "use it or lose it," organizations must always be honing their change-related skills and capabilities. Like math skills, if you don't constantly exercise your mind with some mental gymnastics, you quickly lose the ability. Change is much the same. If an organization only undertakes some form of change every ten years or so, it can easily get out of practice as skills atrophy. For example, a mining company that only develops a new mine every fifteen years is unlikely to have people with the necessary skills set for this type of work. In fact, smart mining companies in this position usually hire outside experienced engineering and construction contractors, such as Bechtel and Varner, to do the job for them.

We believe that there should always be a major change initiative under way within an organization. One would expect that it can't always be deep and culturally related, but it should certainly range from the operational to the strategic. General Electric always ensures that the entire organization is engaged in some form of change, although never more than one or two initiatives at any one time. The "Six Sigma Quality" change campaign was followed quickly by a focus on digitizing the entire company. The key is to maintain the organizational skills and know-how required to drive change so that when a major change is required, the ramp-up time is minimal because people understand what they have to do and how they must behave. Thus, equilibrium should not be a sought-after objective. Rather, a constant state of disequilibrium is what is required and desirable, for there is always something to change, sometimes big and sometimes small.

## 5. Maintaining a Limited and Focused Strategic Agenda

We have discussed throughout this book the importance of focusing on two or three major initiatives at any one time. A greater number might result in a lack of adequate resources, or an organization could become incapable of managing day-to-day operations effectively and efficiently at the same time. So, if there is always something to change, then the change must be very focused.

It may also be important, a certain point, to refine or add to the organization's capacity for change. The focus of a major change initiative may itself be something that significantly enhances the organization's ability to change rapidly. For example, General Electric's digitization campaign not only created new digital businesses such as GE Exchange, but also digitized their core businesses. The "holy grail" was a digital dashboard that provided real-time information on all of their businesses that sat on the desktop of each senior executive. As a result, the level of knowledge and competence with the Internet across the employee base was raised, which added to the company's asset base of change capabilities.

With respect to maintaining a focused agenda for change, an "unbalanced" scorecard may be more useful than a *Balanced Scorecard* for signaling which particular areas require focus.[5] In the example provided above, the scorecard needed to heavily weigh in favor of the learning component and away from some of the others. A *Balanced Scorecard* might in fact send the wrong signals altogether.

## 6. Ensuring Rapid Strategic Decision-making and Deployment

In maintaining a capacity for change, organizations must be vigilant in removing the "white spaces" in their various decision-making processes. They must also constantly benchmark their performance against that of other exemplars, competitors in particular. Oftentimes, new processes start off well and somehow add bureaucracy along the way. We have found that anytime someone or a group "owns" a process, it quickly becomes elaborate.

This is exactly what happened to the strategic planning processes in organizations when the Strategic Planning Department was responsible for the process. The best of intentions to obtain precision and to ensure that the department was perceived to be adding value translated into more and more time required to execute the process. The same thing happened in many organizations that adopted the Stage-Gate approach to new product development. Typically, the Quality Department became responsible for the process and, again with the best of intentions, added more gates and stages and quickly lengthened the time from start to finish quite substantially. In addition, the criteria for each gate became so onerous that nothing passed all the way through until the window of opportunity had passed. As an example of how this process can go awry, in one high-technology company, the final gate required that all product documentation be translated into twenty-three different languages prior to launch. Finally, the company scrapped the entire process and created a much more streamlined version.

We have noted repeatedly that rapid deployment relies on having the necessary resources, both human and financial. On the human capital front, change-oriented organizations need to ensure that they have a pool of talent capable of leading change programs and projects. At the limit, every manager should be so capable. At a minimum, there must be a core of capable change champions; more will be said on this front under the subtopic of leadership.

In terms of financial resources, change programs require funding and funding that is typically not linked to an annual budgeting cycle. We talked earlier in the book about having a program budget allocated to major investment and change projects, and many organizations successful on the change front have now adopted a budget of this kind that cannot be reduced to satisfy short-term operational demands.

## 7. Expanding the Human Flywheel of Commitment

A capacity for change implies that an organization can quickly engage employees around any change initiative. In order to do this, the cogs of the human flywheel must be capable of being engaged very quickly. Like the gears in a fine timepiece, the component parts must be close together, but not touching, so that when the hour needs to be changed, the clockworks engage quickly.

Steven Kerr, former chief learning officer of General Electric, understood this need for proximity of the various parts of the organization and parts that weren't necessarily well linked via a formal organization chart. In fact, Kerr and other change specialists recognize that all parts of the organization need to be hooked up, regardless of their position on the organization chart. Kerr often refers to himself as a "plumber" to signify the hooking-up function he fulfilled within General Electric.[6] The vehicle through which he hooked up the various pipes was the company's Crotonville education center, where executives and managers involved in training and education activities created the informal relationships and networks that could be quickly leveraged to create critical mass across the organization for any new initiatives.

Over time, the human flywheel is also an integral part of increasing an organization's capacity for change. Most organizations are constrained in their ability to change rapidly because they have a limited pool of employees who can lead change initiatives, particularly large ones. It's always the same old faces who are being asked to lead and be part of the project teams. Part of sustaining and enhancing the organization's capacity for change is to expand the pool of potential change leaders through on-the-job training and selective recruitment.

## 8. Identifying and Managing Sources of Resistance

Any change initiative will experience resistance, no matter how change oriented the organization is. What can be done, however, is to reduce the percentage of employees who will typically resist change. This is achieved primarily by ensuring that recruitment policies and criteria reflect change-oriented attributes that can be made part of the selection criteria for new employees. Employee-development activities that deal with change skills can also help. Over time, such policies can shift the balance of the 20-70-10 principle to something that more closely resembles 40-55-5.

Although, over time, a larger percentage of employees will be part of the "true believer" category, there will still be a significant group that will be perceived as resistant, to some degree, to specific proposed changes. What's different about this group in change-oriented organizations, however, is that when they resist, it is usually the case that they have valid reasons or that they simply aren't well informed about the proposed change. Either way, their views should be listened to and addressed.

Finally, to ensure a capacity for change, the percentage of saboteurs should become smaller as better recruitment processes work their magic and weed out these change arsonists before they set foot inside the organization. Nevertheless, no recruitment process is perfect, and people will continue to succumb to the "dark side" of the change world. As such, there will always be a requirement to ensure that the saboteurs are identified and dealt with appropriately.

### 9. Following through on Organizational Enablers

There are numerous enablers of change capacity, and almost every aspect of an organization must be assessed as to whether it helps or hinders continuing change efforts. Increasing capacity and developing a change-oriented culture require that the key enablers—recognition and rewards, education and training, infrastructure and policies—are properly aligned.

#### Performance Rewards and Recognition

The first of these enablers is the performance rewards related to change. Successful change leaders tie individual compensation and career progression to change leadership. In fact, in many organizations, specific accountabilities for change initiatives are now routinely a part of each executive's annual performance contract with the CEO. Jack Welch, when launching "Six Sigma Quality," informed his senior executives that there would be no career progression opportunities for those who were not six-sigma black belts, a high designation. The key to using rewards and recognition effectively is to ensure that these are tied to demonstrated behaviors, like black belt standing, and not merely verbal support.

#### Education and Training

Even those employees who are most keen about change may lack the requisite skills and capabilities for the initiative. There may also be new employees who seek out change but are unsure of how the process works within their particular organization. To cover both of these situations, organizations that are serious about building a capacity for change need to be equally serious about funding and maintaining some sort of corporate education facility where change is a major focus of the curriculum. General Electric has the famous Crotonville facility, and scores of other organizations from Motorola to Trilogy Software have their own versions. Trilogy Software, a Texas-based software development company, uses Trilogy University to accomplish several tasks: acculturation of new employees into Trilogy's competitive culture, training on Trilogy's unique disciplined approach to software development, and as a source of new venture ideas. At the end of three months at Trilogy University, "Trilogians" are fully functional in Trilogy's fast-paced, high-tech world.[7]

Specific change-related skills that need to be covered in any education program include project management, teamwork, and informal influence. In fact, when Doug Harrison launched major change at Acklands-Grainger, he discovered that many employees didn't know the basics of project management. This deficiency was causing significant delays in several of the change projects. The situation was rectified when Harrison mandated that every person within the company complete project management training within one year. Teamwork training is critical because it doesn't come naturally to many people, and they are expected to be high performing in sometimes very diverse teams. Similarly, much of getting the change job done relies on one's ability to use informal influence to convince people of the merits of your position and/or requirement like great salespeople do. Training in this area can help immensely with success and needs to be addressed.

### Infrastructure

Organizational infrastructure can include many structures, systems, and processes that enable change. Two of the most important are the communications infrastructure and project management.

Like the "red phone" that used to ring on the President's desk only when there was a very serious matter, organizations also need some communications mechanism that kicks in when a new change is required. In today's world, organizations need to think about their own red phone equivalent. For some organizations, this may be a special internal Web site. For others, this may be "town hall" meetings. Other approaches include company-wide closed-circuit television, used to great effect by Bank of America, Wal-Mart, Unisys, and General Electric. The key here is some special communication forum that, when utilized, sends a clear signal to everyone that the message is serious.

Project management is another critical element of a sustained capacity for change. In some organizations, project management is almost a freestyle activity—everyone has their own approach. This ad hoc style of management usually results in a high degree of variability in execution effectiveness. Organizations that are serious about change, however, take the time to develop and implement a well-thought-out methodology for managing and leading projects, from proposal and development of a charter, through development and start-up, and ultimately to a postaudit to capture the learning. The best of these systems recognize that what's needed for small projects is much simpler than the processes required to implement large, strategic projects. For example, small projects usually do not require steering committees. We have not gone into great detail on project management because there are numerous texts and articles that provide excellent references for this topic.[8]

### Policies

In addition to the enablers discussed above, organizations can use corporate policies to enhance their capacity for change. These can include policies on the availability of seed funding for change initiatives, on risk taking and failure, and on time to work on change initiatives. Borrowing a page from 3M's book of innovation, in which they insist that up to 15 percent of an employee's time be spent working on innovative projects, why not implement a policy that insists that employees spend at least 10 percent of their time on change-related projects?[9] But policies are useless unless reinforced through a performance management system. As one would expect, 3M does just that and annual performance reviews evaluate each employee's application of the 15 percent rule.

Who makes policy? That is a role for senior executives. These are the individuals who have the ultimate decisions on whether a capacity for change is built, maintained, and enhanced. That is where leadership comes in, and it is the subject of the final section of this chapter and the book.

### 10. Demonstrated Leadership Commitment—The Role of the Chief Change Officer

Appropriate and relentless leadership is critical to change. In fact, change cannot be someone's part-time job if a capacity in this area is to become institutionalized. Perhaps a new role is required in corporations to ensure effective formulation and deployment of major change initiatives. Most organizations, public and private sector alike, have chief operating officers. Maybe it's now time for a complementary role, that of the chief change officer (CCO). Is there a need for a senior executive designated to bring together and integrate the necessary skills and resources to develop and sustain the pace of change demanded by a rapidly changing environment?

Some people may argue that change is an integral part of the role of every executive and that to create a role around the function takes away from the accountability of the executive team for driving the process. However, we have seen that most executives have relatively little time to devote to change. Even most CEOs are able to devote less than 25 percent of their time to change activities. Shouldn't there be at least one senior executive who devotes his or her full time and energy to driving the change agenda forward? Most large companies do have a senior executive with responsibility for strategic planning, a key element of the change process, but this role may well be too narrow. Given the pervasiveness and continuous nature of change, there is much to be said for making this portfolio but one element of a broader senior executive change port-folio, reporting to the CEO.

There is a parallel. A number of years ago, corporations started to realize that having a vice-president of research and development was not enough to develop an innovative stance within the corporation. The role was too limited in scope, and the individual in the role usually did not have sufficient power to bring together the resources required for successful innovation to occur. Corporations responded to this need by creating a new role, the vice-president of technology, who was accountable for the technology strategy of the organization. This role has a broad internal and external mandate that encompasses research and development, engineering, intellectual property, commercialization activities, relationships with the scientific community, and often the recruitment and development of appropriate skills.

The role of the CCO would not include direct responsibility for specific change initiatives that lie within the line responsibilities of individual executives because this would not work in any case. Rather, the CCO would be responsible for building and maintaining a change capacity within the organization. The measurable indicator of performance for the CCO's office would be the overall ability of the corporation to identify, implement, and secure results from change initiatives as required. To enable this performance, the CCO would be accountable to the CEO for the key process elements that drive change forward, including:

- Strategic planning—developing the game plans for change.
- Project management—ensuring that the process for delivering specific change initiatives is effective.
- Organization development—specific initiatives designed to improve overall organizational performance.
- Recruitment and development of required change skills, such as facilitation, project leadership, etc.
- Maintaining an external network of consultants and resources capable of supporting the corporation's change initiatives.
- Ensuring that appropriate champions and coalitions are in place for change initiatives.
- Monitoring the performance of key change initiatives.
- Identifying and monitoring leading indicators for change.

The CCO will essentially be an internal change consultant, but with specific executive powers and responsibilities. Such an individual would act as a sounding board for the CEO and other executives on key change initiatives and would also be likely to play an integrating and aligning role through participation in the strategic planning activities of business units and departments. The CCO would also have a key role to play in supporting the Human Resources function in the development of appropriate compensation and recognition plans.

We believe that the CCO need not be a separate individual, depending on the nature of the organization. Ray Lane, formally designated as the COO of Oracle, was in reality the executive responsible for leading significant turnaround within that firm. He essentially acted as a CCO. Larry Ellison, the CEO at the time, had neither the temperament nor the skills to lead the required massive change.

At General Electric, the CCO role was actually fulfilled by four individuals who worked very closely together to drive successive change initiatives through the company. These four were: Jack Welch the CEO; Steven Kerr, the chief learning officer (and author of "On the Folly of Rewarding *A* while Hoping for *B*"); Gary Reiner, the CIO; and William Conaty, the senior vice-president of human resources. Together, they built the capacity for change and prepared and motivated the organization to shift. More common in midsize firms is that the CEO acts as CCO. Doug Harrison, president and CEO of Acklands-Grainger, continues to be the driver and champion for change within his company, spending minimal time on operational matters but focusing almost exclusively on change and strategy.

What makes a great CCO? What attributes must this individual possess? In our research and experience, we have been struck with the similarities between great change leaders and successful entrepreneurs, both of whom appear to exhibit the following characteristics:

- Energetic and persistent.
- Demonstrated change orientation.
- Willingness to undertake personal sacrifice.
- Team building and hero making inclination.
- "Helicopter mind"—ability to conceptualize (see the forest) and sweat the details (the trees).
- Results orientation.
- Patient yet demanding.

Like successful entrepreneurs, rarely does one person possess all of these attributes. Rather, they are typically embodied by two or three individuals who, in combination, are successful in launching and managing new ventures. We believe change leadership is much the same.

But most important, we firmly believe that to be successful in the future, organizations must become proficient at launching and managing major organizational change efforts. The requirement to do so will become more frequent as the drivers of change, technology, globalization, and demographics, to name just a few, continue their relentless march forward. Sustainable organizations will be required to change more, and more often than ever before. The best will ensure that change becomes a part of their DNA and that they are in fact "built to change."

# Notes

## Introduction

1. Mike Doyle, Tim Claydon, and Dave Buchanan, "Mixed Results, Lousy Process: The Management Experience of Organizational Change," *British Journal of Management* 11 (2000): S59–S80. This study also suggested that these outcomes have been more highly pronounced in the public than in the private sector in the United Kingdom.

2. Robert E. Quinn, *Deep Change* (San Francisco: Jossey-Bass, 1996).

3. Rosabeth Moss Kanter, *When Giants Learn to Dance* (New York: Simon and Schuster, 1989).

4. Michael Beer, Russell A. Eisenstat, and Bert A. Spector, "Why Change Programs Don't Produce Change," *Harvard Business Review* 68, no. 6 (1990).

5. Rosabeth Moss Kanter, Barry A. Stein, and Todd D. Jick, *The Challenge of Organizational Change* (New York: Free Press, 1992).

6. In fact, there are very few articles on the topic. Some recent examples include work by Andrew M. Pettigrew, E. F. Ferlie, and L. McKee, who discussed speed as a factor in their book *Shaping Strategic Change* (London: Sage, 1992); E. H. Kessler and A. K. Chakrabarti, who examined issues around the speed of innovation in "Innovation Speed: A Conceptual Model of Context, Antecedents and Outcomes," *Academy of Management Review* 21, no. 4 (1996): 1143–1191; and C. Gersick, who examined the pacing of change in a new venture in "Pacing Strategic Change: The Case of a New Venture," *Academy of Management Journal* 37 (1994): 9–45.

7. Andrew M. Pettigrew, "Linking Change Processes to Outcomes," in *Breaking the Code of Change* (Cambridge, Mass.: Harvard Business School Press, 2000), pp. 243–265.

8. James Brian Quinn, *Strategies for Change: Logical Incrementalism* (Homewood, Ill.: Richard D. Irwin, 1980).

9. John Kotter, *Leading Change* (Cambridge, Mass.: Harvard Business School Press, 1996).

10. James B. Quinn, *Strategies for Change*.

11. Robert E. Quinn, *Deep Change*.

12. See, for example, D. Holman, C. Axtell, C. Clegg, K. Pepper, P. Waterson, I. Cantista, and M. Older-Gray, "Change and Innovation in Modern Manufacturing Practices: An Expert Panel Survey of U.K. Companies," *Human Factors and Ergonomics in Manufacturing* 10, no. 2 (2000): 121–137.

### Chapter 1

1. Jeffrey Pfeffer, *New Directions for Organization Theory* (New York: Oxford University Press, 1997).

2. Many works extol the virtue that small is beautiful; see, for example, A. Hosmer, "Small Manufacturing Enterprises," *Harvard Business Review* 35, no. 6 (November–December 1957): 111–122.

3. Richard L. Daft, R. H. Lengel, and L. K. Trevino, "Message Equivocality, Media Selection and Manager Performance: Implications for Information Systems," *MIS Quarterly* 11 (1987), 355–366.

4. We use this title to acknowledge the impact on our work of the seminal article by Michael Beer, Russell A. Eisenstat, and Bert A. Spector, "Why Change Programs Don't Produce Change," *Harvard Business Review* 68, no. 6 (November–December 1990): 158–169.

5. Diagnosis has been written about in a number of books and articles on organizational change. However, many approaches are insufficiently comprehensive or take far too long to implement. Discussions of diagnosis can be found, for example, in N. Piercy, "Diagnosing and Solving Implementation Problems in Strategic Planning," *Journal of General Management* 15, no. 1 (autumn 1989); and Tony Grundy, *Implementing Strategic Change* (London: Kogan Page, 1993).

6. There are a number of useful references with respect to the importance of learning in organizational change. See Arie P. De Geus, "Planning as Learning," *Harvard Business Review* 66, no. 2 (March–April 1988): 70–74; and Peter Senge, *The Fifth Discipline: The Art and Practice of the Learning Organization* (New York: Doubleday, 1990).

7. The establishment of a sense of urgency is discussed at some length by John P. Kotter in chapter 3 of *Leading Change* (Boston: Harvard Business School Press, 1996).

8. See our chapter, "Strategic Focus: Defining and Measuring the Critical Few as Parameters of Strategic Performance Evaluation," in *Performance Measurement: Theory and Practice*, Papers from the First International Conference on Performance Measurement, The Centre for Business Performance, Cambridge, 1998.

9. Resistance to change is discussed extensively in, for example, Christopher Argyris, *Overcoming Organizational Defences: Facilitating Organizational Learning"* (Boston: Allyn and Bacon, 1990); and John P. Kotter, "Leading Change: Why Transformation Efforts Fail," *Harvard Business Review*, 73, no. 2, (March–April 1995): pp. 54–67.

10. Suggested readings on change leadership include Michael Beer and Nitin Nohria, eds., *Breaking the Code of Change* (Boston: Harvard Business School Press, 2000); Kotter, *Leading Change*; and Andrew M. Pettigrew and R. Whipp, *Managing Change for Competitive Success* (Oxford: Blackwell, 1991).

11. This topic is best discussed by T. J. Larkin and Sandor Larkin, in "Reaching

and Changing First Line Employees," *Harvard Business Review* 74, No. 3 (May–June, 1996): 95–104.

### Chapter 2

1. The first reference to force-field analysis, from which we draw our approach, is Kurt Lewin's landmark book, *Field Theory in Social Science* (New York: Harper Row, 1951).

2. Chester Barnard, *The Functions of the Executive* (Boston: Harvard Business School Press, 1938).

3. D. C. Hambrick and P. A. Mason, "Upper Echelons: The Organization as a Reflection of its Top Managers," *Academy of Management Review* 9 (1984): 193–206.

4. S. Finkelstein, and D. C. Hambrick, "The Effects of Ownership Structure on Conditions at the Top: The Case of CEO Pay Raises," *Strategic Management Journal* 16, (1995): 175–194.

5. D. C. Hambrick, "Guest Editor's Introduction: Putting Top Managers Back in the Strategy Picture," *Strategic Management Journal* 10, special issue (1989): 5–15.

6. See P. Lawrence and J. Lorsch, *Organization and Environment* (Boston: Harvard Business School Press, 1967); and J. Galbraith, *Organization Design* (Reading: Addison-Wesley, 1977).

7. E. Murray, *Bridging Two Solitudes: An Examination of Shared Understanding between Information Systems and Line Executives*, Ph.D. diss., University of Western Ontario, London, Ontario, 1998.

8. Ibid.

9. Elspeth J. Murray and Peter R. Richardson, "Strategic Focus: Defining and Measuring the Critical Few as Parameters of Strategic Performance Evaluation," *International Journal of Business Performance Measurement* vol. 2 nos. 1/2/3 (2000): 5–14.

10. Arie P. De Geus, "Planning as Learning," *Harvard Business Review* vol. 66 no. 2 (March–April 1988): 70–74.

11. Elspeth J. Murray and Peter R. Richardson, "Measuring Strategic Performance: Are We Measuring the Right Things Right?" in *Performance Measurement 2000—Past, Present and Future*, ed. A. D. Neely and D. B. Waggoner (Cambridge: Fieldfare Publications, 2000)

12. M. Fishbein and I. Azjen, "Attitudes towards Objects as Predictors of Single and Multiple Behavioral Criteria," *Psychological Review*, 81 (1974): 59–74.

13. This is discussed by Henry Mintzberg, in "Strategy Making in Three Modes," *California Management Review* 15. no. 4 (winter 1973): 44–53.

14. Chris, Argyris, "Double Loop Learning in Organizations," *Harvard Business Review* 55, no. 5 (September–October, 1977): 115–125.

15. See Murray and Richardson, "Strategic Focus."

16. Ibid.

17. Richard L. Daft, R. H. Lengel, and L. K. Trevino, "Message Equivocality, Media Selection and Manager Performance: Implications for Information Systems," *MIS Quarterly* 11 (1997): 355–366.

18. S. Kerr, "On the Folly of Rewarding *A* while Hoping for *B*," *Academy of Management Journal* 18, no. 2 (December 1975): 769–783.

19. See Daniel Goleman, *Emotional Intelligence* (New York: Bantam Books, 1995).

20. Michael Beer and Nitin Nohria, eds., *Breaking the Code of Change* (Boston: Harvard Business School Press, 2000).


### Chapter 3

1. See important works by Igor Ansoff, *Corporate Strategy: An Analytic Approach to Business Policy for Growth and Expansion* (New York: McGraw-Hill, 1965); Peter Lorange, ed., *Strategic Planning Process* (Dartmouth, Vt.: Dartmouth Publishing Company, 1994): Balaji Chakravarthy, and Peter Lorange, *Managing the Strategy Process*, (Englewood Cliffs, N.J.: Prentice Hall, 1991); and Arnaldo C. Hax and Nicolas S. Majluf, *The Strategy Concept and Process: A Pragmatic Approach* (Englewood Cliffs, N.J.: Prentice Hall, 1991).

2. Henry Mintzberg, *The Rise and Fall of Strategic Planning* (New York: The Free Press, 1994).

3. Michael E. Porter, *Competitive Advantage: Techniques for Analyzing Industries and Competitors* (New York: The Free Press, 1985).

4. Gary Hamel and C. K. Prahalad, *Competing for the Future: Breakthrough Strategies for Seizing Control of Your Industry and Creating the Markets of Tomorrow* (Boston: Harvard Business School Press, 1994).

5. Arie P. De Geus, "Planning as Learning," *Harvard Business Review* 66, no. 2 (March–April 1988): 70–74.

6. Peter Senge, *The Fifth Discipline: The Art and Practice of the Learning Organization* (New York: Doubleday, 1990).

7. Gary Hamel, "Strategy as Revolution," *Harvard Business Review* 74 no. 4 (July–August 1996): 69–83.

8. See Elspeth J. Murray and Peter R. Richardson, "Strategy as Action," *Working Paper* 98–07, Queen's University, March 1998.

9. One of the few references we can find specifically on the topic of using strategic planning to drive organizational change is Stephen Huntsman, "Using Strategic Planning to Drive Organizational Change," *Long Range Planning* 27, no. 1 (1995): 50–55.

10. Wanda J. Orlikowski, "Improvising Organizational Transformation Overtime: A Situated Change Perspective," *Information Systems Research* 7, no. 1 (1996): 63–92.

11. Sumantra Ghoshal and C. A. Bartlett, *The Individualized Corporation: A Fundamentally New Approach to Management* (New York: Harper Business, 1997).

12. Michael Beer and Nitin Nohria, eds., *Breaking the Code of Change* (Boston: Harvard Business School Press, 2000).

13. Most books on strategic management discuss these concepts, but they are most comprehensively discussed in Andrew Campbell and Laura L. Nash, *A Sense of Mission: Defining Direction for the Large Corporation* (Reading, Mass: Addison-Wesley, 1993).

14. Robert S. Kaplan and David P. Norton, *The Balanced Scorecard* (Boston: Harvard Business School Press, 1996).

15. Senge, *Fifth Discipline*.

16. Jeanne Liedtka and J. W. Rosenblum, "Shaping Conversations: Making Strategy, Managing Change," *California Management Review* 39, no. 1 (1996): 141–157.

17. See, for example, Francis J. Aguilar, *General Managers In Action* (New York: Oxford University Press, 1988).

18. A good discussion of this and related techniques can be found in De Geus, "Planning as Learning."

19. This presents us with an opportunity to cite the pioneering work of two of our colleagues at Queen's School of Business; see R. Brent Gallupe and William H. Cooper, "Brainstorming Electronically," *Sloan Management Review* 34, no. 4 (fall 1993): 27–36.

20. Porter, *Competitive Advantage*, and Michael E. Porter, *Competition in Global Industries* (Boston: Harvard Business School Press, 1986).

21. Ibid.

22. Experience curve analysis was the product of work by the Boston Consulting Group. The source reference, still one of the best discussions of the concept, is *Perspective on Experience* (Boston: The Boston Consulting Group, 1972).

23. Robert D. Buzzell, B. T. Gale, and Ralph G. M. Sultan "Market Share—A Key to Profitability," *Harvard Business Review* 53 no. 1 (January–February 1975): 97–106.

24. Gregory Watson, *Strategic Benchmarking* (New York: John Wiley, 1993).

25. Hamel and Prahalad, *Competing for the Future.*

### Chapter 4

1. See, for example, Stanley M. Davis and Christopher Meyer, *Blur—The Speed of Change in the Connected Economy* (Cambridge, Mass.: Perseus Press, 1998).

2. This topic receives some discussion in Robert G. Cooper, *Winning at New Products: Accelerating the Process from Idea to Launch* (New York: Addison-Wesley, 1986).

3. Hirotaka Takeuchi and I. Nonaka, "The New New Product Development Game," *Harvard Business Review* 64, no. 1 (January–February 1986): 137–146.

4. Amar Bhide, Hustle as Strategy, *Harvard Business Review* 64 No. 5 (September–October 1986): 59–65.

5. Michael Hammer and James Champy, *Reengineering the Corporation* (New York: HarperCollins, 1995).

6. Elspeth J. Murray and Peter R. Richardson, "Speed—The New Challenge of Strategic Change: Building Momentum through Shared Understanding and Rapid Deployment," *Working Paper* 99–10, Queen's University, November 1999.

7. Takeuchi and Nonaka, "New New Product."

8. Leonard A. Schlesinger et al., *Transformation at Ford*, Published Case Study, Harvard Business School, 15 November 1991.

### Chapter 5

1. For an interesting short article that explores the transition from planning to implementation, see William Dandy, "Avoid the Breakdowns between Planning and Implementation," *The Journal of Business Strategy* 12, no. 5 (1991): 30–33.

2. An interesting concept of strategic plans as contracts can be found in Y. Allaire and M. Firsirotu, "Strategic Plans as Contracts," *Long Range Planning* 23, no. 1 (1990): 102–115.

3. Good discussions of the role of the "team" in strategy deployment can be found in Steven J. Heyer, Daniel H. Marcus, and Reginald Van Lee, "Making Strategy Work: The Team Approach," *Outlook* 1, no. 12 (1988): 17–23; and in Jon R. Katz-

enbach and Douglas K. Smith, "Why Teams Matter," *The McKinsey Quarterly* (1992, no. 1): 93–27.

4. The role of the executive team in strategy making and deployment has been thoroughly explored by Donald C. Hambrick. For an insightful discussion of the critical role of this team in deployment, see his article "The Top Management Team: Key to Strategic Success," *California Management Review* 30, no. 1 (1987): 88–108.

5. The importance of consensus in strategy deployment is discussed in Steven W. Floyd and Bill Wooldridge, "Managing Strategic Consensus: The Foundation of Effective Implementation," *Academy of Management Executives* 6, no. 4 (1992): 27–34.

6. For a discussion of the role of top management in establishing organization processes, see Sumantra Ghoshal, "Changing the Role of Top Management: Beyond Structure to Processes," *Harvard Business Review* 73, no. 1 (January–February 1995): 86–96. The role of systems in deployment is discussed in Malcolm R. Schwartz and Frank A. Petro, "The Role of Systems in Implementing Strategy," *Outlook* (1985, no. 9): 46–51.

7. For a discussion of the role of education and training, see D. E. Hussey, "Implementing Corporate Strategy: Using Management Education and Training," *The Best of Long Range Planning* 18, no. 5 (October 1985): 73–82.

8. When we identified seven habits, we felt it only right to acknowledge Stephen R. Covey, *7 Habits of Highly Effective People: Powerful Lessons in Personal Change* (New York: Simon and Schuster, 1990).

9. For a great discussion of what it means to be a "living company," see Arie P. De Geus, *The Living Company* (Boston: Harvard Business School Press, 1997).


### Chapter 6

1. Michael Seely, president, Investors Access Corporation.

2. Insightful discussions of diversification and categories of acquisition can be found in Philippe C. Haspeslagh and David B. Jemison, *Managing Acquisitions: Creating Value through Corporate Renewal* (New York: The Free Press, 1991); M. S. Salter and W. S. Weinhold, *Diversification through Acquisition* (New York: The Free Press, 1979); and R. P. Rumelt, *Strategy, Structure and Economic Performance* (Boston: Harvard Business School Press, 1982). A thoughtful overview of the value creation potential of nonsynergistic acquisitions can be found in P. L. Anslinger and T. E. Copeland, "Growth through Acquisitions: A Fresh Look," *Harvard Business Review* 74, no. 1 (January–February 1996): 126–135.

3. See Richard P. Rumelt, "Diversification Strategy and Profitability," *Strategic Management Journal* 3 (1982): 359–369.

4. Haspeslagh and Jemison, *Managing Acquisitions.*

5. Excellent discussions of the postacquisition phase of acquisitions can be found in J. P. Walsh, "Top Management Turnover following Mergers and Acquisitions," *Strategic Management Journal* 9 (1988): 173–183; P. Pritchett, *Making Mergers Work: A Guide to Managing Mergers and Acquisitions* (Homewood, Ill.: Dow Jones-Irwin, 1987); A. F. Buono and J. L. Bowditch, *The Human Side of Mergers and Acquisitions: Managing Collisions between People, Cultures and Organizations* (San Francisco: Jossey-Bass, 1989); and P. Pritchett, *After the Merger: Managing the Shockwaves* (Homewood, Ill.: Dow Jones-Irwin, 1985).

6. Rumelt, "Diversification Strategy."

7. Salter and Weinhold, *Diversification.*

8. Haspeslagh and Jemison, *Managing Acquisitions*.

9. R. N. Ashkenas, L. J. DeMonaco, and S. C. Francis, "Making the Deal Real: How GE Capital Integrates Acquisitions," *Harvard Business Review* 66, no. 1 (January–February 1998): 165–178.

10. Haspeslagh and Jemison, *Managing Acquisitions*.

11. Further discussion of these approaches can be found in Ashkenas et al., "Making the Deal Real."

### Chapter 7

1. See, for example, James C. Collins and Jerry I. Porras, *Built to Last: Successful Habits of Visionary Companies* (New York: HarperCollins, 1994); Hirotaka Takeuchi and I. Nonaka, "The New New Product Development Game," *Harvard Business Review* 66, no. 1 (January–February 1986): 137–146; and Robert G. Cooper, *Winning at New Products: Accelerating the Process from Idea to Launch* (New York: Addison-Wesley, 1986).

2. Excerpted from a presentation by the Eastern Technology Seed Investment Fund (ETSIF) at Queen's University, November 2000.

3. For more information on Nortel Networks' Time to Market process, see www.nortelnetworks.com.

4. Joshua Lerner, "Xerox Technology Ventures: March 1995," Case Study 9-295-127, Harvard Business School Publishing, 1998.

5. Cooper, *Winning at New Products*.

6. "Creative destruction" was coined by Joseph Schumpeter in his monumental work *Socialism, Capitalism and Democracy* to illustrate the two sides of radical innovation—on the one hand, creating new industries; on the other, destroying old ones.

7. An incubator is an organization that provides investment capital and a range of functional services to help build start-ups. One of the best-known incubators is garage.com, founded by entrepreneur Guy Kawasaki. For more information, see www.garage.com.

8. Excerpted from a presentation by the Eastern Technology Seed Investment Fund (ETSIF) at Queen's University, November 2000.

9. W. Cohen and D. Levinthal, "Absorptive Capacity: A New Perspective on Learning and Innovation," *Administrative Science Quarterly* 35, no. 1 (1990): 128–152.

10. Takeuchi and Nonaka, "New New Product."

11. The video "Eureka Ranch" is available through the Canadian Broadcasting Corporation's *Venture* television program website at www.cbc.ca.

12. Gary Hamel, "Bringing Silicon Valley Inside," *Harvard Business Review* 77, no. 5 (September–October 1999):

13. Mitchell M. Waldrop, "Dee Hock on Management," *Fast Company* 5 (October 1996): 79.

14. Edith Penrose, *The Theory of the Growth of the Firm* (Oxford: Basil Blackwell, 1955).

15. Jeffry A. Timmons, *New Venture Creation: Entrepreneurship for the 21st Century* (New York: IRWIN/McGraw-Hill, 1999), 221.

16. William Sahlman, "How to Write a Great Business Plan," *Harvard Business Review* 75, no. 4 (July–August 1997): 98–108.

17. For more information on Second Chance, see www.secondchance.com.

## Chapter 8

1. P. Pritchett, *New Work Habits for a Radically Changed World* (Dallas: Pritchett and Associates, 1994).
2. The Standish Group, 1994.
3. Ernst & Young, Center for Innovation, 1997.
4. S. L. Huff, D. G. Copeland and E. J. Murray, "Western Mining Corporation: The Operations Management System," Case Study 9A95E003, Ivey Business School Publishing, 1995.
5. Ernst & Young, Center for Innovation, 1997.
6. Shoshana Zuboff, *In the Age of the Smart Machine* (New York: Basic Books, 1988).
7. E. Murray, *Bridging Two Solitudes: An Examination of Shared Understanding between Information Systems and Line Executives*, Ph.D. diss., University of Western Ontario, London, Ontario, 1999.
8. Ernst & Young, Center for Innovation, 1997.
9. For more information, see the Project Management Institute's Web site at www.pmi.org.


## Chapter 9

1. William K. Hall, "Survival Strategies in a Hostile Environment," *Harvard Business Review* 58, no. 5 (September–October 1980): 75–85.
2. Nina Disesa, chairman and chief creative officer, McCann-Erickson; quoted by Regina Fazio Maruca, in "Masters of Disaster," *Fast Company*, 1 April 2001, 81.
3. See Elspeth J. Murray and Peter R. Richardson "Measuring Strategic Performance: Are We Measuring the Right Things Right?" in *Performance Measurement 2000—Past Present and Future*, ed. A. D. Neely and D. B. Waggoner (Cambridge: Fieldfare Publications, 2000).
4. See, for example, Charles W. Hofer, "Turnaround Strategies," *Journal of Business Strategy* 1 (1980): 19–31. Hofer argues that operating turnarounds can take the form of revenue growth, cost cutting, or asset reduction or a combination of these. He suggests that strategic turnaround can involve either changing strategic groups within an industry or becoming more effective within a given group.
5. See Donald Hambrick and S. M. Schecter, "Turnaround Strategies for Mature Industrial-Product Business Units," *Academy of Management Journal* 26 (1984): 231–248.
6. The positive impact of restructuring and narrowing the business focus is demonstrated by Constantinos C. Markides in "Diversification, Restructuring and Economic Performance," *Strategic Management Journal* 16 (February 1995): 101–118.
7. Edward H. Bowman, Harbir Singh, Michael Useem, and Raja Bhadury, "When Does Restructuring Improve Economic Performance?" *California Management Review* 41, no. 1 (winter 1999): 33–54.
8. See Peter R. Richardson, *Cost Containment: The Ultimate Strategic Advantage* (New York: The Free Press, 1988).
9. S. Kerr, "On the Folly of Rewarding *A* while Hoping for *B*," *Academy of Management Journal* 18, no. 12 (Dec. 1975): 769–783.
10. See, for example, Gary J. Castrogiovanni, B. R. Baliga, and Roland E. Kidwell,

"Curing Sick Businesses: Changing CEOs in Turnaround Efforts," *Academy of Management Executive* 6, no. 3 (August 1992): 26–41.

### Chapter 10

1. See Danny Miller, "The Architecture of Simplicity," *Academy of Management Review* 18 (1993): 116–138.

2. D. A. Gioia, "Pinto Fires and Personal Ethics: A Script Analysis of Missed Opportunities," *Journal of Business Ethics* 11 (1992): 379–389.

3. B. Virany, M. L., Tushman, and E., Romanelli, "Executive Succession and Organization Outcomes in Turbulent Environments: An Organization Learning Approach," *Organization Science* 3 (1992): 72–91.

4. Michael Beer and Nohria, Nitin eds,, *Breaking the Code of Change* (Boston: Harvard Business School Press, 2000).

5. Jay R. Galbraith, *Designing Organizations* (San Francisco: Jossey-Bass, 1995).

6. Miller, "Architecture."

7. Karl E. Weick, *Sensemaking in Organizations* (Thousand Oaks, Calif.: Sage, 1995).

8. Elspeth J. Murray, and Peter R. Richardson, "Measuring Strategic Performance: Are We Measuring the Right Things Right?" in *Performance Measurement 2000—Past, Present and Future*, ed. A. D. Neely and D. B. Waggoner (Cambridge: Fieldfare Publications, 2000).

9. S., Kerr, "On the Folly of Rewarding A while Hoping for B," *Academy of Management Journal* 18, no. 12 (December 1975): 769–783.

10. Michael Beer, R. A. Eisenstat, and B. Spector, *The Critical Path to Corporate Renewal* (Boston: Harvard Business School Press, 1990).

11. Andrew M. Pettigrew and R. Whipp, *Managing Change for Competitive Success* (Oxford: Blackwell, 1991.

12. Beer and Nohria, *Breaking*.

13. Weick, *Sensemaking*.

14. N. M. Dixon, "The Hallways of Learning," *Organizational Dynamics* 25, no. 1 (spring 1997): 23–34.

### Chapter 11

1. Chris Argyris, "Double Loop Learning in Organizations," *Harvard Business Review* 55, no. 5 (September–October, 1977): 115–125.

2. For more information on NORAD, see www.spacecom.af.mil/norad/.

3. Clayton M. Christensen, *The Innovator's Dilemma* (Boston: Harvard Business School Press, 1997).

4. Arie De Geus, "Planning as Learning," *Harvard Business Review* 66, no. 2 (March–April 1988): 70–74.

5. A scorecard is certainly required to measure progress on the change agenda. However, a Balanced Scorecard as advocated by Robert S. Kaplan and David P. Norton in *The Balanced Scorecard* (Boston, Mass.; Harvard Business School Press, 1992), may not be what's required. Apart from the time required to develop this, and its relative inflexibility, "balance" may not be what's required. Rather, a scorecard that is skewed toward the key dimensions of change may be more appropriate.

6. From an interview with Steven Kerr.

7. Robert D. Austin, "Trilogy," Case Study 9-699-034 (Boston: Harvard Business School Press, 1999).

8. For more details on project management, see the Project Management Institute's Web site at www.pmi.org.

9. For more details on various aspects of 3M's innovation success, see www. mmm.com. It is also extensively discussed in James C. Collins and Jerry I. Porras, *Built to Last* (New York: HarperCollins, 1994).

# Index